Managing the Canadian Business
Chris Bovaird

Custom Publication for
University of Toronto Scarborough

Group Product Engineer: Jason Giles
Product Developer: Corinne Mohr

Front cover photograph copyright of: Gary Mulcahey
Back cover photograph copyright of: Susanne Jeffery
Interior Photographs: Susanne Jeffery, Steffi Kirsh Rotstein, Ken Jones
Content copyright of Chris Bovaird

ACKNOWLEDGEMENTS & DEDICATION

Chef Tina Moorey manages On The Side Gourmet Food Inc. Chef Tina works to meet customer needs, every day. She plans the purchase of food, organises its preparation, leads kitchen and serving staff, and controls the presentation of meals. She manages these things so successfully that her business is the largest employer in the town where it is located. Gary Mulcahey is a photographer. Gary runs a photography gallery, undertakes commissions, and illustrate books. Entrepreneurial people, who work hard and manage thriving businesses, interest me. They are the subject of this book.

I am grateful for the help, support, and encouragement supplied by Susanne Jeffery. Susanne painstakingly edited every chapter. She supplied most of the photographic images. She provided the environments, in the UK and Canada, where I could write this book. I dedicate this book, with much love, to Susanne.

TABLE OF CONTENTS

CHAPTER 1

CHAPTER 2

CHAPTER 3

CHAPTER 4

CHAPTER 5

CHAPTER 6

OPERATIONS: MAKING THE THINGS THAT PEOPLE WANT 95

CHAPTER 7

CHAPTER 8

CHAPTER 9

UNDERSTANDING FINANCIAL STATEMENTS   142

CHAPTER 12

PREFACE

PREFACE

<u>Managing The Canadian Business,</u> this book, is a sequel. It is assumed that readers of this book will have read, and now understand the material in its companion volume <u>Introduction to Canadian Business</u>.

<u>Introduction to Canadian Business</u> was written to provide readers with a basic vocabulary about business as a particular kind of organisation. Assuming that the reader now knows what a business is, this volume turns its attention to the internal workings of a business. In other words, this book is about how businesses are managed.

WHAT YOU SHOULD ALREADY KNOW

Readers of this book should already know the following:

Every business is an organised effort to provide things that people need and want. At the same time, businesses try to make a profit. You should therefore understand what is meant by goods and services, customers, revenue, expenses, profit and loss.

Businesses use a combination of fundamental parts known as the factors of production. Labour, capital, and natural resources come together to create a business under the guiding hand of entrepreneurs.

Canada is a mixed market economy. This means entrepreneurial behaviour and business ownership are encouraged. However, there is a positive role for the government. Governments collect taxes for the financing of public services. Governments create and enforce the laws which protect a country's citizens, including citizens who own businesses. Governments also provide the regulation and oversight which allow businesses to operate in a stable environment.

While the market system is intended to give consumers choice, not every market has a large number of suppliers. You should understand the nature of markets and the characteristics of each of the various degrees of competition.

Canada's mixed market system has served Canadians well. Canada has one of the largest economies in the world, as measured by GDP. We are among the wealthiest people in the world, as measured by GDP per capita. Our economic system does well in its ability to encourage people to participate in the labour market, find employment, and generate prosperity.

"Entrepreneur" describes a personality type, it is not a job title. You should know the common psychological, personality and demographic characteristics that distinguish entrepreneurial people.

Most Canadian businesses fall into one of five types of ownership structure. Each of these forms of organisation have their advantages and disadvantages, their benefits and costs.

Experts advise all would-be business owners to write a "business plan". You should understand the purpose of business planning, in particular the importance of identifying the human and capital resources needed to get the business up and running.

You should understanding the role played by financial intermediaries in locating, collecting, packaging, and redistributing capital from savers and investors into the hands of entrepreneurs and existing businesses.

Once created, businesses need both purpose and direction. You should understand the importance of leadership and strategy, and you should be familiar with a variety of strategic analysis models and tools.

Finally, Canada is an open economy. You should know the importance of international trade, the costs and benefits of imports and exports, and of trade protection.

All of the foregoing, the material presented in <u>Introduction to Canadian Business</u>, is intended to provide background and context to this book. This book turns its attention to a subject barely touched by its predecessor: How businesses actually work.

THE SUBJECT OF THIS BOOK

Businesses take factors of production and turn them into the goods and services that people need and want.

A Business Turns Factors of Production into Products

This is a good description of a business in terms of business theory. However, from this description, a business remains a black box. "Black box" is a term often used in science and engineering to describe a device or system where we can observe the inputs and the outputs but we have no knowledge of its internal workings. This book attempts to illuminate the interior of the black box.

CHAPTER

1

MANAGING AND MANAGERS: WORKING TO ACCOMPLISH A TASK

CHAPTER OVERVIEW

A businesses is an organised effort, formed for a purpose. Responsibility for defining the purpose, and setting the business' direction lies with its leaders. The term commonly used to describe the business' purpose and direction is mission.

There are more than two million business enterprises in Canada, none of them exactly the same. Whatever the particularities of their mission and, if they have one, their mission statement, all businesses exist in order to satisfy customer needs and wants, and also to make a profit. In a well-run business the particular purpose and direction should be clear, especially to the business' owners, employees and customers.

How this is accomplished is through a process called managing. Managing is the name given to the process of planning, organising, leading and controlling resources in order to accomplish a task. In this chapter you will begin to learn about managing, and managers.

Managing is the process, and managers are the people responsible for the functioning of organisations.

LEARNING OUTCOMES

As a result of reading this chapter, you will learn:

- Managing is a process. Management involves planning, organising, leading and controlling resources in order to accomplish a task.

- Planning involves determining what needs to be done to accomplish a task, and deciding the best way to accomplish it.

- Organising means assembling and preparing the resources necessary to complete the task.

- Leading is the art of guiding and encouraging other to accomplish a task

- Controlling is a three stage process. First, set a standard. Then measure the performance and compare it to the standard. Finally, if necessary, take steps to improve or correct the performance to bring it up to the standard.

- The managing process is not confined to the world of business. Parents, teachers, military officers and coaches all manage.

- Individuals manage themselves.

- Managers who work in businesses organisations plan, organise, lead and control the resources available to them, in order to realise the business' mission.

- A business takes the factors of production as inputs. Then, it adds to or transforms those inputs in some way, thus adding to their value or utility. The purpose of doing so is to turn the inputs into a good or service that will satisfy a customer's needs and wants.

WORKING TO ACCOMPLISH A TASK

A businesses is an organised effort, formed for a purpose. Responsibility for defining the purpose, and setting the direction lies with the business' leaders. Typically a business' leaders are its owners. If the business has many owners, for example a partnership with many partners or a corporation with many shareholders, the responsibility of leadership is typically delegated to others, such as directors or senior employees.

The term commonly used to describe the reason why a business exists, and the goals that it is trying to accomplish is **mission**.

Mission: The reason why a business exists, and the goals that it is trying to accomplish.

In recent years, many businesses have chosen to articulate that purpose and direction through the creation of a publicly enunciated mission statement. Many of these are, quite rightly, mocked for their high-minded emptiness. A recent article in the prestigious Harvard Business Review was entitled "If I Read One More Platitude-Filled Mission Statement I'll Scream"[1] Nevertheless, most businesses strive to communicate, briefly and clearly, the reason they exist and the goals they are trying to accomplish. Here's a small sample of the mission statements of three well-known business organisations:

> IKEA: We shall offer a wide range of well-designed, functional home furnishing products at prices so low that as many people as possible will be able to afford them.

> Subway Restaurants: To provide the tools and knowledge to allow entrepreneurs to compete successfully in the Fast Food industry worldwide, by consistently offering value to consumers through providing great tasting food that is good for them and made the way they want it.

> Maple Leafs Sports and Entertainment: We are the parent company of the Toronto Maple Leafs (NHL), Toronto Raptors (NBA), Toronto FC (MLS), and Toronto Marlies (AHL). Our talented group of professionals are accountable for delivering everything our teams need to win.

Whatever the fine words in the mission statement, all businesses exist in order to satisfy customer needs and wants, and also to make a profit. In a well-run business the particular purpose and direction should be clear to all stakeholders, especially shareholders, employees and customers.

A math tutoring business exists in order to help high school students better understand algebra and calculus, and to help those students perform better on their exams. A restaurant exists in order to prepare and serve tasty meals in a pleasant atmosphere, and send home happy customers who will return. A shoe store exists to sell footwear to people who want to feel comfortable and stylish in their shoes and boots.

THE PROCESS OF MANAGEMENT

How each of these things is accomplished is through a process called managing. **Managing** is the process of planning, organising, leading and controlling resources in order to accomplish a task.

---

[1]   Greg McKeown, Harvard Business Review, October 12, 2012

Managing: The process of planning, organising, leading and controlling resources in order to accomplish a task.

Managers are the individuals responsible for planning, organising, leading and controlling resources in order to accomplish a task.

Managers: Individuals responsible for planning, organising, leading and controlling resources in order to accomplish a task.

Perhaps the best way to demonstrate what managers do, and how they perform the activities that make up the managing process, is through a simple example of an outstanding manager, who does her job extraordinarily well.

The Perfect Manager

It is 9.00 a.m. on a Saturday morning. You are lying in your bed, asleep. Your manager opens the door to your bedroom and says, in a cheery voice "Good morning. I hope you had good sleep. Now, today is your Grandma's birthday. So, I need you to be a good helper. We are going to your Grandma's house for lunch."

"I need you to be neat and tidy, wear your best clothes, and be polite to all of your Grandma's friends. We want to make your Grandma very proud, and show her we love her."

"Can you do that for me?"

While your manager is pulling back your curtains she says "I've run you a bath. I need you to jump in it, and give yourself a good scrub."

"I'll go downstairs now and make your breakfast. When you are out of the tub, I want you to get dressed. I've ironed your shirt. I've put out your clean shorts. They are on your chair. I've polished your shoes and put them by the front door."

"Can you be standing beside the car at ten o'clock? If you are ready by ten, we can be at your Grandma's house by eleven. Today is her birthday, so we don't want to be late..."

PLANNING

Planning means determining what needs to be done to accomplish a task, and the best way to accomplish it.

Planning: Determining what needs to be done to accomplish a task, and the best way to accomplish it.

In the example, the manager has identified the mission: Get to your Grandma's house on time and make a nice impression. In order to do this, she has identified a sequence of discrete, logical steps:

- "I've run you a bath.
- "I need you to jump in it,
- "Give yourself a good scrub."
- "When you are out of the tub, I want you to get dressed."
- "Can you be standing beside the car at ten o'clock?"

and finally

- "If you are ready by ten, we can be at your Grandma's house by eleven."

Each of these things are necessary if the organisation, your family, is to accomplish the task.

ORGANISING

Organising means assembling and preparing the resources necessary to complete a task.

Organising: Assembling and preparing the resources necessary to complete a task.

In the example above, your manager organises a number of the resources necessary for you to make a nice impression on your Grandma.

- "I've ironed your shirt."
- "I've put out your clean shorts."
- "They are on your chair."
- "I've polished your shoes and put them by the front door."

Not only must you have a bath and get dressed in order to make a nice impression on your Grandma. You must have an ironed shirt, clean shorts, and polished shoes into which to get dressed. These must be put in an easy to find and easily accessible location.

The Perfect Manager – Part 2

Two hours later, you arrive at your Grandma's house. You are excited to see your Grandma, but a little nervous because there are lots of grown-ups there, too.

Your manager turns to you and says "We want to make your Grandma really proud, and show her we love her. So, I need you to make a nice impression and be really polite."

"You will be meeting lots of grown-ups. The proper way to meet someone is to shake hands and say 'Hello uncle, it's very nice to see you'. When you meet one of your aunts, to make a good impression you should kiss her on the cheek and say 'Hello auntie, you look very nice".

"You just watch how I do it, and you do the same as me."

Your manager then walks into your Grandma's sitting room and heads straight over to a very old man with a moustache.

You watch her as she says "Hello Uncle Boris. It's very nice to see you." She then kisses the old man on the cheek – even though he has a moustache.

Your manager then walks over to an elderly lady and says "Hello Aunt Gertrude. You look very nice". You then watch in horror as she kisses the old lady on both cheeks – even though she also has a moustache!

LEADING

Previously, you learned that leadership is the art of guiding or inspiring others to follow. If the organisation is to accomplish its chosen task, or mission, people will need to participate, and make their contribution. A manager's responsibility is to show others the way, and inspire them to want to contribute to the cause.

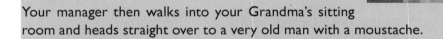

Leading: The art of guiding or inspiring others to follow.

In this case, your manager guides you by providing instruction:

- "The proper way to meet someone is…."
- "To make a nice impression, you should…"

In addition, notice that your manager is displaying leadership not by telling you what to do, but by showing you what to do. Your manager shows you the proper way to do something by doing it herself. This is leading by example:

- "Just watch how I do it, and then you do the same as me."

The Perfect Manager – Part 3

An hour after you arrive at your Grandma house, your manager says in a very loud voice "Okay everybody, we're going to start lunch in five minutes. If you'd like to come into the dining room we can start Grandma's birthday party!"

Then she takes you aside and says "It is good manners to wash your hands before eating. Your Grandma has made a very special lunch for you. Go into the bathroom. I want you to scrub your hands clean. If you have clean hands, it will make a nice impression on your Grandma. She will be proud of you."

You go into your Grandma's bathroom. There's a china figurine on a shelf. There's some black and white photos of some old people. There's a couple of magazines. You look around for a couple of minutes. Then you walk out of the bathroom and toward the dining room. Your manager stops you, and asks "Did you give your hands a good scrub?"

You don't say anything.

Your manager says "Let me see your hands."

You stick your hands out.

"Let me see the other side."

You turn your hands over.

"Your hands aren't clean. We want to make a nice impression on Grandma. Go back into the bathroom. This time use soap and hot water."

CONTROLLING

Controlling begins with setting a goal or an intended result of an activity. The term used for this goal or the intended result is the **standard**. In business, a standard might be expressed as a quantity or value of inputs. Examples of inputs are:

- "We want to sell 24,000 boxes of our product this month."
- "We want each of our salesmen to make 20 sales calls per month."

Of course, a standard can also be expressed as an output or a desired result:

- "By selling 24,000 boxes we want to generate $960,000 in revenue."

- "We want our salesmen to generate $2,000,000 in revenue per month."

Standard: The goal or the intended result for the performance of an activity.

The second stage of the control process is to measure the actual performance of the activity. The performance is then compared to the standard.

- "We sold 12,000 boxes, just half of our target. Revenue is only $480,000."
- "All our salesmen are making 20 sales calls per month, which is what we asked of them. Our sales are averaging $2.4 million per month,"

Then, if necessary, managers can take action to improve or correct performance, to bring it into line with the standard.

- "The people who buy our product give in good reviews, but our sales are only half of our target. Perhaps we need to put more effort into advertising and distribution."

Of course, if the standard is being met, people can be rewarded and further encouraged:

- "Our sales people are working hard. They are meeting their targets, and sales are above forecast. Let's thank them, and give them a bonus."

Controlling: Setting a standard, measuring performance against the standard and, if necessary, taking action to bring the performance into line.

People perform control activities frequently, and in all walks of life. People who wish to lose weight, for example, can set weekly or monthly weight-loss targets, then weigh themselves to see how they are doing. If they fail to meet their target, they must redouble their efforts by taking more exercise.

In the case study in the preceding pages, your manager was setting a standard when she told you "I want you to scrub your hands clean".

Having set the standard, your manager monitored the actual performance: "Let me see your hands."

Then, she compared it with the standard: "Your hands aren't clean".

Finally, she took action to correct the performance: "Go back into the bathroom. This time use soap and hot water."

The purpose of the control function is to get people and other resources to perform in a manner that will achieve the organisation's goals: "If you have clean hands, it will make a nice impression on your Grandma. She will be proud of you."

Mid-Term Tests as a Method of Control

A mid-term test is a method to control studying habits, and academic performance.

Suppose a student decides to take a first year course, outside of his program, as an elective. He has heard from a friend that the course is easy, and that he should get a good grade without too much effort. The student wants to get 80% or better.

Six weeks into the semester, the student writes a mid-term test, worth 35% of his final grade. Before the mid-term the Professor announces "The mid-term will let you know how you are doing on the course".

When the student gets his mid-term back, his mark is 73%. This is less than he wanted, and much less than he needs to assure himself of getting an A as a final grade.

His grade on the mid-term tells the student that the course is not as easy as he thought. If he wants to get a final grade of A, he will have to work much harder.

The student resolves to change his behaviour. He decides to go to every remaining class, attend tutorials, and seek the help of the Professor if there is material that he does not understand.

Two months later, having changed his classroom attendance and study habits, the student sits the final exam. When the final grades are posted, he calculates that he must have attained 85% on the final exam, because his final grade on the course is 81%.

MANAGEMENT IS A UNIVERSAL PROCESS

As the examples in the preceding pages demonstrate, management is a universal process. Management occurs in all fields of endeavour, and in all walks of life.

Management occurs in families. The "mission" of the family organisation is to raise and nurture children to become healthy, happy, and productive members of society. To accomplish this task, parents must manage the feeding, clothing, education and socialisation of their children. This means planning their daily activities, organising the meals they must eat, guiding and educating them to acquire social skills and manners, and monitoring their progression from infancy into adulthood.

Management occurs in the military, where generals plan, organise, lead and control campaigns. Management occurs in sporting arenas and on playing fields, where point guards and quarterbacks must manage ball possession and the clock. Finally, of course, management does occur within business organisations.

It probably occurs to you that the description of managing offered in the preceding pages sounds very much like leading. It ought to. Managing and leading are synonymous. Parents both lead their children and manage them. Generals both manage their troops and lead them.

While leading and managing are synonymous, "leadership" is more often applied to managers who have a longer term orientation. When we speak of leaders, we normally mean people whose concern is to plan, organise, and control resources for several years into the future.

Leaders Manage and Managers Lead
Leaders Manage Further Into the Future

When we speak of managers, we normally associate the term with people who are planning, organising, leading and controlling resources over the next month, or the next week.

While the basic processes are identical, the managing done at the top of the organisation inevitably involves greater resources, and greater risks. The Field Marshal of an army must plan, organise, and control to win a war, and lead hundreds of thousands of soldiers. A General must plan, organise, and control a campaign within the war, and lead tens of thousands of soldiers. A Brigadier might be responsible for a battle within a campaign, and lead thousands of soldiers. Inevitably the number of variables which will impact on the former's success will be larger than the latter's. Inevitably, the quantity of resources to be organised will be larger, and the sequence of steps to be organised will be longer, and more complex.

WHAT DO BUSINESS MANAGERS MANAGE?

One way to understand the internal workings of a business is to recognise that a business is a **system**. A system is a series of connected parts or connected activities. The parts are organised for a common purpose, and work together.

System: A series of connected parts or connected activities. The parts are organised for a common purpose, and work together.

In the case of a business, the system involves planning, organising, leading and controlling labour, capital and natural resources to transform them into the finished goods and services that people need and want.

The idea of the business as a system was most famously articulated by Michael Porter, a Professor at Harvard Business School. In his influential 1985 book "Competitive Advantage", Porter described the system of activities within a business as a **value chain**.

Value chain: The system of activities which a business must manage in order to transform factors of production into finished goods and services.

Most organisations engage in dozens, even hundreds of activities in the process of transforming factors of production into goods and services.

Observe what happens the next time you go to a sandwich shop. It typically requires three employees to take your order, make your sandwich, hand it to you, collect your payment and make change. There are at least two dozen steps involved in producing a sandwich that is custom made to your order. Each activity that the sandwich shop's employees perform bring the raw ingredients closer to being a sandwich for which a customer will pay. See for yourself:

The System for Creating a Sandwich

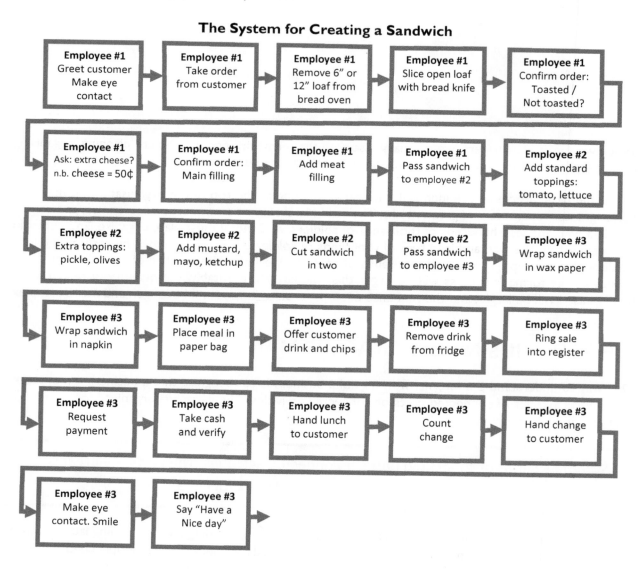

Every one of these activities involves the expenditure of time or other resources. But every one of these activities moves a loaf of bread and a variety of other inputs (including paper napkins, sheets of wax paper, and paper bags) into a finished product for which you, as the customer, will pay several dollars. For individual businesses, the idea is to add as much value as possible, as quickly and cheaply as possible, at every step of the way.

In his conception of the value chain Michael Porter distinguished between two types of activities.

Primary activities are those that are directly involved with making the good or the service that the business provides to its customers. They involve engaging with the business' customers, determining their needs, making the product, packaging and delivering the product into the customer's hands, and taking payment.

Primary activities: Activities that are directly involved with making the good or the service that the business provides to its customers.

The sandwich shop's employees need to engage with customers, and find out what they need and want. The sandwich needs to cut, sliced, assembled and wrapped. It needs to be delivered, with a polite small. Then payment needs to be collected and the correct amount of change needs to be made.

None of these activities, alone, is hugely time consuming or expensive. But each activity requires planning and organisation, and each brings the raw materials closer to being the completed product. Businesses create value by adding time, effort, skills and expertise to the goods and services they are creating for their market.

In addition, every business engages in a wide variety of activities that don't directly involve customers or the making of the business' end product, but which are necessary for the organisation to function. Porter called these the **support activities.**

Support activities: Activities that don't directly involve customers or the making of the product, but which are necessary for the organisation to function.

Before it opened up for trade, the sandwich shop had to negotiate a lease with the owner of the building where it is located. This required planning and organisation. The business needed to recruit experienced managers to run the day-today operations of each store. This, too, required planning and organisation. The business may have needed a loan from its bank. Without these sorts of support activities, the business could not have made one single sandwich.

Support activities underpin the smooth functioning of the business. They allow the primary activities to take place. Support activities include such business functions as:

Leadership and Strategy: In a small organisation, strategy and leadership activities will be performed by the entrepreneur who is the business owner. You will recall from Introduction to Canadian Business that Steve and Maria, the founding owners of the MAST Corporation, not only designed websites, but they concerned themselves with reorganising the business' ownership structure so as to acquire more capital, ensuring that the business had suitable office space, and hiring new employees in anticipation of growth. As a business becomes more complex, the owner(s) may see fit to hire dedicated employees to perform these functions.

Human Resource Management: Businesses need people. Essential to the functioning of any business therefore, are all of the activities involved with recruiting, hiring, training, developing, and compensating employees. Recall that, in order to cope with the MAST Corporation's growth, the founding partners offered Carol, a valuable part-time employee, a full time job. In addition, to reward Carol for her previous loyalty they gave her shares in the corporation. Her share ownership served as an incentive and as a reward.

Financial Management: Businesses need capital. They need capital to buy or rent office space. They need capital to pay the wages and salaries of employees. They need capital to buy equipment, software and other resources. An essential part of any business is finance. Remember finance involves planning the business' capital needs, locating sources of capital, negotiating the terms and conditions for its use, and managing the organisation's relationship with financial intermediaries. You will recall that, among their responsibilities as the leaders of the MAST Corporation, Steve and Maria negotiated a mortgage with their bank.

THE ORGANISATION OF THIS BOOK

The approach taken in this book is that a business begins with an entrepreneur's idea, set of skills or area of expertise. The business founders' must begin by identifying target customers, then validate their idea through market research. Market research will help the business refine and improve the idea, by making it more acceptable to the needs and wants of the target market. The business then creates the good or service. Next, the business must make the product known. It must try to interest and excite potential customers, and of course, make it available to them. Finally, the business needs to collect information on how well it is doing. It needs to measure its performance against its goals, adjust and improve, and begin the whole process again, continuously.

Primary Activities

| Identify and Research Target Market | Develop Product and Set Price | Operations create products | Promote and Distribute Products | Measure and Control |

Strategy & Leadership

Human Resource Management

Financial Management

Support Activities

The diagram above encapsulates all of the major processes or areas of activity carried out by a typical business. The commonly used term for these areas of activity is **business function.**

Business function: A process or activity that is routinely carried out by a business.

This text identifies and describes seven key business functions. These are:

Marketing: The activities involved with interacting with customers and potential customers.

Operations: The activities involved with transforming factors of production into the goods or services that customers want.

Information Management: The development of systems for collecting for collecting data that can be organised in such a way that it produces information of use to the managers of a business.

Accounting: The system for collecting, analysing and communicating financial information

Strategic Management: The activities undertaken by an organisation's senior leadership to determine the organisation's long terms goals and objectives.

Financial Management: Planning, organising, leading and controlling the use of capital.

Human Resource Management: All of the activities involved with planning, organising, leading and controlling an organisation's people.

SELF-ASSESSMENT QUESTIONS FOR REVIEW

1. A lemonade stand is a business. Make a list of all the raw materials that you would need to assemble in order to make a pitcher of lemonade. How many are there?

2. Make a list of all the pieces of capital equipment (jug, knife, spoons, etc.) you need in order to assemble and operate a lemonade stand. How many are there?

3. Calculate what it would cost you, in terms of time and money, to go to a grocery store to buy a loaf of bread, a chicken breast, some cheese, tomatoes and lettuce. How much would you pay to have someone deliver all of these things to your front door?

4. Calculate what it would cost you, in terms of time and money, to slice a loaf of bread, cook and then slice a breast of chicken, cut a block of cheese into thin slices, slice a tomato, and shred a head of lettuce. How much would you pay to have someone do all these things for you?

5. Suppose you shared an apartment with four other students. Every Wednesday, you were responsible for making supper for the five of you. How far in advance do you begin planning to buy the groceries and cook the food?

DEFINED TERMS

- Controlling
- Human Resource Management
- Inbound Logistics
- Infrastructure
- Leading
- Management
- Marketing and Sales

- Materials Management
- Operations
- Organising
- Outbound Logistics
- Planning
- Primary Activities
- Service

- Standard
- Support Activities
- System
- Technological Development
- Value Chain

MARKETING: SATISFYING CUSTOMER
NEEDS AND WANTS

CHAPTER OVERVIEW

All businesses begin with an idea. An entrepreneur perceives a gap in a market, and identifies an opportunity to satisfy an unfulfilled need. Perhaps you have found yourself walking around your neighbourhood and thought "I wish there was a pizza restaurant in this part of the city" or "There ought to be a hair salon closer to the campus".

A business idea can only be turned into a business reality if it can find a market. In other words, the business must identify potential customers who need and want what it proposes to offer, and who are willing and able to buy. The business function concerned with interacting with customers and potential customers is called marketing.

Not every consumer necessarily needs or wants the products that the business proposes to offer. The marketing process begins when the business attempts to identify potential customers through a process called segmentation. Target customers' needs, wants and preferences are identified through the conduct of market research. All of this is done so that the business can create products with features and benefits that people want, and at a price that they are willing to pay.

This chapter concludes by introducing the result of all of this segmentation and research: the creation of a marketing mix that best suits the business' customers.

LEARNING OUTCOMES

As a result of reading this chapter you will learn:

- The meaning of the phrase "marketing concept" philosophy adopted by businesses which focus o customers first, and products second.

- The importance of target markets. No business ca hope to sell everything to everybody.

- Market segmentation is the means by which targe markets are identified.

- There are several ways in which a market can b segmented. You will learn and be given examples the most common means of market segmentatior demography, psychography, and geography.

- The best way to satisfy customers is to under stand them. Businesses therefore need to conduc research.

- A business can collect and review existing marke data, an activity called secondary research. Alterna tively, a business can collect its own, original data an activity called primary research.

- Market research aims to collect both quantitativ and qualitative data, which are used to provide dif ferent information about potential customers.

- Market researchers use a variety of techniques fo collecting data, each with their own advantages an disadvantages, and each suitable for collecting dif ferent data for different purposes.

- The purpose of market research is to help the busi ness refine its concept. Marketers have identifie four key areas that must be perfected in order t satisfy customer needs and wants. These are re ferred to as the "4Ps".

TURNING A CONCEPT INTO SATISFIED CUSTOMERS.

A business is like a bicycle. A bicycle must be going forward in order to stay upright. At the same time, a bicycle must stay upright in order to go forward. A business must satisfy customer needs in order to make a profit. A business must make a profit in order to satisfy customer needs.

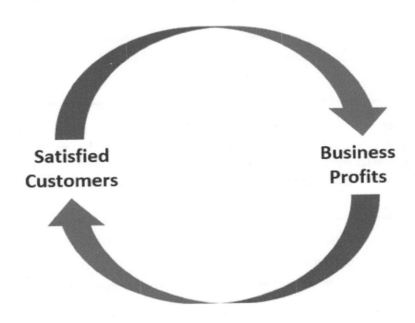

Satisfied Customers

Business Profits

You will recall that it was Adam Smith, the founder of liberal economic thinking, who wrote that "the butcher, the brewer and the baker did not pursue their trades out of benevolence or love for humanity". Rather, these businessmen made their products satisfying out of their own self-interest.[1]

Without customers to buy the product, the business will generate no revenues and therefore no profits. At the same time, without the profit motive entrepreneurs will have no incentive to produce the goods and services that customers want.

The business function concerned with planning and organising the creation of a product, determining a price that people will pay, making the product known, and making it available to customers is called **marketing**. The purpose of marketing is to create exchanges, so that customers get what they need and want, and the business owner makes a sale. Thus, everyone benefits.

Marketing: The business function concerned with planning and organising the creation of a product, determining a price that people will pay, making the product known and making it available to customers.

1 — Adam Smith, An Inquiry into the Nature & Causes of the Wealth of Nations, Vol 1

THE MARKETING CONCEPT

When a business focuses its energy on selling what it has, this is an orientation known as **product focus**. If a business is product focused, it pours the greater part of its resources into making existing goods and services look better, perform better, or achieve better results. A product focused business assumes that it understands the market's needs and strives to meet them as effectively as possible by building on its proven expertise.

Product Focus: An orientation toward producing improved goods and services for which an organisation has proven expertise.

Alternatively, a business can focus its resources on selling customers what they want, an orientation known as **customer focus**. If a business is customer focused, it pours its resources into determining new or emerging needs in its market and developing the goods and services to meet these needs. A customer focused business does not assume it knows what customers want. Rather, it strives to discover what they want.

Customer Focus: An orientation toward determining the needs and wants of customers in the market and developing the goods and services that meet those needs.

The idea that a business should focus its energies on customer needs is often attributed to the American professor, author and consultant Philip Kotler (1931-). Kotler is widely regarded as one of the most influential marketing thinkers in the world. In 2003, the Financial Times newspaper summed up Kotler's contributions to marketing and to management, as follows:

"First, he has done more than any other writer or scholar to promote the importance of marketing, transforming it from a peripheral activity, bolted on to the more "important" work of production. Second, he continued a trend shifting emphasis away from price and distribution to a greater focus on meeting customers' needs and on the benefits received from a product or service. Third, he has broadened the concept of marketing from mere selling to a more general process of communication and exchange." [2]

Kotler believed that there had been an evolution in the strategic management of businesses. In the 19th century most business' resources had been directed on production, in other words making goods and services. In the first half of the 20th century the emphasis had shifted toward sales, persuading customers to buy those goods and services. By the middle of the 20th century Kotler argued that the business' resources should primarily be directed toward serving customer needs. Kotler called this "the **marketing concept**".

Marketing concept: A business philosophy that stresses that the business' resources should primarily be directed toward serving customer needs.

---

2 Witzel, Morgen, August 6, 2003, "First Among Marketers", Financial Times

The marketing concept suggests that if a business provides customers with what they want, those customers will respond by making a purchase, from which will spring the business' revenues and profits.

The Bovairds Try to Buy a Used Car

Some years ago, Professor Bovaird needed to buy a new car. His wife had suggested that car dealers in the suburbs just outside of Toronto would probably sell cars slightly more cheaply than their counterparts in the centre of the city. So, one day, they drove their 8-year old Jeep Cherokee to the Whitby-Oshawa area.

Since the car that they had been driving was a Chrysler product, the Bovairds went to a Chrysler dealer first. They drove to the dealership, parked in the customers parking area and walked into the showroom. Immediately, a well-dressed, well-groomed smiling young woman walked up to them, her hand extended in a friendly gesture.

"Good morning" said the saleswoman "are you looking to buy a new car?"

"Well, new to us." said Professor Bovaird "We're wondering if you have any used SUVs, models that are two or three years old, with maybe 35,000 kilometers on them, or less."

"Oh! You don't want a used car" said the sales woman "Come, let me show you this year's models"

"I don't think we can afford this year's models" said Mrs. Bovaird "our budget is about $23,000."

"No problem" said the sales woman "we have new models starting at $25,000. That's within your price range."

"Can we look at your used models first?" asked Professor Bovaird.

The sales lady ignored Professor Bovaird's question. Soon she was standing beside a nice looking Jeep. "This is our latest model. It comes with automatic sun roof, central locking, air- conditioning and leather seats. This is priced at $32,000. But I could let you folks have it for $28,000".

"I think we need to go for a cup of coffee" said Mrs. Bovaird.

   *   *   *

Half an hour later, the Bovairds were standing outside a GM dealership, right across from the Chrysler dealership where they had just been.

A paunchy, middle-aged man in a black leather jacket ambled slowly out of the dealership. "Hi folks" he said "Do you want to buy a car or are you just browsing?"

"We're buying" said Professor Bovaird "We're wondering if you have any used models that are two or three years old, with maybe 35,000 kilometers on them, or less."

"Used models? Two or three years old? Yes, we have three or four of those. What's your budget?"

"We'd prefer not to spend more than $23,000" said Mrs. Bovaird

"Sure, we can do that. Let me show you a 2 year-old GMC Jimmy. It's got 32,000 kilometres on the clock. New, this was a $36,000 vehicle. We've got it listed at $21,999. But I might be able to give it to you for $21,000."

On the way to see the Jimmy, the Bovairds noticed a mid-sized 4-door Sedan. That's a nice looking little car." said Mrs. Bovaird.

"That's a Corsica" said the salesman. "It's six years old, and has 54,000 kilometers on it. We're only asking $12,000. It would make an inexpensive second car for a two car family. Would you like to take it for a spin?"

*   *   *

An hour later, after test driving both cars, the Bovairds were in the dealership's office.

"Would you give me $30,000 for both cars?" said the salesman.

They did.

TARGET MARKETS – IDENTIFYING THE CUSTOMER

There are about 7 billion people on the earth. No business, even the largest business in the world, can reasonably hope to sell to every one of them! When entering into a market, in other words, when attempting to locate, interest, and excite potential buyers, a business must recognise that the vast majority of people will have some reason NOT to buy a product.

Common sense tells us, for example, that illiterates are unlikely to buy books. Likewise, vegetarians don't buy meat. Pacifists don't buy weapons. Bald people don't need shampoo. These are trivial or obvious examples, of course. However, a more thoughtful consideration of target markets will suggest that the demand for almost any product will vary according to peoples' age, gender, ethnicity, socio-economic status or geographic location. Marketing managers therefore must not waste time or valuable resources trying to sell products to people who don't need a particular good or service, don't want it, can't afford it, or don't understand it. Rather the business should concentrate its efforts on identifying and communicating with people who are mostly likely to need and want what it offers.

A particular group of people who share a number of similarities and have similar needs and wants, and are most likely to buy a product is called a **target market**.

Target market: A group of similar people who have similar needs and wants, and are most likely to buy a product.

Target markets are groups of individuals that are separated by distinguishable and noticeable aspects. For example, Mr. Big-and-Tall sells to men who are taller and heavier than average.

IDENTIFYING TARGET MARKETS: SEGMENTATION

To help themselves identify potential customers, marketers begin by carving up the total population into groups or categories of people called segments. The members of a market segment share some common characteristics, habits or behaviours that are likely to give them common needs. This act of dividing up the market is known as **market segmentation**.

Market segmentation: Dividing a total population into groups or categories of people who share common characteristics, habits or behaviours which give them common needs.

Three of the most common means by which marketers segment a population are on the bases of: demographic characteristics, psychological traits, and geographic location.

DEMOGRAPHIC SEGMENTATION

Demographic segmentation involves identifying people based on some external characteristics that they share. Examples of some of the more obvious external characteristics are: age, gender, race and ethnicity. Although the term race and ethnicity are often used interchangeably, race refers primarily to physical and physiognomic characteristics, for example skin colour, hair colour, the shape of one's eyes, nose and lips. Ethnicity refers to characteristics of language and culture. Most Quebecers share the same race as most other Canadians, they look Caucasian. However, Quebecers' language, politics and culture make them ethnically different from Albertans.

Demographic segmentation: Identifying people based on some external characteristics that they share, for example age, gender, race or ethnicity.

Also included under the heading of demographics are the social and economic characteristics that distinguish groups of people. These include, for example, marital status, as well as income, education and other determinants of social class.

A market can be segmented using just one characteristic. For example, a product may be aimed at everyone aged 20 to 34. Alternatively, a market can be segmented using several characteristics, For example, a product may be aimed at university-educated, 20-34 year old females, who earn more than $40,000 per year.

A Selective List of Demographic Characteristics and Groups	
Age:	Under 5, 5–11; 12–19; 20–34; 35–49; 50–64; 65+
Education:	Less than high school; some high school; graduated high school; some college or university; college diploma or university degree; advanced degree
Family life cycle:	Single under 21; young married no children; married with young children; married with teenaged children, empty-nesters
Household size:	1, 2–3, 4–5, 6+
Income:	Under $20,000; $20,000–$49,999; $50,000-$89,999; $90,000 +
Race:	White, Black, First Nation, East Asian, South Asian,
Ethnicity:	Irish, Italian, Brazilian, Scottish, Jamaican
Religion:	Buddhist, Catholic, Hindu, Jewish, Muslim, and Protestant
Gender:	Male, Female
First Language:	English, French, Italian, Ukrainian, German

PSYCHOGRAPHIC SEGMENTATION

While demography refers to an individual's external characteristics, those that might be visibly apparent, psychography refers to the opposite: an individual's internal traits. Put simply, **psychographic segmentation** separates people according to what goes on in their minds, their hearts and in their guts.

A general list of psychographic traits would include people's attitudes, beliefs, values, and motivations. A specific list might include the following:

- Religious or unbelieving
- Extroverted or introverted
- Sentimental or unemotional
- Adventurous or cautious
- Proud or humble
- Disciplined or uninhibited
- Generous or uncharitable

Psychographic segmentation: Identifying people according to their internal traits, such as their attitudes, beliefs, values, and motivations.

While political parties and charities are not businesses, these types of not-for-profit organisations will make particular use of psychographic segmentation. They will address themselves to people who are for gay marriage or against it, "pro-life" or for "a woman's right to decide", consumerist or environmentalist, and so on.

For many years Petro Canada described itself as "Canada's gas station" and Molson sold its Canadian brand of beer using the slogan "I am Canadian". These businesses believed that the people in their target market were likely to be patriotic.

Apple's famous slogan "Think different" was meant to appeal to consumers who considered themselves to be innovative, adventuresome, and willing to try new things.

GEOGRAPHIC SEGMENTATION

Geographic segmentation involves distinguishing people according to where they live, from countries to neighbourhoods.

Often, people who live in different locations buy different products, for different reasons. It seems likely that people who live in mountainous British Columbia will purchase more ski equipment than people who live in Saskatchewan. Residents of Newfoundland and Nova Scotia are more likely to buy sailboats than the citizens of landlocked Alberta.

Geographic segmentation: Distinguishing people according to where they live.

Research consistently shows that Quebecers have different tastes, attitudes and behaviour from residents of the rest of Canada. Quebecers live more in the moment than other Canadians, and save less.[3] The same research showed that the simplicity of products and ease of use was more important to Quebecers than to other Canadians. 60% of Quebec Francophones consider themselves to be very brand loyal. Only 44.3% of Anglophones in the rest of Canada feel the same way.[4]

MARKET RESEARCH

Once a business has identified its target market, it then needs to discover its prospective customers' customer needs. What's the best way to do that? It should ask them. **Market research** is the study of what buyers need, and how best to meet those needs,

---

Market Research: Systematic study of what buyers need and how best to meet those needs

---

Market research can be performed at almost any point in a product's existence. Most commonly, however, it is undertaken when a new or altered product is being considered. Ultimately, its role is to increase

---

3 Headspace Says It Knows What Quebec Consumers Want" Caroline Fortin, Marketing Magazine, May 16, 2013
4 "Target take note: Quebec market tricky for outsiders" Susan Krashinsky, The Globe and Mail, March 4, 2013

the business' competitiveness by better understanding target customers. Marketing researchers use a variety of methods to obtain, interpret, and use information about customers.

SECONDARY AND PRIMARY MARKET RESEARCH

The quickest and easiest way to collect information on a subject is to refer to research or data collection that someone else has already done. The Canadian and US governments, as well as the governments of most wealthy countries, collect vast amounts of statistical, financial and operational data about every imaginable subject. They do this for reasons of tax planning, policy formation, and to understand the effectiveness of existing laws and regulations.

Much of the information in this book comes from sources such as Statistics Canada, Industry Canada and Transport Canada, and US sources like the Department of Commerce and the US Bureau of Labour Statistics.

Research that is collected from already published material is referred to as **secondary market research**. The adjective secondary refers to the fact that it is second-hand information, in other words, collected by someone else, at some other time for some other purpose.

Secondary Market Research: Collecting information from already published sources

---

These days of course most secondary research is done on-line. The digitisation of academic journals means that there is a great deal of high-quality research available at little or no cost. A business will typically begin researching its market or industry by establishing what information has already been collected.

Secondary market research is intended to inform business mangers by learning from what others have already learned. Secondary data will help the business to answer general questions such as:

- Is there a market for goods and services such as this, elsewhere?
- What did consumers buy last year?
- What were our rival's sales?

Secondary research does not answer the specific question:

- Will consumers buy this specific product?
- Will consumer pay this price?
- Will consumer buy it this year?

To answer that specific question, the business must conduct its own, primary, research. **Primary market research** is original research conducted or commissioned by the business itself. Primary research is done so that the business can obtain timely answers to its specific questions, for example:

- What features do you want?
- What price will you pay?
- What promotional media will reach you?
- Where do you want to get it?

Primary market research: Original research conducted or commissioned
by the business itself.

RESEARCH METHODS: OBSERVATION AND COMMUNICATION

The two basic types of methods used by market researchers are **observation** and **communication**

Probably the oldest form of research is to simply observe what is happening. Observation is the market research technique that involves viewing or otherwise monitoring consumers' behaviour.

Observation: A market research technique that involves viewing or otherwise monitoring
consumers' behaviour.

The advantages of observation as a research methodology are that it can be done easily and at very little cost. For example, a retail business can station an employee outside of the store and ask him to observe and record the following:

- The number of people who enter the store at various times of day
- The age of shoppers
- The gender of shoppers
- The mode of transport by which they arrived, i.e. by car, on foot or by public transportation
- The number of people who left with a purchase

This information can help the retailer to improve its customer service provision or shop amenities by, for example:

- Increasing the number of salespeople at the busiest time of the day
- Providing wheel chairs for older shoppers, or baby changing facilities for younger shopper
- Providing more men's or women's washrooms
- Expanding the car parking facilities, building a bus shelter outside of the store, or installing a direct line phone to a local taxi service
- Investigating why, once many shoppers were inside the store, they did not make a purchase

Observation as a research method also avoids the problem of **interviewer bias**. Interviewer bias is the name given to the idea that many people will feel that an interviewer is pleading, flattering, or intimidating them, in order to influence their response.

Interviewer Bias: The risk that an interviewer will plead with, flatter or intimidate a respondent thus influencing the response to a question.

In earlier times, when a store owner notices that customers were buying red children's wagons, not green ones, the owner reordered more red wagons, the manufacturer's records showed high sales of red wagons, and the marketing department concluded that customers wanted red wagons. But observation is now much more sophisticated. For example, electronic scanners in supermarkets allow marketers to "observe" consumers' preferences rapidly and with tremendous accuracy.

In addition, some businesses are adopting video equipment to observe the behaviour of the consumers who visit their stores. This is known as video mining. Retailers can use the video files to compare the percentage of shoppers that buy as opposed to the percentage that merely browse. Retailers can do this by comparing the number of people seen entering the store against the number of purchases made.

When you watch someone, you can see what they do. However, without asking them, you don't know why they do it. The deficiency of observation as a research method is that you can't probe the subject's motivation. You can't ask "Why...?" or "What if...?" Observation also has limited use if the proposed good or service offering is brand new.

The other way to obtain information from prospective customers is to **communicate** with them. This can be done by writing to them, or by talking to them. Sometimes marketers need to ask questions of prospective customers. The way to get answers is to ask them.

Because no firm can afford to survey everyone, marketers must be careful to get a representative group of respondents when they do surveys. They must also construct the survey questions so that they get honest answers that address the specific issue being researched. Surveys can be expensive to carry out and may vary widely in their accuracy. In the past, surveys have been mailed to individuals for their completion, but online surveys are now gaining in popularity because the company gets immediate results, and also because the process is a less intrusive way of gathering data.

Communication: Asking consumers directly about their needs and preferences.

When a business' market researchers communicate with potential customers it gives the business an opportunity to give samples, it also allows researchers to follow-up on closed-ended responses by asking the important question "Why?"

One obvious potential disadvantage of communicating directly with potential customers is interviewer bias. As previously noted, interviewer bias is the tendency for respondents to feel pressured into giving a response that they believe an interviewer wants to hear. Friends, family and colleagues might give false encouragement to enthusiastic, optimistic entrepreneurs who believe in their product.

RESEARCH METHODOLOGY - SAMPLING

Obviously, it would be prohibitively time-consuming, expensive and difficult for a business to talk to every member of the target market. Research that attempts to collect data from every member of a population is known as a **census**.

Census: Research that involves collecting data from every member of a population

---

Researchers who try to collect data from everyone in a population will obtain an accurate picture of that population. However, it would be a difficult, expensive and time consuming project to attempt. Most research therefore involves collecting data from selected members of a population. This is known as a **sample**. To give you a simple example, if there are 120 people enrolled in your third year psychology course, that is a population. On a particular Wednesday afternoon, your Professor takes a poll of the 84 students who are attending that lecture. That is a sample.

Sample: Research that involves collecting data from a selected number of the members of a larger population

---

A sample is not as accurate as a census. However, a sample that involves a large enough percentage of the target population may be good enough to give researchers a pretty good idea as to what the entire population is thinking. Research by sampling is a lot easier to perform.

When market researchers are selecting a sample to survey, they must be careful to ensure it is a **random sample**. That is, each person in the population must have an equal chance of being selected.

Random sample: A sample taken from a larger population where each person has an equal chance of being selected.

Your psychology professor might ask the 84 people attending a Wednesday afternoon class "I was thinking of scheduling the mid-term during one of the Wednesday afternoon lectures. Does that suit everyone?" Obviously those who are in class for the survey find it relatively easy or convenient to attend class on Wednesday afternoons. Equally obviously, those who have to work on Wednesday afternoons, or baby-sit on Wednesdays, but faithfully watch all of the lectures on line, are not being consulted.

If market researchers working for a sportswear manufacturer go to a swimming pool and ask "Do you buy swimwear?" they will come away with a biased answer. Perhaps 100% of the population will say "Yes". Market researchers must therefore strive to conduct their research using a random sample.

QUANTITATIVE AND QUALITATIVE RESEARCH DATA

Ideally, market research should collect two kinds of data: **quantitative** and **qualitative**.

Quantitative research is designed to collect facts and numbers, and data which can be analysed statistically. Quantitative research is intended to yield information like the following:

- 60% of respondents....
- $7.95 average price...
- 3 times per year...
- 5 out of 7...

Quantitative data: Data that consists of facts and numbers which can be analysed statistically.

On the other hand, qualitative research is intended to collect opinions, ideas and impressions. These ideas and impressions may be subjective, but they are intended to give researchers insight into consumers thought processes, and their emotional responses to a product's features or benefits. Through the collection of quantitative data, researchers hope to answer the question: "Why?"

Qualitative data: Data that consists of opinions, ideas and impressions

---

Qualitative data is particularly important for the business that is segmenting its target market on psychographic grounds. In this case, it is particularly important for marketing managers to understand the target consumers' thoughts, beliefs, motivations and emotions.

MARKET RESEARCH TECHNIQUES

There are many ways in which market researchers can collect data about actual and potential customers. Below, is a selective sample of some of the most commonly used techniques, including several with which you may have personal experience.

To collect quantitative data, researchers can choose between various types of **survey**. A survey is an investigation about the characteristics of a given population by means of collecting data from a sample of that population.

Survey: An investigation about the characteristics of a given population by means of collecting data from a sample of that population.

With most surveys, the questionnaires are structured – the questions are asked in the same order, the same way, and only the pre-defined answer choices can be given.

Postal Surveys

Despite the wide array of technologies that allow businesses to communicate electronically with anyone, anywhere, a surprisingly large number of businesses continue to use good, old-fashioned snail mail.

Putting a survey into an envelope and sending it by post has the advantage that it is relatively low cost, and can be sent anywhere.

Using the post avoids any risk of interviewer bias. Respondent can't feel bullied, pleaded with or flattered by someone writing a survey weeks before, in a different city or province.

The disadvantages of mail surveys are the poor response rate, the inability to ask follow-up questions, and often, a slow turnaround time

Telephone Surveys

Telephone surveys are familiar to most of us. A bored-sounding caller, reading from a script, disturbs us just as we are sitting down for dinner.

Telephone surveys can reach respondents practically anywhere at very little cost. The caller can ask a few screening questions, for example "Are you over the age of 25?" and "Do you own or drive a car?" These screening questions helps ensure that the respondent is qualified to answer. If the respondent stays on the line long enough, he or she may be willing to answer supplementary questions that probe deeper, and provide the researcher with more insight..

The disadvantage of phoning people at home is that each call takes an equivalent amount of the caller's time and is therefore labour intensive. Most people decline to participate, or get bored and hang up. Thus, telephone surveys yield a very low response rate, Finally, most people, even if they are willing to participate, have little time to think about the questions being asked, so their answers to the interviewer's questions may be superficial or the first thing that comes to mind.

Man in the Street Surveys

Man in the street surveys have the advantage of researchers interacting with respondents where they work or shop, as opposed to disturbing them at home, at night, when the products or services that the business proposes to offer is the last thing on their mind.

In addition, researchers can quickly and easily do a visual demographic classification. If the intended target market for the business' product is 18 – 30 year-old females, they need only stop and attempt to survey people who appear to fall into that demographic.

In addition, man in the street surveys allow researchers to combine data collection by communication with data collection by observation. Researchers can quickly and obviously see whether consumers arrived at a destination on foot, by car, or by public transport. They can note the time of day without having to ask. They can observe whether consumers are shopping in groups, as a family, or on their own.

Personal interaction allows potential customers in a target market the chance to see, feel, or sample the product. Finally, if the research is conducted in shopping malls, airports, train or bus stations the respondents may have time on their hands, and be willing to engage in a detailed conversation.

The disadvantages of this means of data collection include the obvious potential for interviewer bias, and the labour intensity. In addition, unless the business has the means to send interviewers across the country or across the province, the sample is likely to be limited in its geographic scope.

Internet Survey

This increasingly common research methodology attaches a survey as a link to an e-mail. Internet surveys are low cost to design, and free to send. There are many on-line survey design businesses. A short list of the better known such businesses includes Survey Monkey, SurveyGizmo, SurveyShare, and Google Forms.

These businesses have designed the back-end algorithms for analysing data and presenting it in spreadsheet or tabular form. If the survey is relatively short and looking to collect a limited amount of quantitative data, internet surveys are easy for respondents to complete. Ease of completion, of course, increases response rates. The use of the internet as the means of communication means businesses doing the research can also attach links to brochures, images, and the business' website.

Like any research method designed primarily to collect quantitative data, internet surveys don't allow the researcher to ask follow-on questions or to probe. Once upon a time, surveys conducted over the internet would have delivered a fairly skewed demographic sample: Only geeks and nerds would reply. Today, of course, nearly everyone is computer literate and on-line. However, there is still the risk that only technophiles will respond to internet surveys.

IN-DEPTH INTERVIEWS AND FOCUS GROUPS

To collect qualitative data, researchers will use interviews or focus groups. Unlike surveys, interviews and focus group are often, by intention, unstructured. The purpose of an interview is to learn by listening.

In-Depth Interviews

An in-depth interview is a method of collecting qualitative data, in which the researcher sits down for an extended, open-ended discussion with the respondent. The interviewer needs to take notes, or record the conversation. In-depth interviews are most typically done face-to-face, but can be done via telephone.

In-depth interview: A method of collecting qualitative data, in which the researcher sits down for an extended, open-ended discussion with the respondent.

In-depth interviews are different from surveys in that they are less structured. The interviewer will normally have a general plan of inquiry, however he or she has no specific set of questions that must be asked with particular words and in a particular order. Ideally, the respondent does most of the talking while the interviewer listens, takes notes, and guides the conversation in the direction it needs to go.

This research method is most appropriate when the business is offering sophisticated or complex products, with many features. The respondent must be carefully chosen: an industry expert say, or the purchasing manager of a large target customer. The interview format allows the researcher to probe, by asking "If we were to include this feature, what would you think…" or "Why don't you like this aspect of the service…?. For this reason, in-depth interviews tend to yield a lot of qualitative data.

In-depth interviews are labour intensive, because one interviewer will devote several hours to planning scheduling and conducting a single interview. This means of data collection also runs the risk of interviewer bias.

Focus Groups

A focus group typically consists of a small group (normally in the range of 6 to10) people who do not know each other. The participants are selected because they are members of the target market, or they are considered by the researchers to be well informed about the product, the business or the industry.

Focus groups are led by a moderator. That is, someone working for the research team plays the role of group discussion leader, and creates an environment that encourages everyone to speak, offer their opinions, and points of view. The participants are not usually told who is sponsoring the research. The focus group is intended to get people talking, to generate information about how groups of people think or feel about a topic, an issue or a product, and to provide insight into why people feel as they do.

As noted above, the purpose of a focus group is to learn by listening. Focus group discussions are normally tape recorded and sometimes filmed. At their most sophisticated, focus groups are occasionally observed from behind one way glass. The researchers then go through the transcripts of the discussion carefully, looking for common themes or points of view generated by the group.

Focus group: A small group of people brought together to discuss selected issues in depth.

Focus groups are particularly useful for generating qualitative data about how the participants might react to a product or service offering, or what they hope to obtain from a product. A focus group may help the researchers to discover new or unexpected points of view. This is particularly useful in helping the business to improve the planning or design of new goods or services.

However, focus groups require a good deal of lead time to find a find and select an appropriate sample of willing participants, transport them to the interview site and, often, to provide them with cash or a small gift to compensate them for their time. To obtain the opinions of just 6 to 10 people will require several days of preparation by the moderator, and the labour of a film or sound recording crew.

THE MARKETING MIX

The purpose of all of the market research is to give the business' managers the information they need to create a plan to meet the target market's needs and wants. Marketing, therefore, begins when a company identifies a consumer need and develops a product to meet it.

In 1960, US marketing theorist Jerome McCarthy suggested that the many decisions and variables that go into a marketing plan could be boiled down to four essential points that have come, famously, to be known as "The Four Ps". McCarthy encapsulated the marketing function into four essential elements that the business needed to perfect. The 4Ps of marketing, collectively known as the **marketing mix** are:

- Product,
- Price
- Promotion
- Place

Marketing Mix: The specific combination of product features and benefits, price, promotional and distribution methods used to a sell a product to a target market.

Understand these four essential elements and the business is well placed to satisfy its target customers' needs and wants. The next chapters take a much closer look at product, price, promotion and place.

SELF-ASSESSMENT QUESTIONS FOR REVIEW

1. Make a list of 4 items that one your parents might buy from time to time, that are of no interest to you. What is difference between you, and your parent's circumstances or characteristics that makes them need or want a product that you wouldn't consider buying?

2. Make a list of 4 items that one your friends or classmates might buy from time to time, that are of no interest to you. What is difference between you, and your friend's circumstances or characteristics that makes them need or want a product that you wouldn't consider buying?

3. Suppose you wanted to establish a small business, teaching, coaching or tutoring others people in something that you are good at or enjoy doing. What market research would you do, to see if there was a market for your services? What 3 key pieces of information would top your list of research questions?

4. In the chapter, you learned about interviewer bias. Has a teacher or a professor ever asked you a question about a course, and you felt pressured to give them the "correct" answer? Did you tell a white lie, so as not to cause offence or embarrassment?

DEFINED TERMS

- Census
- Communication
- Customer Focus
- Demographic segmentation
- Focus group
- Geographic segmentation
- In-depth interview
- Interviewer bias
- Marketing

- Marketing concept
- Market Research
- Market segmentation
- Marketing Mix
- Observation
- Product Focus
- Primary Research
- Psychographic segmentation

- Random sample
- Qualitative data
- Quantitative data
- Random Sample
- Sample
- Secondary Research
- Survey
- Target market

CHAPTER

3

PRODUCTS: THE THINGS CONSUMERS NEED AND WANT

CHAPTER OVERVIEW

In the previous chapter you were introduced to some of the basic principles that underpin marketing. Without customers, a business can make no sales, generate no revenue, and make no profit. In the latter half of the 20th century, as living standards and incomes for most consumers rose, it was no longer enough for a business merely to produce products. Businesses began to embrace the idea that customers increasingly knew what they wanted, and could increasingly afford to be demanding.

Today's businesses recognise that they must carefully target customers, and must engage with those customers. Businesses need to observe their prospective customers, survey them, and interview them. By doing so, customer oriented businesses can precisely understand customers' needs, and constantly improve and refine the products that are on offer.

The purpose of this targeting and research is to allow the business to create the business' marketing mix of:

- Product
- Price
- Promotion
- Place

The first of the "4 Ps" is Product. A business needs to have the right product before it can shape and tailor the other elements of the mix. This chapter looks at the characteristics and attributes of products, and introduces you to some key theories that help us to better understand the development and differentiation of products.

LEARNING OUTCOMES

As a result of reading this chapter, you will have learned:

- A product is anything that is capable of satisfying customer needs and wants.

- Customers view products as a combination of functions, features, and benefits upon which they place a value.

- Not all of the functions, features and benefits within the value package are tangible. For some products, little or nothing is tangible, and much of the benefit is intended rather than actual.

- Products, like people, have finite lives. The product life cycle theory suggests that every product goes through four stages from birth to death. The stages of the life cycle are introduction, growth, maturity, and decline

- Recognising the existence of the life cycle, businesses work to extend the lives of existing products and also work to develop new products to replace those in decline.

- A key reason why many businesses do not survive is that they fail to extend or replace products that are surpassed by new tastes, new attitudes, or new technologies.

- An important means of sustaining a product's revenue and profitability is branding, an activity designed to increase a product's visibility and encourage customer loyalty.

PRODUCTS: FILLING NEEDS AND SATISFYING WANTS

Every day, every single person on earth needs or wants something. Young or old, rich or poor, urban or rural, the earth's people need food, clothes, shelter and diversion. The range of human needs and wants are infinite, and an attempt to list the goods and services bought and sold could fill this textbook and a dozen others. There is no limit to people's hopes and dreams, tastes, and fancies.

A **product** is therefore whatever a purchaser hopes to get, or believes they are getting whenever they purchase a good or service off of another individual or organisation.

Product: A good or service that fills a buyer's need or satisfies a want.

In filling a need or satisfying a want, most products deliver three elements:

- Functions
- Features
- Benefits

A product's **function** is what it is intended to do. A car is intended to provide a means of transport. A hotel is intended to provide accommodation for the night. A pair of shoes is intended to provide protection for one's feet

---

Function: What a product is intended to do.

Function describes a good or service at its most minimal. Describing all cars as means of transport places no distinction between a car that has air conditioning, heated leather seats, and a sun roof and a car that does not. Describing all hotels as places of accommodation places no distinction between a city centre hotel, with two restaurants, a coffee shop, a wine bar, gym, swimming pool and 24-hour concierge and a hotel that offers none of these features. A **feature** is an additional attribute or offering which contributes to the product. Features are intended to improve the usefulness or experience of a good or service.

Features: Additional attributes or offerings which contributes improved usefulness or experience to a product.

A feature might be the use of better quality or more durable materials in the construction of a good. Another feature could be to make the product bigger, more powerful, or longer lasting. Features give a good greater versatility. A car without air-conditioning can get you to your destination. A car with air conditioning will make the journey more comfortable on a hot summer day.

Features of services might include greater convenience of location, longer hours, better décor, or more carefully trained staff. Service features make the experience of the service easier, faster, or more pleasant. An economy class airline ticket can transport you from Toronto to Rome. A first class ticket will offer you tastier food, a larger choice of films to divert you, a wider seat, and more leg room.

A business chooses to build features into its products so as to attract different segments of a target population. The same automobile manufacturer can offer the same model of car with few if any features, or it can offer the car "loaded up". Airlines transport three segments or "classes" of passenger: economy, business and first class.

Products provide much more than just their obvious function and visible features. The acquisition of a car gives its purchaser greater mobility, and independence. A car allows people greater flexibility in the scheduling of their day. Having a car allows its owner to offer a lift to a friend, and provides the owner the pleasure of being generous, and a sense of status. In buying a product, consumers are also buying an image and a reputation. These are a product's **benefits**.

Benefits: The advantages that are derived from purchasing a product.

Benefits are very difficult to measure, since perceptions of "benefit" often occur inside someone's head. The sum of thoughts, feelings, comfort, convenience, and sense of achievement that a purchaser obtains from buying a product are unique to each purchaser's circumstance.

Elizabeth Arden, the founder of the cosmetics business which bears her name, understood that she was selling much more than jars of cream. She gave voice to this idea of marketing benefits when once, famously, she said "I don't sell cosmetics…I sell hope".

Together the three elements of function plus features plus benefits give a product its **value**.

Product Value = Function + Feature + Benefits

Value is the regard with which a product is held by potential buyers, most commonly expressed as its financial worth, i.e. what people are willing to pay.

Value: The regard with which a product is held by potential buyers,
expressed as its financial worth.

Together, as a bundle, the tangible and intangible functions, features and benefits created by a business are known as the **value package.**

Value package: The bundle of tangible and intangible functions, features and
benefits that a business offers to buyers of a product.

The purpose of the marketing function in any business is to understand what makes potential customers place value on a product, and to augment that value by adding the extra something: improved functionality, more features, or the intangible benefits that come from pride of ownership and status.

UNDERSTANDING DIFFERENT PRODUCTS AND THEIR CONSUMERS

One way to gain a better understanding of products, and how and why people buy them, is to recognise that not all products attract the same number, or kind of buyers. Another way of better understanding products is to recognise that some products engage us more than others. That is, there are certain goods and services which we will buy only after much research, much comparison shopping, and after the expenditure of both time and emotional investment.

Let us begin by differentiating products according to expected buyers. We can readily distinguish between two groups of purchasers: buyers of **consumer products** and buyers of **industrial products**.

Consumer products are purchased for consumption by the end user, for personal use. Consumer products are the end result of production and manufacturing and are what the average consumers sees in a store. Clothing, books, magazines and food are all examples of consumer products.

Consumer Products: Products purchased by the end user, for personal use.

Boxes of breakfast cereal are purchased by tens of millions of consumers. They are purchased with the intention of being eaten by the purchaser, or the purchaser's family. Because of this, boxes of breakfast cereal must be colourfully and attractively packaged in order to attract the shopper's attention. The cereal manufacturer must work closely with grocery store chains to ensure that the product is prominently displayed on store shelves. They must be advertised so that millions of consumers, and their children, are aware of the name. Although consumers aren't entirely uninterested or uninformed about how the final product was made, or the parts and ingredients that go into the product, they are unlikely to be experts. Therefore, rather than any detailed technical expertise, consumer choices are more likely based on taste, habit, or the ability to recall a product name.

Industrial products are the parts, ingredients materials, and supplies that are bought by one business from another in the process of making consumer goods.

Industrial Products: The parts, ingredients materials, and supplies that are bought by one business from another in the process of making consumer products.

A manufacturer of breakfast cereals, Kellogg's or General Foods for example, must buy tons of cardboard with which to make cereal boxes. They must buy tons of waxed paper into which to pour the cereal before inserting the paper bag into the box. They must buy ink, and glue for the making and printing of the box. They must buy machinery that cuts and folds cardboard, and other machinery that can pack 500 boxes of cereal onto a wooden pallet and wrap it securely for transportation.

Industrial products aren't purchased by the end consumer, they contribute as inputs to the making of the consumer product. Because industrial products are purchased for different reasons than consumer products, the way that they are marketed also differs.

Industrial goods are sold to a much smaller number of buyers. While there are millions of breakfast cereal eaters, there is a much smaller number of breakfast cereal manufacturers, perhaps a few dozen. Industrial products like ingredients and supplies don't need to be colourfully packaged. Buyers are likely to be more interested in the supplier's ability to meet technical specifications and delivery timetables.

When designing the functions, features and benefits into a product, the business must bear in mind whether the purchaser is likely to be another business or the end user.

Just as we can distinguish between consumer products and industrial products, the former can be further divided into three categories that reflect buyers' degree of engagement when making the purchase.

Convenience products, also known as fast moving consumer goods (FMCGs) are inexpensive goods and services which are purchased relatively frequently and with little expenditure of time and effort. Convenience products are consumed quickly and regularly. Examples of convenience products or FMCGs include newspapers, disposable razors, deodorants, a cup of coffee on the way to work, and a chocolate bar on the way home.

Convenience products: Inexpensive consumer goods or services which are purchased frequently and with little expenditure of time and effort.

The key to marketing convenience products is that they must be inexpensive, easy to find and perform their function well.

Shopping products are more expensive and purchased less frequently than convenience products. Shopping products also tend to have more features than convenience goods. As a result, consumers are willing to spend more time and effort evaluating alternatives in terms of style, performance, colour, price, after sales service, and other criteria. Examples of shopping goods are cars and laptops. Examples of services, include life insurance or a contractor to remodel your kitchen.

Shopping products: Products that are moderately expensive, and purchased infrequently causing consumers to spend time comparing features, benefits and price.

The key to selling shopping products is that they must offer good value in terms of the features that they offer.

Specialty products are goods and services for which a customer will spend a good deal of both time and effort to find exactly what they want. Specialty products will justify the time and effort because they are goods and services to which consumers will attach a great deal of importance. An example of a specialty good is an engagemnet ring. A specialty service will be the catering for a wedding reception. Consumers expect to buy these goods or services just once, and will long remember the features, benefits and attributes that come with the purchase.

Specialty products: Products to which consumers will attach a great deal of importance and for which they will spend a good deal of both time and effort to find exactly what they want.

The key to selling specialty products is to stress the benefits that will come from using a particular supplier.

The reason that businesses need to be aware of the difference between industrial and consumer products, or convenience versus shopping versus specialty products, is that the nature of the buyer, and their degree of knowledge, interest and commitment, will affect all aspects of the business' marketing mix. Depending on the nature of the good or the service, industrial buyers may be more or less price sensitive. Depending on the good or the service, advertising and other forms of promotion will be more or less important. Depending on the good or the service, delivery times and schedules may be more or less important to the buyer.

PRODUCT OBSOLESCENCE

People are naturally curious, and inventive. Engineers are constantly inventing new products, and marketers are constantly designing new services to satisfy customer needs and wants. The theory of the product life cycle, which is discussed two pages from now, suggests that products, technologies, and industries have finite lives. The **diffusion of innovations theory** seeks to explain how, over time, an idea or product gains momentum and spreads through a population. The theory was developed by Everett Rogers, an American professor of communication studies, in his book *Diffusion of Innovations* published in 1962.

Diffusion of innovations theory: Explains how an idea or product gains momentum and spreads through a population.

Rogers argued, and subsequence research has shown, that people who are the first to try a new product are different from people who try the new product much later.

Rogers identified five categories of people, based on their willingness to try something new. He argued that a business needs different strategies used to appeal to each category of consumer.

Innovators – This small percentage of the population are people who actively want to be the first to try something new. These people are willing to take risks. Little, if anything, needs to be done to appeal to this group.

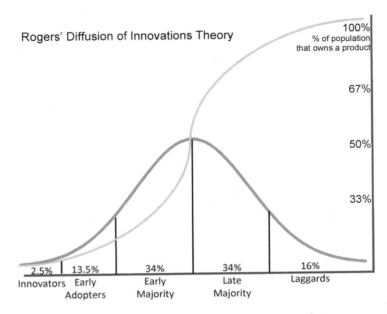

Rogers' Diffusion of Innovations Theory

Early Adopters - These people are aware of the need to change and are comfortable adopting new ideas. Strategies to appeal to this population include how-to manuals and information sheets on implementation. They do not need much information to convince them to change.

Early Majority - This large segment of the population aren't taste leaders, but they are willing do adopt new ideas, or try new products, before the average person. That said, they typically need to see evidence that an innovation works before adopting it. Strategies to appeal to this population include success stories and evidence of the innovation's effectiveness.

Late Majority - These people are skeptical of change, and will try something new only after it has been tried by the majority. Strategies to appeal to this segment of the population include information on how many other people have tried the innovation and have used it successfully.

Laggards - These people are bound by tradition and conservative in their tastes. They are skeptical of change and are the hardest group to bring on board. Often they will purchase a new product or new technology after the previous versions have become obsolete.

THE PRODUCT LIFE CYCLE

Building on the diffusion of innovations theory, marketers must also understand that products, technologies, and industries — like people - have finite lives. New products or new technologies get launched into the world and are unknown. Sales are low, profits are weak, then they begin to grow, subsequently mature and ultimately decline. This passage is known as the **product life cycle.**

Product life cycle: The introduction, growth, maturity, decline and ultimate demise of products and industries, as technologies and tastes change.

The product life cycle can be visualised on a two dimensional diagram. The two dimensions are growth and time

The purpose of the model is to help us to understand, as time passes what happens to a new product or new industry's growth.

There are many ways to measure the growth of a person. As we "grow up" we gain height. We gain weight. We gain strength. We gain cognitive ability. Most people, as they near the end of their lives, begin to lose these things.

Equally, the growth of a business can be measured in many ways. If you were running a business that tutored math, there are several measures that you could use to show whether the business was growing. Three obvious measure are:

- number of students being taught
- $ value of revenue
- $ value of profits

To that list, you could add "number of hours taught per week".

A manufacturing business can measure its growth through the number of units produced in any given period, or the number of units sold. A chain of shops or restaurants could measure its growth through the addition of new of locations. Any business with employees could claim to be growing if it hired more people.

Likewise, "time" can be measured in several ways: weeks, months, years, or decades. Some products have very short lives. Movies go from theatres, to DVDs, to late night movies on television in about one year. Nothing is more out-of-date than last year's fashions. Technology businesses launch next generation smartphones at roughly 12 month intervals.

Life Span of Successive Apple iPhones

Launched	Model	Discontinued	Lifespan
June 2007	iPhone (8GB)	July 2008	12 months
July 2008	iPhone 3G (16 GB)	June 2009	12 months
July 2008	iPhone 3G (8GB)	June 2010	24 months
June 2009	iPhone 3GS	June 2010	12 months
June 2010	iPhone 4	October 2011	16 months
October 2011	iPhone 4S	September 2013	23 months
September 2012	iPhone 5	September 2013	12 months
September 2013	iPhone 5C	September 2014	12 months
September 2013	iPhone 5S	current	
March 2014	iPhone 5C 8GB	current	
September 2014	iPhone 6	current	
September 2014	iPhone Plus	current	

Conversely, some products have very long lives. Coffee, bread, and pencils are purchased in the same way today as they were 150 or 200 years ago. Whatever the length of a product's life, whether short or long, the birth, growth, maturity and death of virtually every product, technology or industry that you can think of conforms to the same shape, as shown below.

The Product Life Cycle

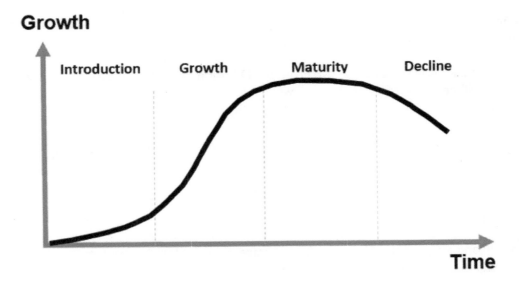

INTRODUCTION STAGE

The first stage of the product life cycle is called the **Introduction** or Start-Up stage.

During the introduction stage, the product, or the technology that created it, is new and little known. Because potential purchasers in the market will be small. The products themselves are likely to be expensive and difficult for most consumers to find.

Introduction: The stage of the product life cycle when the product, or the technology that created it, is new and little known.

Examples of products or industries at the introductory stage of their life cycle would include desk-top personal computers in the 1980s, digital photography in the 1990s, e-commerce retailing and smart phones at the turn of the century.

In the current decade, products which entered the introduction stage of their cycle are mass produced and affordable plug-in electric cars. These were discussed merely as theoretical concepts prior to 2010.

Characteristics of the introduction stage of the life cycle are that the vast majority of the population will be unfamiliar with the product concept. Product price will be high initially, due to the absence of economies of scale. Because the product is expensive, it is unlikely to be found in many stores.

At this stage of the life cycle only a small number of producers will understand, or have access to the technology to produce the product.

At this stage of the product's life cycle, marketing's primary responsibility will be to educate customers, build channels of distribution, and perfect the product design

Because the product is new, sales are low. From the Diffusion of Innovation categories, the small number of customers will be innovators. Innovators will be willing to pay a high price, but because they are few in number the business is unlikely to be making a profit.

An example of a product, which is new, little known, expensive, and hard to find might be virtual reality headsets.

GROWTH

This is the second stage of the life cycle. At this stage, demand for the product, particularly from first-time users, will expand rapidly as many new consumers enter the market.

Growth: The second stage of the life cycle, when demand for a product expands rapidly as many new consumers enter the market.

In time, the product or technology becomes better known, more popular, and more available. As consumers become more familiar with the product or technology, they will become more knowledgeable, and more demanding. This might describe smart phones over the past several years, and electric cars in the decade to come.

During the growth phase of the life cycle, production costs should begin to fall as producers begin to enjoy economies of scale. Lower production costs means producers can lower their selling price. This brings growth products into the financial range of more consumers, increasing demand and sales even more.

The pull of growing demand leads to rapid development of distribution channels. In other words, to satisfy the growing number of consumers, producers build more warehouses, ship to more stores, and take a variety of measures to make the product more easily and more widely available. The more stores that stock a product, the more familiar it becomes to the average consumer. The easier it is to purchase, the more will be purchased, and so on.

Despite falling prices, dramatically increased sales means higher profit for the producer. The profile of the typical consumer goes from innovators to early adopters and the early majority.

MATURITY

Explosive growth cannot be maintained forever. The rate of growth for any product or service will begin to slow. It is inevitable that, once the late majority has purchased the product, the industry's sales will peak.

Maturity: The third stage in the product life cycle, when sales peak.

When a market has reached maturity it is also said to have experienced **saturation**. A sponge reaches saturation when it can absorb no more water. Similarly, once every family owns three televisions and two cars, it is difficult for TV and car makers to sell more. The only purchases that consumers make are replacements. If there are new customers, they will be the small percentage of the population known as laggards.

Saturation: When a market can absorb no more products

It is human nature that we don't always see the end of a good thing coming. We expect to stay young forever. Businesses, no matter how clever their management, become accustomed to fast growing revenues and large profits. Managers look at the past trends, and continue to add productive capacity, extrapolating prior demand. However, actual sales will soon begin to lag behind capacity.

Businesses with excess capacity will be forced to lower prices to maintain demand, and to keep the additional capacity working. With prices falling and demand staying flat, profits will stabilise. This will drive the less efficient firms from market. Businesses will focus on reducing their costs, there will be little new product development, and the number of suppliers in the market will drop. The surviving low cost producers will attempt to capitalise on the loyalty of existing customers.

Businesses at this stage of the cycle tend to be oligopolies. Examples of Canadian industries in their maturity stage are banking and brewing.

PRODUCT EXTENSION

What does a business do when everyone in the target market knows about the product, and everyone in the target market already buys the product? One tactic is to launch a new variation or an update. This is known as life cycle extension.

Over the past fifty years, sales of TV sets have been continuously revitalised by a constant series of innovations: the introduction of colour, increased portability, miniaturization, and stereo capability. In fact, businesses can extend product life through a number of creative means. Coca-Cola's many flavours are prime examples of product extensions.

By re-packaging, re-launching or slightly updating a well-known product, marketers try to keep products in the maturity stage as long as they can.

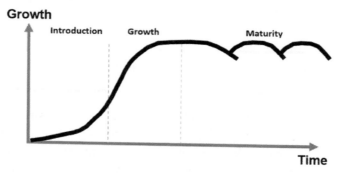

DECLINE

The final stage of the product life cycle is called decline. At this stage, growth becomes negative. Industry revenues fall. Profits fall. The number of customers falls, as the product or technology is old fashioned.

The cause of industry decline is often the introduction of newer and better technologies that can perform the same function better, faster, or more cheaply. Other reasons for industry decline might be changing social attitudes, or changing demographics

Within the past 75 years, we can observe the full product life cycle being played out by half a dozen different technologies for playing music. A partial list of the dominant technologies includes the following products:

Era	Technology
1930s, 40s and 50s	78 rpm records
1950s, 60s, mid 70s	33 rpm records
Early 1970s to mid-1970s	8 track cassettes
Mid-1970s to mid-1990s	16 track cassettes
Mid-1980s to mid-2000	CDs
2000 onwards	downloads?

When products or technologies go into decline, **barriers to exit** become important. Previously you learned about barriers to entry, characteristics which make a business or industry difficult, time-consuming or expensive to enter. At the end of the product life cycle, businesses are at risk of failing if they do not have an exit strategy and an industry is difficult, time consuming, or expensive for a business to leave.

Barriers to exit: Characteristics which make an industry difficult, time-consuming or expensive for a business to leave.

Recent and well known examples of businesses that failed because technology passed them by are Blockbuster Videos and Kodak.

RESEARCH & DEVELOPMENT

A business can't extend an existing product's life forever. Eventually, changing tastes or new technologies will render a product obsolete. To safeguard their future, most businesses devote some effort looking for innovations and ideas which will lead to the next generation of products. The name given to these efforts is **research and development** or "**R&D**".

Research and Development (R&D): Looking for innovations and ideas which will lead to the next generation of products.

In the U.S., a typical industrial business spends about 3.5% of revenues on research and development.[1] Rapidly changing or technology intensive business like pharmaceuticals, software and semiconductor makers often spend four or five times that much. A 2014 article in Fortune Magazine[2] identified the world's leading R&D spenders. Here's what they found:

---

1 European Commission, http://iri.jrc.ec.europa.eu/scoreboard13.html, "The 2013 EU Industrial R&D Investment Scoreboard"
2 "The 10 biggest R&D spenders worldwide", Fortune Magazine, Michael Casey & Robert Hackett, November 17, 2014

Businesses with the Largest R&D Expenditure

Rank	Business	Industry	R&D Spend ($ billions)	R&D as % of revenue
1	Volkswagen	Automobiles	$13.5	5.2%
2	Samsung	Electronics	$13.4	6.4%
3	Intel	Microchips	$10.6	20.1%
4	Microsoft	Software	$10.4	13.4%
5	Roche	Pharmaceuticals	$10	19%

It is perhaps not surprising that Volkswagen and Samsung lead the list. In the developed world, at least, automobiles and consumer electronics are mature products. Much of Volkswagen's research is going toward developing new technologies to replace the carbon burning internal combustion engine. Volkswagen hopes to make breakthroughs with electric cars and self-drive technology. Much of Samsung's R&D efforts are going toward the development of smart TV monitors and smart TV features.[3]

In Canada[4] the leading research and development spenders are:

Business	Industry	R & D Spend ($ billions)
Bombardier Inc.	Airplane manufacturer	$2.2
BlackBerry Limited	Smart phones	$1.3
Magna International	Car parts and assembly	$0.6

BRANDING

Developing products and product features is only part of a marketer's job. Marketers must also design and package products so that consumers recognise them. Three important tools for this task are branding, packaging, and labelling.

Branding is the use of logos, colours or symbols to identify a product and differentiate it in the mind of target consumers. Branding is intended to help consumers, particularly those who have tried and liked a product, to remember its name.

Branding: The use of logos, colours or symbols to identify a product and differentiate it in the mind of target consumers.

Businesses want customers to develop **brand loyalty**.

---

3 Ibid.

4 Canada's Top 100 Corporate R&D Spenders, Research Infosource Inc., Toronto, 3 November 2014

Brand loyalty: Customers' recognition of, preference for, and insistence on buying a product with a certain brand name.

Creating brand loyalty is a three stage process. First, marketing managers must work to get customers to recognise the product's name, logo, colours or design, so that when they need a particular good or service, they will look for any of these. This is known as **brand awareness**. If you are hungry and you need a quick, inexpensive meal, you might look for some golden arches, or perhaps for the face of a Kentucky colonel, with a goatee and string tie.

Brand awareness: A consumer being able to recognise a product's name, logo, colours or design, so that when they need a particular good or service, they will look for any of these.

Next, marketers must attempt to get consumers to develop a favourable attitude toward the product, and to choose it over competitive offerings. This is known as **brand preference**.

Brand preference: Consumers develops a favourable attitude toward a product, and chooses it over competitive offerings

---

Finally, **brand insistence** involves persuading consumers to demand a product, and make them willing to go out of their way to get it.

Brand insistence: Consumers demand a product, and are willing to go out of their way to get it.

Widely known and admired brands are valuable because of their power to attract customers. Brand loyalty can have a major impact on a business' profits. Academics, researchers, and accountants go to great lengths to calculate the additional revenue and profit that flows to a well-known business because of the success of its branding efforts.

Consulting firms, advertising agencies, and business magazines all perform annual rankings of the world's most popular, or valuable brands. While their precise methodologies may differ, there is consistency across all of these rankings as to which brands appear at the top. One such recent survey, published in Forbes Magazine, identified the world's most valuable brands as follows:

World's Most Popular Brands - 2014

Business / Brand	Value of the Brand	1-year % change
Apple	$145	17%
Microsoft	$69	10%
Google	$66	16%
Coca-Cola	$56	0%
IBM	$50	4%
McDonalds	$40	-1%

Source: Forbes Magazine, The World's Most Valuable Brands 2014

PROTECTING THE PRODUCT

Businesses undertake research and development in order to create new products that better satisfy customer needs. The effort can be time consuming and expensive. Businesses therefore want to ensure that their inventions and creations are protected.

The name given to the ideas, inventions, and other creations that belong to a business is **intellectual property.**

Intellectual property: Ideas, inventions, and other creations that belong to a business.

The three most common forms of intellectual property are:

- Trademarks
- Patents
- Copyrights

A business does not want another business using its name and confusing consumers into buying a substitute product. Businesses apply to the Canadian government and receive a **trademark**, the exclusive legal right to use a brand name.

Trademark: Exclusive right to the use of a name

Trademarks are granted for 15 years and may be renewed for further periods of 15 years. Businesses with well-known names like Xerox, Coke, Jello, and Scotch Tape work hard to enforce their trademarks.

A **patent** gives its owner the exclusive right to the use of an invention or technological innovation, for a period of 20 years. To obtain a patent the inventor must go through a fairly lengthy, and sometimes expensive process of providing drawings, blueprints, and workings models to the Canadian Patent Office. The individual or business applying to obtain the patent must prove that they were the first to design and develop a working invention. For this reason, the process can take up to three years. A Canadian patent confers exclusive right to use the invention only in Canada. If the business wants to prevent competitors in the US from using its invention, it must go through the same long and costly process to obtain a patent from the US Patent Office.

If an individual or a business believes that it has come up with a truly ground-breaking innovation, it has four options as to how best to exploit its inventiveness:

- Do not patent the invention. Instead, keep the innovation or process secret for as long as possible. This gives the inventor a monopoly until a rival can duplicate the discovery. Coke has never patented its formula.

- Obtaining a patent, and keep the right to be the only organisation legally entitled to make the product or use the process to which the patent applies. This gives the owner of the patent a 20 year monopoly.

- Obtain the patent, then sell the right to use the invention to others. This gives the owner of the patent an immediate stream of revenue from the discovery.

- Announce the product to the world, with great flourish. Before doing so, the business should ensure that it has the productive capacity, and the sales and delivery capacity to produce and distribute the product widely. If the innovation is truly valuable and catches on, the inventing organisation will become the market leader when the product becomes the industry standard.

Patent: Exclusive right to the use of an invention or technological innovation.

A **copyright** gives ownership rights to the creators of books, articles, designs, illustrations, photos, films, music, and computer programs. Copyrights apply to the tangible expressions of an idea.

Copyright: Exclusive right to the use of words, designs, illustrations, photos, films, and music that are the tangible expression of an idea.

In Canada, the copyright process is relatively simple. The individual who creates the "copy" need only assert his or her ownership of the intellectual property, and assert their exclusive right to grant anyone else the right to copy it. Thus, we have the term "copyright".

The creator typically affixes the copyright symbol © and the date, and claims ownership or authorship to their work. Copyrights are given to the creators for the duration of their life, and then to their heirs for another 50 years.

PACKAGING & LABELLING

Almost all products, with the exception of some industrial products, need some form of **packaging** so they can be transported to the market. For consumer products packaging helps to make the product attractive, displays the brand, and identifies the product's features. Packaging is the marketer's last chance to say "buy me" to the consumer.

Packaging: The physical container in which a product is sold.

PRODUCT: CONCLUSION

At the outset of this chapter, you read that "a business needs to have the right product before it can shape and tailor the other elements of the mix". Products are intended to fill a buyer's need to satisfy a want. They do so by offering functions, features and benefits.

However, marketers must recognise that people's tastes and aspirations change. New technologies, and new innovations come along, offering superior functionality, more features, and enhanced benefits. The first job of marketers is to create products that people want to buy. In the coming chapters, we will look at the other elements of the marketing mix.

SELF-ASSESSMENT QUESTIONS FOR REVIEW

1. Identify a product that you purchased recently without spending any time or effort comparison shopping. Did you take it to the cashier without even bothering to look at the price? Why was that?

2. Identify a product that you have purchased recently where you shopped around, compared features, and took advice. If you had a choice between two or three competing products, what were the key determinants behind your final choice?

3. Have you ever purchased a good or a service after you had shopped around extensively, and taken a great deal of time negotiating and specifying the features? What was the good or service and what features or intended benefits made you so choosy?

4. Is there a product that you have purchased recently without doing much comparison shopping because you have purchased that brand previously, and you know you like it? Are you consciously brand loyal?

5. Identify a product that you were excited to get, or was new to you 5 years ago, that you now consider to be obsolete or common.

DEFINED TERMS

- Barriers to Exit
- Benefits
- Brand insistence
- Brand loyalty
- Brand preference
- Brand awareness
- Branding
- Convenience products
- Copyright
- Decline
- Features
- Function
- Growth stage
- Intellectual Property
- Introduction
- Luxury goods
- Maturity
- Packaging
- Patent
- Product life cycle
- Saturation
- Shopping products
- Specialty products
- Trademark
- Value
- Value package

CHAPTER

4

PRICING STRATEGIES &
BREAK-EVEN ANALYSIS

CHAPTER OVERVIEW

Previously, you learned the importance of businesses embracing the marketing concept. A business must dedicate itself to satisfying customer needs and wants. If it does so, those customers will respond by purchasing products. Purchases generate revenue, and revenue generates profit. Without customers, a business can make no profit.

However, satisfying customers is only one half of the reason that a business exists. A business must also make a profit in order to survive. A business cannot afford to sell a product at, literally, any price.

The second of the 4Ps in the marketing mix is "price". Marketing managers must determine a price that will not only attract and satisfy customers, but will generate a profit for the business' owners.

There is no precise formula to help managers decide a product's price. The decision as to what price to charge, the fine balance between satisfying customers and generating profits, is a matter of judgement. In this chapter, you will be introduced to some of the key concepts that assist and guide managers in the art of setting a price.

LEARNING OUTCOMES

As a result of reading this chapter you will learn:

- There is no precise formula by which a business can calculate the "correct" price for a product.

- Since a business must make a profit, managers set prices by first understanding the business' costs.

- Most prices are set by adding a "markup" to a product's variable cost.

- The size of the markup is a matter of choice, and competitive positioning.

- Skimming involves a decision to add a large mark-up to costs, setting the price of a product high. By using the skimming strategy, a business hopes to make a profit from a small number of high margin sales.

- Penetration involves a decision to add a small mark-up to costs, setting the price of a product low. By using the penetration strategy, the business hopes to make its profit from a large number of small margin sales.

- Break even analysis helps managers understand the volume of sales the business must attain in order to make a profit, at any given price.

- People aren't always rational, so businesses use a variety of stratagems to induce consumers to make a purchase.

WHAT DETERMINES A PRODUCT'S PRICE?

A business exists for two purposes. On the one hand, a business must satisfy customer needs. On the other, it must make a profit. When a business' managers set a price for each of its products, they must try to balance these two competing interests. Because of this, there is no precise formula to tell managers exactly what the price of each product should be. Setting a price necessarily involves tradeoffs between the business' two fundamental purposes.

Broadly speaking, two things determine the business' ability to set its price:

- The degree of competition
- The business' costs

In addition, marketers should recognise that consumers aren't necessarily rational, and that there are a variety of tricks and tactics which a business can use to induce consumers to make purchases.

HOW COMPETITION AFFECTS PRICE

Previously you learned that there are four degrees of competition. The degree of competition within a market determines whether a business has any flexibility when it comes to setting a price for its products.

Pricing in a Perfectly Competitive Market

A perfectly competitive market is characterised by a large number of small sellers, offering more-or-less the same product. In a perfectly competitive market, buyers enjoy a good deal of choice. In a market with this degree of competition, a buyer has the right to walk away from any seller and look for a better deal. When a business is offering a relatively inexpensive product that is similar in most respects to those offered by competitors, it has limited ability to dictate the product's price. Individual businesses must therefore charge what everyone else charges. This is called the **market price**. At any particular time, the market price is the prevailing price to which buyers and sellers agree.

Market Price: At any particular time, the prevailing price to which
buyers and sellers agree.

Perfectly Competitive Goods

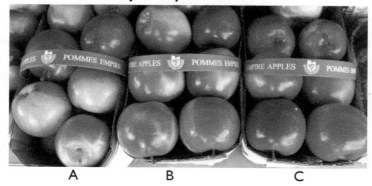

A   B   C

With little or no ability to influence a product's price, businesses that choose to offer perfectly competitive products can increase profits only by keeping a keen eye on their costs.

Pricing in an Oligopoly Market

In an oligopoly, the small number of competitors watch each other closely. If one supplier in an oligopoly raises or lowers its price, these changes are swiftly matched by the others. Oligopoly businesses tend to compete, therefore, on the basis of differentiation. That is, they try to convince potential customers that their product is different or better in some way. As you learned in the last chapter, one way of doing this is by branding. Oligopoly businesses want consumers to associate their product with colours, designs and logos that become symbols for the product's reliability. Of course, this requires that each business spend money on branding, advertising, and other forms of promotion.

Oligopoly Goods are Differentiated and Branded

Would you pay more for one of these baskets?

Pricing in a Monopolistically Competitive Market

In a monopolistically competitive market most of the many sellers are small. Most sellers do not have a big share of the market or a large number of shops. However, a monopolistically competitive market also has a small number of large sellers. These few large sellers can differentiate their products. They will try to differentiate themselves, so they can charge more than most. Many hundreds of businesses produce golf shorts, but only Nike shirts can display the familiar "swoosh" symbol. Because it is a larger, and better known business than most of its rivals, Nike can charge more than most.

Pricing in a Monopoly Market

Finally, there are some products or services for which there is only one available seller. This is known as a monopoly. As a consumer, when faced with a monopoly, we must sometimes make a difficult decision: We must buy the product or service on the seller's terms, or decide to do without.

Monopoly - No Choice

TO SET A PRICE A BUSINESS MUST UNDERSTAND ITS COSTS

Remember, every time a buyer purchases a product, the seller must give up something in return. So, before determining a product's price, managers must understand what the product has cost. A business has two types of costs. These are:

- The cost that goes directly into making the product.
- The cost of running the organisation that makes the product.

Now, let's consider these two types of costs in more detail. The cost that goes directly into making the product is known by a variety of names, one of which is the **cost of sales**. When a business is selling a tangible good the ingredients, parts and materials that go into making that good are often visible and obvious. So, these costs are even more frequently known as the cost of goods sold.

Cost of Sales / Cost of Goods Sold: The cost of the ingredients, parts, and materials that go directly into making a product.

As an example of the cost of goods sold, consider the cost of making a commonly purchased, inexpensive consumer good, such as a small vegetarian pizza. Every pizza costs money to make, mostly in the cost of the ingredients, as follows:

Pizza crust	$ 1.00
Cheese	$ 1.00
Tomatoes	$ 0.50
Peppers	$ 0.50
Olives	$ 0.40
Mushrooms	$ 0.40
Cardboard box	$ 0.20
=	$ 4.00

If the pizzeria makes and sells one pizza, the cost of goods sold is $4.

In addition to being called the cost of goods sold, the ingredients and parts that go directly into making a product are also known as the **variable costs**. They are given this name because they increase, or vary, in direct proportion to every additional unit of product that is made. If the pizzeria makes 2 pizzas, the cost of goods sold will be $8. If it makes 3 pizzas, the cost of goods sold will be $12.

Variable cost: Costs that increase in direct proportion to every additional unit of product that is made.

The pizzeria's cost of goods sold, or variable costs, can be drawn on a graph, as a straight line rising at a rate of $4 per pizza. A business that makes and sells 10,000 pizzas will spend $40,000 to make them.

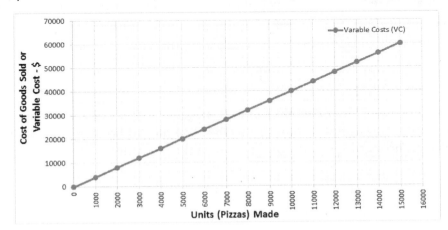

The first constraint for managers setting a product's price is they must charge at least the variable cost. If the business were to sell its pizzas at any price less than $4.00 revenues would be less than the cost of the ingredients. The business would be guaranteed to make a loss. Knowing a product's variable cost, at very least, gives managers a floor for setting a price. The least that the business can charge, and hope to make a profit is $4.01

OPERATING COST OR FIXED COST

The second type of cost that businesses incur is the cost of running the organisation. In addition to the cost of making pizzas, a pizzeria will spend money on a variety of administrative and managerial activities. A take-away pizza business will have to rent a storefront in an area frequented by lots of pedestrians. To run the pizza oven it will need to pay for electricity. The pizzeria's Manager must be paid a salary, and will spend much of his time ordering supplies, hiring and training employees, paying bills, and keeping records. The manager may decide to print a few thousand flyers announcing the pizzeria's "Grand Opening", and distribute them to all the homes and apartments within a 2 kilometer radius.

These costs might be the following:

Rent	$12,000
Electric Utilities	$ 3,000
Manager's Salary	$12,000
Advertising (flyers)	$ 3,000
Part-time employees	$10,000
Total	$40,000

The cost of operating an organisation, as opposed to the cost of making a product, is known as the **operating cost** or the **operating expense**.

Operating Cost / Operating Expense: The cost of operating a business organisation.

Many of a business' operating costs are determined long before the business opens its doors and sells its first product. In our simple example, the pizzeria negotiated a fixed rent on its premises many months before it had its grand opening. Similarly, the Manager was hired weeks before the first pizza was made. For this reason, operating costs are also referred to as **fixed costs**. They are "fixed" in the sense that the owner of the business must pay these whether the business is wildly successful or falls flat. In addition, the operating costs are "fixed" in that they will not increase as the number of pizzas increases.

Fixed Costs: The costs of operating the business, which do not change as the volume of production increases.

The fixed costs will not change whether the business makes ten pizzas or ten thousand. If drawn on a graph, the business' fixed costs would appear as a straight line running horizontally at $40,000. This number should not change, no matter how many pizzas the business makes.

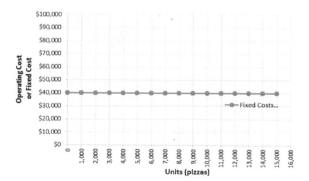

Together, the two types of costs – the variable cost of making pizzas plus the fixed cost of running the organisation – tell the business' managers what their total costs will be, for any level of production.

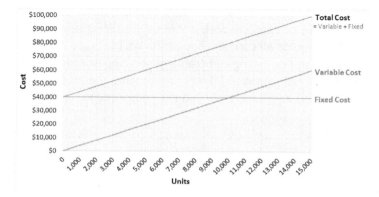

It is only by understanding these costs that managers can now begin to make informed judgements about setting the price of the product. The pizzeria's manager knows that a pizza costs $4.00 to make. He must set the price, at very least, at $4.01.

MARKUP AND MARGIN

The key question for managers is, how much more than $4.00 is the appropriate price? The amount that a business adds, beyond its variable cost, in order to establish its price is called the **markup**.

Markup: The amount that a business adds to the variable cost of making a product, in order to set its selling price.

Variable Cost + Markup = Selling Price

The markup ensures that, with every unit that it sells, the business will generate funds toward the fixed cost of running the organisation. The markup expressed as a percentage of the selling price is known as the **contribution margin**.

Contribution Margin % = $\dfrac{\text{Markup}}{\text{Selling Price}}$

Contribution Margin: The markup expressed as the percentage of the selling price

---

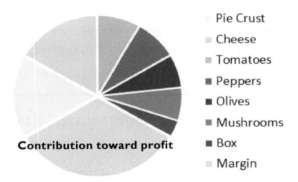

Contribution toward profit

- Pie Crust
- Cheese
- Tomatoes
- Peppers
- Olives
- Mushrooms
- Box
- Margin

For example, if the business did sell its pizza for $4.01, the markup of just $0.01 is equivalent to just 0.25% of the selling price. The remaining 99.75% of the revenue is needed to cover the variable costs. The margin for profit of just 0.25% leaves the business very little room for spoilage or waste in the kitchen and demands hard to attain portion control. One extra slice of tomato, or half an olive too many on a pizza could turn the chance to make a small profit into a loss.

The business' managers must now make a judgement. If they choose a large markup the high price may deter many potential customers. If they choose a small markup, they might attract a large number of customers, but the low price will not generate much contribution towards the business' fixed costs.

The size of the markup that a business adds is a matter of choice. Some large, successful and well-known businesses choose to add a **large** mark-up to their costs. They choose to charge the highest price that customers will pay. Examples of well-known businesses that have taken this strategy are Rolls Royce cars and Rolex watches.

This pricing strategy is popularly known as **skimming**. The term skimming is an analogy. When raw milk comes from a cow the richer, higher fat content milk floats to the top of the milk pail. This is normally too rich for most pallets, and full of butter fat. The richer, fatter content is separated from the lower fat content, by "skimming" the top layer. It can then turned into cream and butter. Skimming as a pricing strategy involves selling to the richer segments of society, and taking fat profits from each sale.

Skimming: The strategy of charging a high price, expecting a
small volume of sales, but making a large contribution from each.

The advantage of skimming is, even though the target market is small, this segment is not price sensitive. **Price sensitivity** means the degree to which consumers' willingness to buy is affected by price.

Price sensitivity: The degree to which the price of a product affects
consumers' willingness to buy.

The disadvantage of the skimming strategy is that the target market for expensive products is small. The number of people who can afford to buy a Rolls Royce or a Rolex is limited.

Other businesses choose to do precisely the opposite. They add a small markup to their costs, and charge a low price. This pricing strategy is known as **penetration**. Penetration pricing brings products within the reach of the largest possible number of consumers.

Penetration Pricing: The strategy of charging a low price, and relying on a large volume of
sales, making a small contribution from each.

Examples of successful, well known businesses whose strategy is to maximise sales by setting low prices are: Casio watches, Bic pens and Walmart.

The disadvantage of the penetration pricing strategy is that the low markup means the business **must** sell a very large number of units in order to make a profit.

Both the high markup strategy ("skimming") and the low mark-up strategy ("penetration") are successfully used by well-managed, profitable businesses. A business can therefore choose its pricing strategy.

Of course, many consumers won't buy the most expensive product whatever its merits. Many won't buy the cheapest whatever its value. Therefore, the most likely pricing policy for the majority of businesses is "somewhere in the middle" influenced by any number of factors.

If the pizza business chooses a markup of $2.00, the selling price will be $4.00 + $2.00 = $6.00. The markup represents $2 / $6, or 33.3%, of the revenue. The business will make a substantial contribution toward profit from each pizza that it sells. The pizzeria would not need to change its price or dramatically alter the recipe for its vegetarian pizzas if the price of onions, peppers or mushrooms should rise.

BREAK EVEN ANALYSIS

The penetration strategy is based on the premise that a low price will attract a large market. A low price does not exclude people with limited incomes or those who are price sensitive. Taking the price penetration strategy to its limit, the business could choose to sell its product for $4.01 per pizza.

The skimming strategy is based on the opposite logic. Although a high price will deter many consumers the business' managers believe that there are enough wealthy, or price insensitive people who aren't put off by an expensive product. The business could choose to sell a small vegetarian pizza for $50.00.

Most businesses of course, won't take a pizza that costs $4.00 and sell it for $4.01. There's too little profit to be made. At the other extreme, pizza can't be considered a luxury product, so it's unlikely that any business will try to persuade customer to pay $50. Guided partly by the price charged by competitors, and party by what the market research suggests customers are willing to pay, most businesses will pick a price somewhere in the middle of these two extremes.

To understand the implications of choosing a slightly higher or lower price, businesses perform **break even analysis**. Break even analysis is a tool that helps managers to understand the relationship between their costs, their chosen price, and the number of units that the business must sell in order to make a profit.

Break even analysis: A tool that help managers understand the relationship between their costs, their chosen price, and the number of units that the business must sell in order to make a profit.

The **break even quantity** is the minimum number of units a business must sell in order to recover all costs and begin to make a profit. In colloquial terms, it has "broken even". Any sales beyond this quantity increases the business' overall profit.

Break Even Quantity: The minimum number of units a business must sell in order to recover all costs and begin to make a profit.

There is a simple formula, which allows managers to calculate how many units they must sell, in order to make a profit at any given price. The break-even point can be calculated, as follows:

$$\text{Break Even Quantity} = \frac{\text{Fixed Costs}}{\text{Selling Price minus Variable Cost}} = \frac{FC}{SP - VC}$$

Using Break Even Analysis to Evaluate Pricing Strategies

Consider the following example. It shows how break even analysis helps a business evaluate three possible pricing strategies:

Penetration Strategy: The Sales Manager argues for setting a low price of $5.00. "Look" he says "once people see what a good deal they are getting, they'll be knocking down our doors! The 'Super Value Everyday Low Price Pizza Deal' will have a huge market, and deliver a high volume of sales."

Skimming Strategy: The Finance Manage argues for setting a high price. "Ladies and gentlemen" he says to his colleagues "we don't want to chase desperately after down-market customers. Our aim is to make a profit for our shareholders. I think that we should charge $14.00 for the 'Limited-Edition Designer Luxury Gourmet Pizza'."

Somewhere in the Middle: The Marketing Manager says "We have to satisfy both customers **and** shareholders. My market research suggests that most people won't buy the most expensive product **or** the cheapest. Setting our price in the middle of the range will attract the "average" consumer, and we won't have to make and sell as many pizzas as we would if our strategy was penetration. Let's consider a price of $8 for the "Family Friendly Pizza."

Scenario No. 1 Penetration Strategy: $5 for the "Super Value Everyday Low Price Pizza Deal"

$$\text{Break-Even Quantity} = \frac{\text{Fixed Costs}}{\text{Selling Price - Variable Cost}} = \frac{\$40,000}{\$5 - \$4} = \frac{\$40,000}{\$1} = 40,000$$

Scenario No. 2 Skimming Strategy: $14 for the "Limited-Edition Designer Luxury Gourmet Pizza"

$$\text{Break-Even Quantity} = \frac{\text{Fixed Costs}}{\text{Selling Price - Variable Cost}} = \frac{\$40,000}{\$14 - \$4} = \frac{\$40,000}{\$10} = 4,000$$

Scenario No. 3: $8 for the "Family Friendly Pizza"

$$\text{Break-Even Quantity} = \frac{\text{Fixed Costs}}{\text{Selling Price - Variable Cost}} = \frac{\$40,000}{\$8 - \$4} = \frac{\$40,000}{\$4} = 10,000$$

Using the penetration strategy, the pizzeria would have to sell 40,000 pizzas to make a profit. That's a lot of pizzas! Using the skimming strategy, the pizzeria would have to sell only 4,000 pizzas. But, are there 4,000 customers who would be willing to pay $14 for a small, vegetarian pizza? With the price set at $8, the business must sell 10,000 pizzas before it starts to make a profit. This third scenario is shown on the graph below.

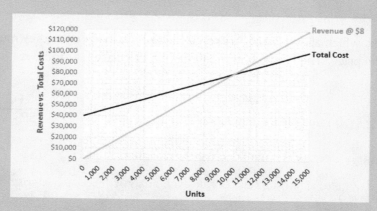

The pizzeria's manager can now evaluate this pricing strategy against his knowledge of how many people are in the market, and against the capacity of the restaurant's kitchen. He can ask himself "Can we realistically make 10,000 pizzas a year?" and "Can we realistically sell 10,000 pizzas a year?"

Break-even analysis allows managers to consider the trade-off between high and low selling price, and the effect it will have on the business break-even quantity.

CONSUMERS AREN'T NECESSARILY RATIONAL

Marketers should remember that consumers, being human, make purchasing decisions which are guided by their emotions as well as the rational parts of their brain. There are, therefore, a number of tactics which the business can use to excite consumers into making purchases. These tactics are collectively referred to as **psychological pricing**.

Psychological Pricing: A range of tactics designed to appeal to consumers' emotions.

The $5 'Super Value Everyday Low Price Pizza Deal' is a strategy that will appeal to those looking for a value. The $14.00 the 'Limited-Edition Designer Luxury Gourmet Pizza' appeals to consumers who purchase products for reasons of status, or perceived quality.

Among the range of psychological pricing tactics are the following.

Odd-Even Pricing

The odd-even pricing strategy involves setting the price of a products just below the whole dollar amount.

Odd-Even Pricing: A strategy of setting the price of a product just below the whole dollar amount.

For example, instead of charging $5 for a product a business might charge $4.95. Buyers tend to associate the price with the first digit that they see, imagining the price to be closer to $4 than to $5.

$500
~~Now just~~
$499.95

The same applies to larger dollar amounts. For example, a home might be priced at $399,999 instead of $400,000. A seller will do this because many buyers will establish price limits in their minds, for example "under $400,000". A house selling for $399,999 satisfies that criterion and thus expands the size of the market.

A 1997 study in the Marketing Bulletin showed that 60% of prices end in the number 9 and another 30% of prices end in the number 5. Just 7% of prices end in the number 0. This leaves just 3% for the other seven digits.

Bundle Pricing

Bundle pricing involves packaging several products together and offering the combined package at a single price that is less than the sum of the parts. Two words that are commonly associated with this pricing strategy are "combo" and "package".

Bundle Pricing: Packaging several products together and offering the combined package at a single price that is less than the sum of the parts.

Bundle pricing is frequently used by fast food companies, and at movie theatres. You have probably experienced going to a movie theatre and intending to buy a large bag of popcorn. The regular price of popcorn is $5.95.

The young woman behind the confectionary counter says, "Would you like a combo package of a large popcorn and a medium drink for just $6.95?"

You glance quickly at the menu on the wall behind her, to see that a large popcorn costs $5.95 and a medium drink costs $2.95. Without doing the precise math, you quickly calculate that you will get the drink for less than half of its regular price. Your emotional response is that you are getting a deal. So you agree, and pay $6.95 for the "combo package".

It's only after you settle into your seat that you think to yourself "Hey, wait a minute, I've paid a dollar more than I was intending, for a drink that I didn't originally want!"

Bundle pricing allows the business to increase revenues by increasing the sales volumes of low margin products.

SELF-ASSESSMENT QUESTIONS FOR REVIEW

1. In the chapter, the example was given of bundle pricing being used at movie theatres. Have you ever purchased a "combo package" and then thought to yourself "Hey, wait a minute, I've paid a dollar more than I was intending, for a drink that I didn't originally want!"

2. The next time you go to a book store, take the time at look at the number of books that are priced at $24.95, $34.95 and so on. How much did you pay for this textbook?

3. Some businesses set their pricing above the market price because of consumers' commonly held perception that higher price means more features or more benefits. When you shop for medium-priced "shopping products" do you associate higher price with higher quality?

4. Some businesses set their price below the market price because of consumers' common help perception that lower price offers better value. Do you always look for the lowest price product?

5. Businesses often offer price reductions — discounts and sales – to interest and excite potential customers. If you see s sign in a store window that reads "SALE!" do you normally go into the store, looking for bargains?

DEFINED TERMS

- Break Even Analysis
- Break Even Point
- Bundle Pricing
- Fixed Costs
- Margin
- Market Price
- Markup
- Odd-Even Pricing
- Penetration Pricing
- Price Sensitivity
- Price Skimming
- Psychological Pricing
- Total Costs
- Variable Costs

CHAPTER 5

PROMOTION & PLACE: MAKING PRODUCTS
KNOWN, EASY TO FIND AND EASY TO GET

CHAPTER OVERVIEW

While many people enjoy wandering through a village market when on vacation, few of us have the time, or the inclination, to do so in our daily lives. Generally, busy consumers in need of goods or services want to know what products are available and they want to know where those products can be found.

The marketing activity that informs consumers about the products that are available is called promotion. Promotion is intended to help consumers become knowledgeable about products. It is also intended to interest them, excite them, and to induce them to buy. This chapter therefore introduces the aims and means of promotion.

Once people make a decision to purchase a product, they have to be able to get their hands on it. Many consumers won't buy what they can't see or sample. They can't see or sample a product if it's hard to find, or hard to get. This chapter concludes by looking at the fourth "P" in the marketing mix, which is distribution or "place".

LEARNING OUTCOMES

As a result of reading this chapter you will learn:

- The marketing activity known as promotion is intended to inform, educate, excite, and persuade potential customers to purchase a product.

- There are four main means of promotion: advertising, personal selling, sales promotion and publicity.

- Each of the four methods of promotion has advantages and benefits and each has shortcomings. Businesses generally use of all four, a combination known as the promotional mix.

- Consumers go through a structured, five stage process when searching for products: they become aware of a need, they gather information, they evaluate alternatives, then they make a purchase and finally they reflect back and validate their decision. Businesses use all four promotional methods because each addresses some part of the customer search, decision making, and acquisition process.

- Once a consumer decides to purchase a product, the business needs to get that product into the consumers' hands or home. This important marketing activity is called distribution.

- The various paths that a product can take from producer to consumer are called the channels. Businesses can choose between a variety of channels to get their products to the end user.

- The ease with which a product can be found, and its relative availability, is called distribution intensity. Businesses can choose between several strategies to make products more or less easy to find.

PROMOTION

Imagine that you are on holiday, somewhere in the developing world. You are wandering through a village market. A rug seller, perceiving you to be a "wealthy" tourist comes running out from his stall. "Sir! Sir! Look at my beautiful carpets! Are you on holiday? Look at the beautiful work! I can sell it to you very cheap!"

"I don't need a carpet."

"Sir! Sir! This is a beautiful carpet. Look at the fine silk thread. I give it to you. Just 1,000 dinars!"

You laugh, and continue to walk.

Two weeks later, you are sitting in your living room at home. You are watching TV. A major multinational corporation breaks into the baseball game you are watching.

"Sir! Sir! Buy my beautiful truck. It has four wheel drive. It has room for five passengers. It has just won the Canadian Automotive Writers' 'Truck of the Year' award!"

You think to yourself "I don't need a truck"

"Sir. My friend! My beautiful truck gets the best gas mileage of any truck in its class. I will give you a truck for just $43,000!"

A business cannot sell a product if the people in the target market don't know about it. Businesses therefore use a variety of techniques to inform, educate and excite potential customers about itself and its products. The name given to these activities is **promotion**. The ultimate purpose of promotion is to induce people to buy.

Promotion: Any technique used to inform, educate and excite potential customers about a business and its products, and to induce them to buy.

Promotion seeks to accomplish four things with potential customers:

- make them aware of products
- make them knowledgeable about products
- persuade them to like products
- persuade them to purchase products

THE BUYER DECISION PROCESS

Before we consider the various methods of promotion, you should understand the process that buyers go through before, and after, making a purchase. Marketers have long understood that buyers go through a structured five stage decision making process. The five stages are:

- Problem or need recognition
- Information search
- Evaluation of alternatives
- Purchase decision
- Post-purchase evaluation

It isn't necessarily the case that all consumers systematically go through every stage in this process. If you feel a sudden urge to buy a convenience product like a chocolate bar, you probably won't spend much time on the information search and evaluation of alternatives stages. You won't think to yourself: "Marcie likes Reece's Pieces, but Rico always buys Mars Bars." or "My Mom says dark chocolate keeps her awake, but milk chocolate doesn't." If you buy an inexpensive convenience product you will probably go straight to the purchase decision.

Likewise, having satisfied your craving for chocolate, you'll probably not spend much time doing a post-purchase evaluation. You won't think "I enjoyed that Kit-Kat. But, I remember, that when I bought a Crunchie bar two weeks ago, I really, really enjoyed it."

Nevertheless, this five stage framework is a useful way to understand how, in general, most consumers decide what to buy. As you learned previously, shopping products and specialty products are distinguished by the time and effort that goes into making the decision as to which product to buy. Marketers need to understand the **buyer decision process.**

The Buyer Decision Process: A five stage process that most consumers go through before and after buying a good or service.

The Five Stage Buyer Decision Process

Problem or Need Recognition

Information Search

Evaluation of Alternatives

Purchase Decision

Post-Purchase Evaluation

Problem or Need Recognition

The first step in the buying process is need recognition. To begin, consumers become aware of some situation in their life that needs solving or satisfying. For example, our body tells us that we are hungry. Alternatively, a need can be suggested by an external stimulus. For example, an advertisement suggests that our lives will be more fulfilled if we buy a particular make of truck, or we will become more socially popular if we wear a particular brand of clothing.

Our need can be satisfied through the purchase of a good or a service that is available. At this stage, marketers must make sure that buyers are aware of their products. As another simple example of need recognition, suppose your three year old phone stops functioning. The business that you purchased it from no longer supports the technology. So, you tell yourself that you need a new phone.

Information Search

Having recognised a need, consumers then search for information as to what goods or services may provide a solution. At this stage, the objective of promotion is inform consumers about available products. Continuing the previous example, as you search to replace your phone, you will probably ask family of friends what brand of phone they use. You might do an internet search, using the words "Blackberry", "iPhone 7" or "Android".

Evaluation of Alternatives

At this stage, consumers evaluate the different products that are on offer, on the basis of each product's function, features, and benefits. This stage of the process is heavily influenced by one's attitude to the provider. If you have had a bad experience with a particular bank, airline or cellphone service provider, you may find yourself reluctant to buy their product, regardless of the features they offer. The goal of promotion is to demonstrate product quality and performance in comparison with competitors' products.

Purchase Decision

This is the fourth stage of the process, when the purchase takes place. If the consumer has spent some time in the information search and evaluation of alternatives stages, they will be fairly committed to a particular product. The goal of promotion is to make the purchase convenient and to give consumers an incentive to buy.

For example, you have decided to buy a particular brand of phone and purchase the time from a particular phone service provider. This decision will be reinforced when you learn that the phone service provider you have chosen is offering a special promotion for a limited time, one that gives you 500 extra long-distance minutes for no extra cost. The promotion offer expires at the end of the month. So, you had better act quickly to take advantage!

Post-Purchase Evaluation

This stage is critical if the business wants to retain customers for future repeat business. After making a purchase buyers will compare what they have received against their expectations. A buyer will ask himself "Did I make the right decision?" or "Was that a good choice?". The answer to these questions will greatly affect the decision process for a similar purchase in the future. At this stage, the business' promotional objective is to create positive post-purchase impression. Customers need to be thanked, and praised for the wisdom they have shown. If customers are satisfied after making a purchase they will develop brand loyalty. For future purchases, the information search and evaluation of alternative stages may be shortened or skipped altogether.

THE PROMOTIONAL MIX

Traditionally there are four types of promotional methods. These are:

- Advertising
- Personal Selling
- Sales Promotion
- Publicity & Public Relations

In deciding how to spend its promotional budget, a business must match each of these methods with the five stages in the buyer decision process:

Promotional mix: The combination of advertising, personal selling, sales promotions, publicity and public relations - that a business uses.

Stage of the Consumer Buying Process	Most Effective Promotional Tool
Need recognition	Advertising
Information seeking	Personal selling
Search for and evaluate alternatives	Sales promotion, Personal selling, Advertising;
Purchase decision	Personal selling, Sales promotion
Post-purchase evaluation	Personal selling, Advertising, Publicity

A recent US survey of 200 large public corporations found that these businesses spend roughly 10% of their revenues on promotion.[1] In the following several pages, you will learn the features of each of the various ways that are used, to help the business to successfully complete a sale.

---

[1] Gartner U.S. Digital Marketing Spending Report 2013

ADVERTISING

Advertising is the promotional method with which most people are the most familiar. It is the promotional method with which we come into contact more often than the others. It is intended to be.

Advertising is paid, non-personal communication. An advertiser buys or rents time or space and uses that time or space to raise awareness about the business and its products.

Advertising: Paid, non-personal communication used to raise awareness about the business and its products.

Most of us are familiar not only with advertising in general, but also with many of the advertisements that we have seen or heard. This is because advertising messages are most effective after they have been repeated and reinforced. An audience is unlikely to remember the message of an ad until they have seen it several times. In addition, we have a short attention span. Recent research suggests that the human attention span is approximately eight seconds, just long enough to remember a slogan or a jingle. Advertisement must therefore be kept short and simple and repeated frequently for their message to register.

Advertising media tend to price their time or space on the basis of the number of viewers or readers who will see an ad. For this reason, if marketers choose advertising as their promotional method, they must pay particular attention to market segmentation. As an example, suppose that a Canadian manufacturer of downhill skis wanted to make its product known. The business could choose to advertise in the Toronto Star. The Saturday Star has a circulation of about 392,000 copies.[2] In contrast, Ski Canada magazine has a paid circulation of just over 32,000 per month, less than one tenth the readership of The Star. However, nearly all of the readers of Ski Canada Magazine have an active interest in skis and skiing. On the other hand, readers of the Toronto Star are more likely to represent a typical cross-section of Canadian society. In any given year, fewer than 10% of Canadians will ski more than twice.[3] Moreover, roughly 60% of Canadian skiers live in British Columbia or Quebec. An advertisement for skis that appears in the Toronto Star will probably be ignored by 95% of the people who see it.

Advertising is useful for raising awareness. On the other hand, given that most TV or radio advertisements last 30 seconds or less, and that we glance at a print ad for much less than that time, advertising is much less effective at educating. Being impersonal, advertising is no use in closing the sale.

Consumers tend to ignore the bulk of advertising messages that bombard them. Marketers must therefore find out who their customers are, which media they pay attention to, what messages appeal to them, and how to get their attention. Thus, marketers use several different **advertising media**—specific communication devices for carrying a seller's message to potential customers in the target market.

Advertising media: The specific communication devices or channel used to carrying a seller's message to the target market.

---

2 Newspapers Canada http://www.newspaperscanada.ca/about-newspapers/faq-about-newspapers
3 2008-2009 *Canadian Skier and Snowboarder Facts and Stats,* September 2009

An effective promotional campaign might use a variety of media to address potential customers at each stage of the purchasing decision process. For example it might use television ads to make its name known to consumers, and newspaper and magazine ads to reinforce that awareness. It could use trade publications to educate them about product features. Finally it might use personal selling to make the sale. An advertiser selects media with a number of factors in mind. The marketer must ask: "Who do I want to reach? What do I want them to learn or to know?"

Businesses choosing to advertise in order to promote their products have a wide array of media from which to choose. The most common media are the internet and television. These are followed, by some margin, by newspaper and radio advertising. These are followed, again by some margin, by magazines and out of door advertising, most familiar to us as signs and billboards.

Television

For the past fifty years, television has been the medium which attracted by far the largest amount of advertising revenue. Television allows advertisers to combine sight, sound, and motion, thus appealing to almost all of the viewer's senses. Information on viewer demographics for a particular program allows advertisers to promote to their target audiences.

TV has been losing its dominance as an advertising medium for the past two decades. Depending on who is measuring precisely what, several recent surveys suggest that TV has given way to the internet as business' preferred advertising medium. With the advent of, first, cable, and then digital and satellite TV, the number of stations that most viewers can watch has grown from four or five, to dozens, to – now – literally hundreds.

Canadian Advertising Revenue by Medium
2012 & 2013

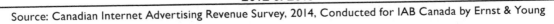

Source: Canadian Internet Advertising Revenue Survey, 2014, Conducted for IAB Canada by Ernst & Young

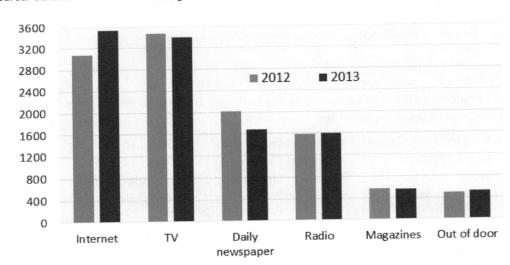

This fragmentation of the TV market means that ads shown on any one station are seen by far fewer viewers than twenty years ago. On the other hand the proliferation of stations, particularly those aimed at particular demographic segments, means that those ads can be better pinpointed to the target audience. Professor Bovaird's wife likes to watch Vision, a station that carries a lot of religious and faith-oriented programs. Professor Bovaird prefers TSN (Television Sports Network) and Sportsnet. Vision carries a lot of advertising by charities. TSN's advertisers are more likely to be promoting beer and deodorant.

In recent years, the technology that allows DVRs (digital video recorders) gives viewers the ability to fast-forward past the ads, to TV shows they have recorded. The brevity of TV ads also makes television a poor medium in which to educate viewers about complex products.

The Internet

From nowhere in the 1990s, the internet has very recently overtaken TV as the largest medium in terms of total advertising spending. Internet advertising offers advantages for both buyers and sellers. For buyers, the internet allows consumers to browse for products, seeing both pictures, videos, and written descriptions without leaving their homes. They can do so 24 hours a day.

For sellers, the advantages of the internet include the ability to access consumers anywhere in the world. In addition, a seller can promote products without having to invest in a "bricks-and-mortar" store.

Despite these advantages, the internet has its weaknesses. The internet is accused of bringing consumers information overload. This means that the internet makes more information available than most consumers can reasonably use or make sense of. In addition, the impersonal nature of internet communication gives rise to consumer concerns about the authenticity of the site, and about matters of security.

Newspapers

In recent years the volume of ads placed in newspapers has declined as advertisers have shifted their emphasis to the internet. Nevertheless, most newspapers are local, offering advertisers the opportunity to tailor their advertisements for different cities or regions. Most newspapers are published daily or weekly, allowing the advertiser the flexibility to change the ad's content frequently. Presented side by side with news, newspaper advertisements tend to acquire credibility. However, newspapers are generally thrown out after one day, and some do not have good reproduction quality.

Magazines

The principle advantage of magazine advertising lies in the astonishing variety of titles published for every possible interest. A very selective list of magazines with the words Canada or Canadian in the title include:

Boating Industry Canada	Canadian Geographic	Canadian Yachting
Canada's History	Canadian Grocer	Dogs in Canada
Canadian Art	Canadian Literature	Education Canada
Canadian Aviator	Canadian Poultry	Firefighting in Canada
Canadian Business	Canadian Screenwriter	Greenhouse Canada
Canadian Cowboy	Canadian Stamp News	Groundwater Canada
Canadian Firefighter	Canadian Theatre Review	Opera Canada
Canadian Florist	Canadian Woodworking	

The many different magazines available provide advertisers with the ability to pinpoint target customers. The person who reads Canadian Cowboy is likely to shop for different goods and services than the reader of Canadian Yachting.

Many special interest magazines devote space to product reviews and forums. This allows advertisers opportunity to provide detailed product information. Magazines have a long life and tend to be passed from person to person, thus doubling and tripling the number of exposures.

Radio

Since most radio stations are programmed locally, radio allows advertisers a high degree of customer selectivity. In addition, content formats vary. Radio audiences can be segmented into listening categories, such as rock, '60s, roll, country and western, jazz, classical, talk shows, news, and religious programming.

The disadvantage of this medium is that radio ads are very short, typically less than 30 seconds per spot, and most people tend to use the radio as "background" while they are doing other things. So, radio's use as a promotional medium tends to be limited to raising awareness.

Outdoor Advertising

Outdoor advertising—billboards and signs – have the advantage of being geographically specific. Roadside signs can be viewed multiple times by potential customers who live or work in the local area. This medium is useful to consumers who are at the "searching for alternatives" stage of the buyer decision process. On the downside, outdoor ads can present only limited information.

PERSONAL SELLING

Personal selling involves a salesperson communicating directly, usually one-on-one, with potential customers. Virtually everyone has done some personal selling. Perhaps as a child you had a lemonade stand or sold chocolate bars to raise money for your soccer team.

Personal selling: Promotional tool in which a salesperson communicates one on- one with potential customers.

When faced with making a purchasing decision, many consumers want someone with whom to interact. A real live human being can answer questions. Personal selling provides this interaction. It therefore helps to instill a level of credibility and trust between a seller and a consumer.

Personal selling is an appropriate promotional method if the products being promoted are complex, or have many features. This is why personal selling is so common in the marketing of cars, houses, life insurance and investment products. A customer can ask questions and get direct, individual responses. Nevertheless, a number of fairly simple, consumer products continue to rely heavily on personal selling. Among the best known are: Avon Cosmetics, Mary Kay Cosmetics, and Tupperware.

The principal disadvantage of personal selling is the cost. Having a sales person meet one-on-one with potential customers is labour intensive. If the sales person is on the road, the cost includes travel, food and lodging.

Personal selling is an effective method for educating potential customers about a product's features. The salesperson can answer specific questions. It is also good for creating enthusiasm, and is therefore often the best method for "closing the sale", in other words getting customers to commit to the purchase decision.

Since personal selling is labour intensive, and normally involves either one-on-one, or one person to a small group, interaction, it is not an effective means of broadly raising awareness.

SALES PROMOTION

Sales promotion includes a variety of short term incentives intended to stimulate immediate interest and excitement in a product, and stimulate sales.

Sales promotion: A variety of short term incentives intended to stimulate immediate interest and excitement in a product, and to stimulate sales.

Whereas advertising is designed to offer reasons to buy a good or service, sales promotion is designed to offer reasons to buy the product now. What all types of sales promotion have in common is to persuade the consumer that they must act soon, in order to get a deal.

Premiums

A premium is a method of sales promotion in which an item is offered free or at a bargain price. Put simply a premium involves: "Buy one get one free". Consumers like to believe that they are getting a deal, and there is no better deal than to get something for free.

Bonus packs

A bonus pack is an item that has an increased quantity (net weight, count, volume) and is sold at the same price as the regular item. A simple example is a package of 6 disposable razors being sold for the price normally charged for 4.

Coupons

A coupon is a method of sales promotion featuring a certificate that entitles the bearer to savings off a product's regular price. Coupons may be used to encourage customers to try new products, to attract customers away from competitors, or to induce current customers to buy more of a product. They appear in newspapers and magazines and are often sent through direct mail.

Finance Deals

This form of sales promotion applies to big ticket items such as cars, or home appliances. The supplier will offer very low cost financing, such as 0% interest on the first three years, as incentive to get customers to purchase a product that they otherwise might not be able to afford.

Advantages and Weaknesses of Sales Promotion

Sales promotions often give people the impression that they are getting a "deal". This method of promotion is therefore good at creating enthusiasm, and good at getting would-be purchasers to close the sale. It is less good at raising awareness, and is no use at educating.

PUBLICITY & PUBLIC RELATIONS

Publicity is any activity that generates news coverage about a business. Because press releases are often presented as news, consumers tend to see publicity as objective and give it more credence than advertising.

Publicity: Any activity that generate news coverage about a business.

The principal advantage of publicity is that it's free. However, the disadvantage of publicity is that it's difficult for the business to control. Not all publicity is good publicity. There is little that Toyota could do to counteract a string of headlines when it was discovered that the brake systems for some of its cars were defective.

Headlines like "US to probe Toyota brake problems", "Toyota's botched response" and "Toyota to recall Prius in US and Japan" will obviously have a detrimental impact on a product's sales.

Public relations are public service activities designed to create goodwill and to enhance the business' image. The most common means of doing this is for the business to sponsor a not-for-profit cultural or charitable organisation, or to sponsor an event.

Public relations: Public service activities designed to create goodwill and to enhance the business' image.

In Canada, the CIBC has managed to raise a good deal of goodwill through its long-standing and high profile involvement with the cancer research fund raising event the "CIBC Run for the Cure".

In this respect, public relations is good at raising awareness of the organisation's name. However, it does nothing to educate consumers about the organisation's goods or services, and therefore does nothing to help complete a sale.

PLACE

Imagine that you bump into one of your friends. You admire the coat that she is wearing. She replies that it is the best winter coat that she has ever owned. When you ask her to tell you more, she says it is made from alpaca wool. Alpaca wool is lighter than sheep's wool, waterproof, has better insulating qualities, and is hypoallergenic.

"Where can I get one" you ask.

"You can't" replies your friend. "I bought it in Peru. The company that makes these coats sells them only in Peru."

The fourth "P" in the marketing mix is **distribution** or "place". This is the area of marketing concerned with getting products from the seller into the hands of the buyer.

Distribution: The area of marketing mix concerned with getting products from the producer to the buyer.

When conducting its market research, a business must ask prospective customers such questions as:

Where do you live?
Where do you shop?
When do you shop?
Where do we find you?
How do we reach you?

DISTRIBUTION CHANNELS

Producers of goods and services have a number of choices as to how best to distribute their products. The principal choices are sending a sales force door to door, owning and operating stores, or selling warehouses full of products to retailers who are then responsible for dealing directly with consumers. The path that the business chooses to get its product into the hands of consumers is called the **distribution channel**.

Distribution channel: The path a product follows from the producer to end user.

Direct selling is also referred to as **direct distribution.** Direct selling occurs when a business sells its products directly to the consumer.

Direct selling or direct distribution: A business sells its products directly to the consumer without passing through any intermediary.

Direct selling can be done by mail order, where the consumer selects the item from a photo and description in a catalogue. This means of distribution is most appropriate when some or most of the target market live in rural areas, away from population centres where sales people can travel efficiently or the population justifies the cost of operating a store. Although Canada's land area is huge and largely empty, it is nevertheless one of the more urbanised countries on the planet. 82% of Canada's population live in cities or towns, the same as the United Kingdom, and a higher proportion higher than that of The

United States, Germany or France.[4] While most major retailers offer sales through catalogues, Canada's densely concentrated population, the excellent transportation system, and the widespread availability of the internet have made this means of distribution an also-ran.

Some businesses rely on door-to-door selling or home parties. The two methods are often used for selling inexpensive household goods and cosmetics. In Canada, well known practitioners of in-home direct selling are Avon Cosmetics, Mary Kay Cosmetics and Tupperware kitchen food containers. These businesses hire and manage their own sales force, who are largely paid on commission, and engage in personal selling to family, neighbours and friends.

Most visibly, businesses can own and manage their own retail stores. In Canada, Canadian Tire sells tools and appliances made by many makers, but emphasises its own line of Mastercraft Tools. Similarly, Shopper's Drug Mart sells its own Life Brand pharmaceuticals through 1200 stores nationwide. Unknown to most consumers Ontario's Beer Stores are owned by Labatt Brewing (49% ownership), Molson Coors (49%) and Sleeman Breweries (2%). Perhaps the most obvious example of direct distribution in towns and cities are the thousands of branches belonging to Canada's "Big 5" banks.

The direct channel is also prominent on the internet. You can purchase airline tickets, books, CDs and an infinite variety of other products and services directly from the supplier, by visiting their internet sites.

When a business sell its products to the public with the aid of an intermediary, it is called **indirect selling** or using **indirect channels**. Indirect selling occurs when the maker of a product does not want to be involved in the costly activity of maintaining its own sales force, or operating its own stores.

Indirect Selling / Indirect Channels: Distribution of a product by selling to intermediary, as opposed to the end user.

Previously you learned that intermediaries are individuals and organisations which help to put buyers and sellers together. A **distribution intermediary** is any businesses which helps another business to distribute its goods or services to the ultimate consumer. Indirect sales includes any chain of distribution that involves retail stores, wholesalers, distributors, brokers or agents. .

Distribution Intermediary: Any business which helps another business to distribute its goods or services to the ultimate consumer.

The most obvious distribution intermediaries are, of course, retail stores. **Retailers** sell products directly to consumers.

Retailers: Intermediaries who sell products directly to end-users.

If you are like most Canadians, you buy nearly all the goods and services you consume from retailers. If you walk into a Hudson's Bay store you can find jeans made by Levis, shoes made by Nike and Adidas, shirts made by Arrow, Lacoste, Ralph Lauren and Tommy Hilfiger.

---

4 The World Bank, 2014

Most retailers are small operations, often consisting of just the owners and part-time help. But there are a few very large retailers, and these account for billions of dollars of sales each year in Canada.

Canada's Largest Retailers, 2012

Retailer	Annual Revenues (billions)
Walmart Canada	$23,435,000 (U.S.)
Costco Wholesale Canada	$15,717,000 (U.S.)
Canadian Tire Corp.	$11,189,800
Shoppers Drug Mart	$10,781,848
Home Depot of Canada	$7,225,000 (U.S.)

In addition to selling its own "Mastercraft" tools, Canadian Tire distributes tools and appliances made by Black & Decker, skates made by CCM, and bicycles made by Schwinn. In addition to selling its own "Life Brand" products, Shopper's Drug Mart sells bandages made by made by Johnson & Johnson, pain relievers made by Bayer, and personal care products made by Proctor and Gamble.

Canadian Tire and Shoppers Drug Mart, like other intermediaries, providing a service. If Canadian Tire buys a drill from Black and Decker for $30, it might charge the end consumer $60. The $30 markup is the revenue that Canadian Tire earns by unpacking cases of electrical drills, displaying them on shelves, and employing sales people to provide customers with in-store help and advice.

Each link in a distribution channel charges a markup. Thus, indirect distribution means higher prices. The more intermediaries in the distribution channel, the higher the final price to the consumer. However, intermediaries provide producers with valuable and necessary services, displaying the product, providing customers with advice, and doing all of the work involved with the final transaction.

NON-STORE AND ELECTRONIC RETAILING

Some of Canada's largest retailers sell all or most of their products without bricks-and-mortar stores. Of course, the biggest development of the past quarter century in product distribution is the rise of on-line shopping.

Electronic retailing or **e-tailing** allows consumers to purchase products directly from their home. This method of reaching customers is expected to increase sharply during the next few years due to its convenience, and as consumers become increasingly confide about making online purchases using credit cards.

The internet represents a cross between a promotional medium and a distribution medium. Many consumers who prefer to see and feel the merchandise in-store will nevertheless go on-line to compare prices and features before making the purchase.

Electronic Retailing: Use of the internet to promote products and services, and allow consumers to purchase products directly from their home.

Internet as Distribution Tool
E-commerce share of total US retail sales
1999 - 2014

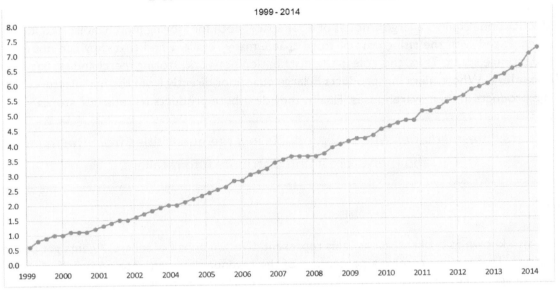

Source: United States Census Bureau, Monthly and Annual Retail Trade Report, May 2015

E-commerce Sales in Canada
2012-2019

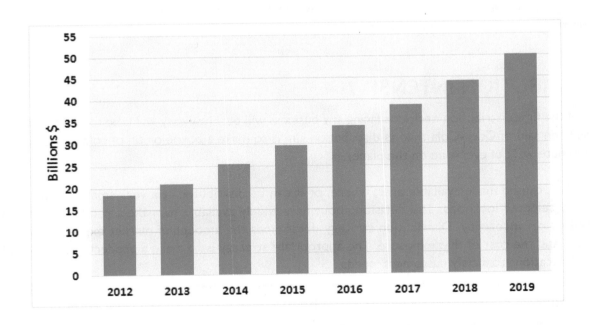

Source: Statista

WHOLESALERS

Retail distribution requires a large amount of floor space, both for storing merchandise and for displaying it in stores. Faced with the rising cost of store space, many retailers find that they can not afford both retail and storage space. Thus, this role in the distribution network, storing merchandise, has been taken by **wholesalers**. Wholesalers buy products in large quantities directly from the manufacturer. They then store the products in their warehouses. Finally, they distribute products to retailers' stores.

Wholesalers: Intermediaries who buy products in large quantities from the manufacturer, and then store it and distribute it to retailers.

Agents

Agents, also known as brokers, act as sales representatives on behalf of sellers. Agents get paid through commissions. That is, they receive a percentage of the revenue they generate on behalf of their clients. The value of agents lies primarily in their knowledge of markets and their expertise at selling.

Agent / Broker: Individuals who acts as representatives on behalf of sellers. They receive of percentage of the revenue in return.

Travel agents, for example, represent airlines, car-rental companies, and hotels. Real estate agents help sellers to find buyers of residential property.

DISTRIBUTION INTENSITY

One of the first distribution decisions facing any business will be: How easy will it be to find the product? It has been said of Coca-Cola that its distribution aim is to make a bottle or tin of coke available within a 10-minute walk of everyone on the planet.

A product can be made available everywhere, or it can be distributed at a very small number of very carefully selected locations. The decision about how widely available to make a product is known as **distribution intensity.** Distribution strategy determines the amount of market exposure the product gets and the cost of that exposure. The appropriate strategy is to make a product accessible in just enough locations to satisfy customers' needs.

Distribution intensity: The decision about how widely available to make a good or service.

Of course, the more widely available a product becomes, the more people see it, become aware of it, and may be tempted to buy. Ubiquity, the characteristic of being everywhere, becomes part of the product's promotion strategy. It's hard not to see the famous Coke logo, and its well-known colours many times a day.

Broadly speaking, there are three distribution strategies:

- Intensive distribution
- Selective distribution
- Exclusive distribution

INTENSIVE DISTRIBUTION

Intensive distribution is a strategy designed to give a product maximum exposure. This is done by making the product available through as many outlets as possible. Intensive distribution is most appropriate for products which consumers won't go out of their way to find, where there are acceptable substitutes.

Intensive distribution: Making a product available through as many outlets as possible, using every possible means of distribution.

Intensive distribution is used by many low-cost consumer goods, such as candy bars and as mentioned by the example of Coke, soft drinks.

The benefit of making a product universally available is that it gains visibility. The downside of such a distribution strategy is, of course, that it adds complexity and cost to the distribution process.

EXCLUSIVE DISTRIBUTION

In contrast to intensive distribution, **exclusive distribution** is a strategy that involves making the product available through a very small number of carefully selected dealers and distributors. Sometimes these distributors will have purchased the right to be the exclusive distributor for a product in a particular geographic market.

Exclusive distribution is most often used for high-cost luxury products for which part of the value package is the aura of exclusivity, or prestige. As an example, there are only four Rolls-Royce car dealerships in all of Canada! Piaget, the luxury Swiss watchmaker sells its products through six locations in Canada: two in each of Toronto and Vancouver, and one store in each of Calgary and Montreal.

Exclusive distribution network reduces a product's visibility, and reduce the size of the market. There are no Rolls Royce dealerships, four example, in Canada's four Atlantic Provinces. However, for a high priced products, where skimming is the chosen pricing policy, the business' overall strategy is to make a large margin from each sale, rather than make a small margin from each of a large number of sales.

Exclusive distribution: A strategy that involves making a product available through a very small number of carefully selected dealers and distributors.

SELECTIVE DISTRIBUTION

Selective distribution falls between intensive and exclusive distribution. A business that uses this strategy carefully selects only retailers who will give special attention to the product in terms of sales effort and customer service.

Examples of businesses that use this type of distribution strategy tend to be medium priced goods with strong branding, for example "Ralph Lauren" and "Black & Decker"

Selective distribution: A strategy that uses a limited number of outlets for a product.

PHYSICAL DISTRIBUTION

Of course, if a business wants to get a product into the hands of a customer, it needs to transport the product to where the customer lives, works or shops. This is known as **physical distribution**. The goals of physical distribution are to make products available when and where consumers want them, and to keep costs low.

Physical distribution: The activities needed to transport a good from the manufacturer to the end user.

The transportation industry is extremely important to a geographically large, sparsely populated country like Canada. Cost is a major factor when a business chooses a transportation method. But cost is not the only consideration. The business must also consider the nature of its products, the distance the product must travel and the timeliness that customer require. A business shipping orchids or other perishable goods will probably use air transport, while a company shipping sand or coal will use rail or ships.

The major transportation modes are rail, water, truck, air, and pipelines. Differences in cost are most directly related to delivery speed.

Planes. Air is by far the fastest transportation mode, and in Canada's far north, it may be the only available transportation. However, air freight is the most expensive form of transportation.

Trucks. The advantages of trucks include flexibility, fast service, and dependability. All parts of Canada except the far north can be reached by truck. Trucks are a particularly good choice for short-distance distribution. Trucks can, however, be delayed by bad weather. They also are limited in the volume they can carry in a single load.

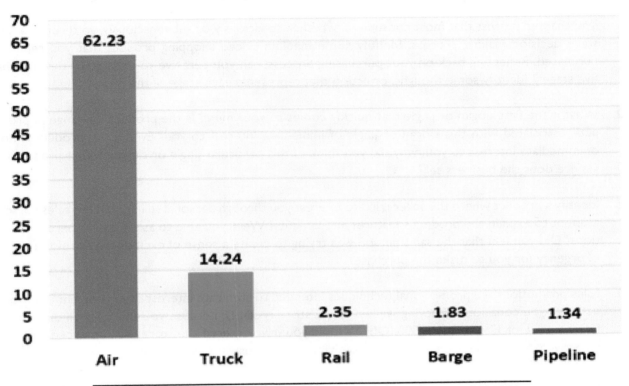

Comparative Transport Costs
(cents per ton mile)

US Department of Transportation, Bureau of Transportation Statisitics, Table 3-21
Average Freight Revenue per Ton Mile (US cents), data for 2004

Railroads. Railroads have been the backbone of our transportation system since the late 1800s. They are now used primarily to transport heavy, bulky items such as cars, steel, and coal.

Water Carriers. Of all the transportation modes, transportation by water is the least expensive. Unfortunately, it is also the slowest.

SELF-ASSESSMENT QUESTIONS FOR REVIEW

1. The chapter suggest that most consumers, whether consciously or subconsciously, go through a five stage decision making process. Identify some medium-priced shopping product that you recently purchased. Reflecting back on your purchasing process, can you perceive yourself going through the five stages? Identify some thought, or action that represents each stage of the process.

2. What is the first slogan or jingle that quickly comes to your mind? Is the product, or range of products, associated with this slogan or jingle of immediate interest to you? Even if the product is not of immediate interest to you, why did you think of this particular jingle or slogan? What product or service does the business sell?

3. Identify a product where the seller tried to interest you through personal selling. Did the sales person attempt to explain the product's features and benefits? Were you able to ask the sales person questions? Did you feel that the sales person was trying to create a sense of excitement and also a sense of urgency for you to make the purchase?

4. Sales promotions are promotional techniques intended to stimulate interest or excitement in a product. Are you conscious of having walked into a store recently, because you saw a sign indicating "2 for the price of 1" or "Sale – 50% Off"? Would you have entered the store had it not been for the incentive to save money on a purchase you hadn't consciously intended to make?

5. Identify a product that you recently purchased that required a special trip to a particular store or location. Now, identify a product that was available in the first store you walked into. Was there a large difference in the price of these two products? Was one product more complex than the other? In retrospect, do the two different distribution strategies make sense to you?

- Advertising
- Advertising media
- Agent
- Broker
- Buyer decision process
- Coupons
- Direct channel
- Direct selling
- Discounts
- Distribution channel

- Distribution Intermediary
- Distribution mix
- Electronic re-tailing
- Exclusive distribution
- Indirect channel
- Intensive distribution
- Personal selling
- Physical distribution
- Premiums
- Promotion

- Promotional mix
- Public relations
- Publicity
- Retailers
- Sales
- Sales agent (or broker)
- Sales promotion
- Selective distribution
- Telemarketing
- Wholesalers

CHAPTER 6

OPERATIONS: MAKING THE THINGS
THAT PEOPLE WANT

CHAPTER OVERVIEW

A business is formed for the purpose of providing people with the things that they need and want. An essential part of any business are the systems and procedures that ensure that it can create products which are satisfactory to the customer.

Managers must dedicate time, effort, energy and resources to ensure that the goods or services that that the business offers are properly planned, organised, assembled, work as they should, and are available in the time, place, and quantity that customers expect. A business can promise the moon, but it must be able to deliver.

The business function that concerns itself with creating goods and services is called operations. Operations involves taking inputs and turning them into the finished products that customers want.

LEARNING OUTCOMES

As a result of reading this chapter you will learn:

- Operations is the part of the business that create goods or services.

- The term used for this function was once know as "production". It is now more widely known a "operations".

- Most Canadian businesses provide intangible ser vices, they don't produce tangible goods.

- There are several reasons why the provision of ser vices is more complex and difficult to manage tha the production of goods, and often requires mor management.

- Operations managers plan the business' capac ity, that is the quantity of goods or services tha the business can produce. Capacity planning mus strike a balance between spending too much on idl equipment and under-used employees, and turnin customers away.

- Operations managers must decide the business' op timum location. A business must take into accoun the location of suppliers, employees, and customers

- Layout planning involves deciding the best way to design the business' factory, store or office.

- A business must provide customers with goods o services when they need them. Operations man agers must determine when activities should take place, so that products are available when needed.

OPERATIONS – PROVIDING THE THINGS THAT PEOPLE WANT

The World's Worst Coffee Shop

Some years ago, while doing some errands near my home, I walked into a coffee shop near the corner of Bathurst and Dupont streets in central Toronto. It was about 10.15 on a weekday morning.

I grabbed a large cup, and placed it under the spigot of the first coffee canister. Initially, about two inches of coffee poured out. Then, the flow became a dribble. Then the dribble stopped. I shook the coffee canister. It was empty.

I moved my cup, which was about one third full, two feet along the counter to the next canister. I can't taste the difference between Colombian and Brazilian coffee, so I continued to fill my cup. Once again, after about two inches of coffee dribbled out lazily, the flow stopped. My cup was now about two-thirds full.

I was frustrated, but hardly distraught. Once again, I moved my cup two feet along the counter, to the next canister. The sign on this canister said "French Vanilla". It's not my favourite tasting coffee – too sweet. So, I moved my cup to the next canister. The sign said "Decaf". I wanted a caffeine hit. However, my cup was two thirds full, and they had run out of the other caffeinated coffees. I tried to top up my cup with decaf. To my horror, it was completely empty!

"Excuse me" I called to the young woman who was working behind the counter. "These two canisters are empty. So is the decaf. You've run out of coffee!"

"Oh, I'm so sorry" she said, apologetically. "It will take me three minutes to make a fresh pot" she added brightly. She quickly began to make fresh coffee. I was in no great hurry, so I waited. Less than five minutes later, the friendly young counter attendant said "Sir, I'll pour you a fresh cup. Cream, milk and sugar are over by the window".

She poured my coffee, then I paid her what I owed.

I strolled over to the window. I don't normally take milk or cream in my coffee. However, I do like to take sugar.

I picked up the round, glass sugar dispenser. I was about to pour its contents into my cup. Then, I noticed - the sugar dispenser was empty!

About one month later I was in the same neighbourhood, once again doing a variety of messages. As I strolled past the coffee shop, I saw that the windows were papered over. A huge "For Lease" sign was inside the door.

The world's worst coffee shop had gone out of business.

You might think that this story is trivial or fanciful. It's not fanciful, it really happened. You might think it's obvious. Surely, a coffee shop ought to have coffee! However, what this story illustrates is NOT that the owners or managers of this coffee shop were necessarily lazy or stupid. No-one pays tens of thousands of dollars to purchase a franchise, thousands in wages, and hundreds of dollars each month in rent, if they are lazy. Obviously, it takes no great insight, nor does it require 30 years of business experience, to recognise that a coffee shop must have coffee.

Rather, the example of the world's worst coffee shop points to the need for businesses to have systems and procedures in place, and for the shop's employees to have appropriate training, work routines, and resources to ensure - something seemingly obvious – that a coffee shop has a plentiful supply of coffee.

Incidents similar to the above happen to all of us. Have you stopped at a cash dispenser and, after inserting your card and PIN number, received the message "Temporarily out of service – try again later"? Have you ever rushed to get to an airport and, when you got there, been told that your plane's departure will be 3 hours late? Do you remember that, not very long ago, Toyota recalled millions of cars because their brakes didn't work and, as a result, people died?

Surely, you tell yourself, a bank should have cash, and a scheduled air flight should leave on time, and a car should come to a stop if you step on the brakes! It seems obvious that a business must be able to make the good or service, or provide it or deliver it, if that is what it promises. The example of the "World's Worst Coffee Shop" demonstrates that when a business fails to delivers what it promises, it will lose customers and fail.

An essential aspect of running a business is that managers dedicate time and effort to ensure that the product the business promises is properly assembled, works as it should, and is available in the time, place, and quantity that customers expect. This function of the business is known as **operations**. Operations take the factors of production, and transform them into the goods or services that customers want.

Operations: The function of the business that transforms factors of production into the goods or services that customers want.

WHY "OPERATIONS" AND NOT "PRODUCTION"

Historically the business function that created products was known as production. The responsibility of managers in this function was called production management. However, during the last quarter of the 20th century, the term production found itself replaced by the word "operations". The word production implies that Canadian businesses "produce" tangible goods like cameras, clocks and clothing. In fact, goods represent less than 20 per cent of Canada's total GDP. This percentage has been falling since the end of the Second World War.

Production operations: Activities that turn inputs into tangible goods.

Canadian GDP by Sector

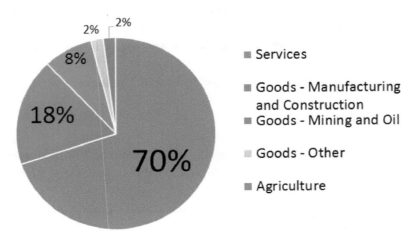

- Services
- Goods - Manufacturing and Construction
- Goods - Mining and Oil
- Goods - Other
- Agriculture

Many of the things that we need or want, from education, to health care, to banking, are services. The term "operations" is more inclusive, and helps to remind us that, like goods, services also require inputs. Those inputs need to be managed.

Generally, the provision of services involves less focus on machinery and technology and a greater emphasis on human input. Many services rely heavily on human interaction. When you eat at a restaurant, your enjoyment of the evening is likely to be as much affected by the friendliness of the waiter as the size of the portions. When you have your hair washed and styled, your satisfaction with your purchase is likely to be affected by the flair and style of the person performing this service.

Service operations: Activities that turn inputs into intangible services.

Canadians consume a vast array of services. Cable and internet businesses pump entertainment and information into your homes and onto your phones. Painting contractors redecorate houses. Airlines take you where you want to go. Movie theatres provide you with entertainment.

In addition to these consumer services, businesses purchase services from other businesses. For example, Tim Horton's hires photographers to take the photo images which decorate menus, in-store signs, and annual reports. Likewise, Tim Hortons hires accountants, PR consultants, legal advisers, architects and restaurant designers. These all provide services.

As you can see from these examples, operations occur in locations other than factories. Operations take place in restaurant kitchens, hotels, movie theatres and health clubs. A health club needs to plan:

- Gyms that are conveniently located. A health club needs to be close to where its members live or work.
- Convenient opening hours. Many people like to work out early in the morning, on their way to work.
- Sufficient number of lockers, so every member is able to store their street clothes and

valuables while working out.

- Sufficient number of personal trainers available when the club is busiest. This means finding staff who will work at 7.00 a.m., at nights and on weekends.
- Running machines and weight machines that are regularly maintained and in perfect working order.
- Large supplies of clean towels, folded and laid out in the locker rooms, and regularly restocked during the gym's busiest hours.
- .... and so on.

All of these things need to be planned, organised, and controlled. The management of the creation of goods and services, and their satisfactory provision to the buyer, is the function called **operations management**.

Operations management: Management of the creation of goods and services, and their satisfactory provision to the buyer

---

Operations managers are responsible for ensuring that the business is producing products that work as they should, at the right time, and in the right quantity so as to satisfy customer needs. At the same time, being mindful of profit, they attempt to do so while using as few resources as are necessary to do the job properly and well.

SPECIAL CHARACTERISTICS OF SERVICES

Service and manufacturing operations both transform inputs into finished products. In service operations the inputs are not wood, plastic, glass or steel. Rather, the inputs tend to be the people who provide help or expertise. In service operations, the finished products or "outputs" are people whose needs have been met. There are several key areas where service operations differ from production operations.

Goods are Made While Services are Performed

One obvious difference between service and manufacturing operations is that goods are produced, whereas services are performed. In many ways, this makes the provision of services more complex than the production of goods.

Goods Can Be Made in Advance, Services are Performed Immediately

Most goods can be made in a different time, and in a different place from their purchase or consumption. A book can be written in Vancouver, edited in Calgary, printed in Montreal, and shipped to a bookstore in Ottawa. All of this can happen many months before a resident of Toronto walks into the Ottawa bookstore, and buys a book that he will read the following week, once he returns home to Toronto.

In contrast, if you are hungry you want to buy and consume a meal immediately, and where you are. Likewise, if it's late at night, the weather is cold, and you are tired, if you want a taxi to take you home, you need it immediately, and where you are. This means that the operations managers of service businesses must do a great deal of precise planning for demand. The "World's Worst Coffee Shop" probably had plenty of coffee an hour before Professor Bovaird walked into the shop. It probably had plenty one hour later. Nevertheless, the coffee shop did not have coffee at the time and place that he wanted to buy a cup of coffee, and it changed his opinion of that business forever.

This characteristic of **immediacy** makes the scheduling of services more complex than scheduling the production of goods.

Immediacy: The quality that makes something important or relevant because it is happening now

---

Many Services Require the Involvement of the Consumer

As a consequence of the above, many services necessarily involve the presence and involvement of the consumer. You can't get a haircut without sitting in the chair. You can't benefit from a taxi ride unless you climb into the back seat of the cab. Services that require the presence of the customer are called **high-contact services**.

High-contact services: Service operations that necessarily involve interaction with the customer.

Not all services necessarily involve the consumer, or require the consumer's presence. Your car can have an engine tune-up, your grass can be cut or your drive cleared from snow, in your absence. These are called **low-contact services**.

Low-contact services: Service operations that don't necessarily involve interaction with the customer.

Customer involvement adds complexity to the operations manager's job. Not only must the business offer consumers sufficient capacity at the right time and place, but employees of service businesses need the interpersonal skills that factory workers may not. An assembly line worker in a factory canning peaches can do her job when she is tired and grumpy. A waitress in a crowded restaurant has to deal with impatient diners with good humour and tact.

High-Contact versus Low-Contact Services

Nursing Home	
Haircut	High-contact
Four star hotel	
Restaurant	
Airline travel	
Management consulting	
Retail banking	
Car repair	
Motel	
Telephone banking	
Dry cleaning	
Fast food	
Insurance	
Cable TV	Low-contact
Internet banking	

Services are Intangible

Manufactured products are tangible. You can see them and touch them. A tin of soup is typically made out of metal, it stands 6 inches tall, is 4 inches wide, and weighs 300 grams. To get the tins to market a manufacturer of soup must put 48 together in a cardboard carton. To attract customers' attention, the soup manufacture will print a bright, eye-catching label onto the exterior of the tin, and so on. In contrast, services are **intangible**. Services are experienced, they cannot be seen or touched,

Intangibility: The characteristic of services that makes them unable to be seen or touched

An important aspect of any service, therefore, is the feeling of pleasure, satisfaction, or improvement that the customer receives as a result of receiving the service. This means that a service business needs to identify, and anticipate what intangible aspects of the service are needed to best satisfy the customer's needs.

For example, when you hire a lawyer to help you to resolve a problem, you purchase not only the intangible quality of legal expertise but also the intangible reassurance that help is at hand. Perhaps the lawyer's office needs to have reception staff who are trained to look, sound and act thorough and professional. The office décor may need to convey the law firm's solidity and gravity. The lawyer needs to convey more than experience and technical expertise, but also a sense of care and concern for her client's interests.

Another example, when you go to your favourite restaurant you purchase not only benefit of having someone else prepare, cook, and serve your meal, you also get the intangible benefit of the sense of occasion that comes with dining out. A restaurant needs to give as much consideration to the lighting, the decor, the sound system, and the design of the menus as it gives to the food.

Services are Customised

In the example of tangible goods given above, tins of soup were described as being 6 inches tall, 4 inches wide, and weighing 300 grams. Most products are standardised in their size, shape and weight. When you go shopping for jeans that have a 32 inch waist and a 28 inch leg, every pair of 32 x 28 jeans should be exactly alike. Goods can be made in long production runs with the machinery and equipment set to produce identical products.

In contrast, services are customised. That is, no two customers need the identical service, delivered in the same way.

Customisation: The characteristic of services that means that no two customers need the identical service, delivered in the same way.

When you have your pet groomed, you expect the groomer to take account of the size, age, and breed of your dog. Likewise, when you have your hair cut, you expect the barber to listen to, and respect your preferences. Some men will want their hair washed, others not. Some clients will want their beard or mustache trimmed, others not. A restaurant that serves lunch to a business crowd on a weekday will want to organise meal preparation and service to get most diners in and out in under an hour. The same restaurant, when accepting a reservation for a party of eight at 8.00 p.m. on a Saturday night, could probably expect that the customers will linger at the table for most of the night.

Customisation means that services are harder to schedule. The operations managers of service business must build flexibility into their scheduling, or they must collect and analyse many customer interactions in order to predict the distribution of "quick", "slow", "simple", "complicated" and "average" service provisions.

Services Can Not be Stored.

Services such as housecleaning, childcare, and landscaping can't be produced ahead of time and then stored. Services typically can't be purchased in bulk. There's no benefit to having the grass on your front lawn cut five times in one week, and then not having it cut again for the rest of the summer!

Now that you have learned about the important role of operations, and of the special considerations faced by the managers of service operations, we can return to a more general consideration of what operation management entails. Like any management process, operations management begins with planning.

THE ACTIVITIES OF OPERATIONS MANAGEMENT

Operations planning involves determining how much the business will be supplying to its customers. As with other functions of the business, operations takes its starting point from the organisation's overall business plan.

The business' owners and strategic leaders will use their prior knowledge and intuition, observation of existing competitors, and market research to develop an idea of the potential size of the overall market. This will allow the business to **forecast** future demand for the business' goods or services.

Forecast: An estimate of the future demand for a business' goods and services.

The operations plan then needs to address:

Capacity: How much of the market should the business prepare to capture?
Location: Where should factories, warehouses, stores or offices be located?
Scheduling: What days of the week and hours of the day will the business operate?
Layout: What's the most efficient way to design factories, shops or offices?
Materials Management: If raw materials and other inputs need to be acquired, from whom should they be bought, what quantities should be obtained, and when must they be ordered?

CAPACITY PLANNING

Observation and research will help the business' managers to estimate future demand. Whether the business builds the facilities and hires the people to capture all of that demand is a matter of choice. The quantity of product that a business plans to produce under normal working conditions is called its **capacity**.

Capacity: The quantity of product that a business plans to produce under normal working conditions.

The capacity of a business depends on the quantity of machinery and equipment that it uses, and on the number of people that it employs. Quite simply, a business can produce more if it buys more, bigger or more modern equipment or if it hires more people. However, equipment is expensive to buy, install, maintain and insure. People are expensive to recruit, train, and employ.

A business whose capacity is too small may have to turn customers away. A business whose capacity is too large is wasting money on unused machinery and under-employed workers. Managers must therefore strike a careful balance between capacity that is large enough to satisfy most customers most of the time, and over-investing in excess capacity.

Two interesting examples of businesses that appear to have made a calculated decision to carefully limit capacity are Apple, and Major League Soccer (MLS). Many people observe that Apple's retail stores are small, and sometimes crowded. However, the busy-ness of an Apple Store creates an atmosphere of urgency and excitement. MLS teams all play in big cities that have large stadiums. However, MLS' policy is to play in soccer-specific stadiums with capacities of 20,000 - 25,000 seats. In 2014, Toronto FC's average attendance was 22,086. This was 96% of the capacity of their packed, exciting, noisy stadium.

LOCATION PLANNING

In the last chapter you learned about the important marketing dimension of "place". This is the business activity concerned with getting products from the seller into the hands of the buyer. "Place" is as important a consideration when the business creates the product as it is when distributing the product to the end user. **Location planning** involves the decision as to where to locate the factory, warehouse, store or office.

Location planning: The decision as to where best to locate the business' facilities and operations.

Choosing the best location for performing operations needs to take into consideration the location and availability of:

- Raw materials
- Employees
- Electricity
- Transportation
- Distribution intermediaries, if needed
- Customers

Previously, you learned that one of Canada's most important industries was the manufacturing of automobiles, many of which were exported to the United States. Remember, much of Canada's competitive advantage in this industry is due to the fact that all of the important inputs are abundantly available in or near southern Ontario. The metals needed to make cars, such as iron and copper, come from Sudbury, Ontario. The iron is turned into steel in Hamilton. The design, engineering and business expertise comes from Ontario's highly-educated work force. Financial capital is available from banks and other financial intermediaries with headquarters in Toronto. Once assembled, cars built in Windsor, Oshawa and Oakville can be transported quickly by road, rail or water to end users in both Canada and the United States.

As noted above, high contact service business must be located close to the customer. There is a well-known saying in the retail business that success depends on three things:

- location
- location
- location

The manufacturer of tangible goods enjoys more flexibility. However, as you learned in the previous chapter, transportation isn't free, and distribution intermediaries add cost to a product. So, even businesses that make tangible goods must strike a balance between locating where the inputs are inexpensively abundant, and locating close to the market.

LAYOUT PLANNING

Once the location is selected, operations managers must plan the optimal design for the factories, offices and stores, an activity called **layout planning**. Customer-facing areas need to be spacious, and easy to locate, so as to effectively attract customers. The goods producing areas in factories must be arranged so that the machinery, equipment, and supplies can be efficiently used to make more than one model or design of product, and can respond quickly to each customer's specific needs.

Layout planning: Designing the business' factories, shops and offices so as to provide maximum efficiency and effectiveness.

Fast food restaurants are an interesting hybrid between a service business and a goods producing business. When you buy a submarine sandwich, you are paying for the service of someone else making it. You therefore expect the counter staff to be pleasant. But a fast food counter is not a restaurant and customers are primarily paying for the tangible product – the sandwich – which they expect to be made quickly, and to individual specifications. Earlier in this book, the two dozen – or more – steps involved in producing a submarine sandwich were described. Observe them the next time you buy a sandwich for your lunch. It typically requires three employees to take your order, make your sandwich, hand it to you, collect your payment and make change. And yet, due to the careful layout behind the counter, the three employees can be making three sandwiches at once, never moving more than one or two paces, in an area smaller than the average bedroom. The sandwich follows one continuous flow from right to left, and no employee needs to move more than two or three steps to complete the order.

Layout Planning in a Sandwich Shop

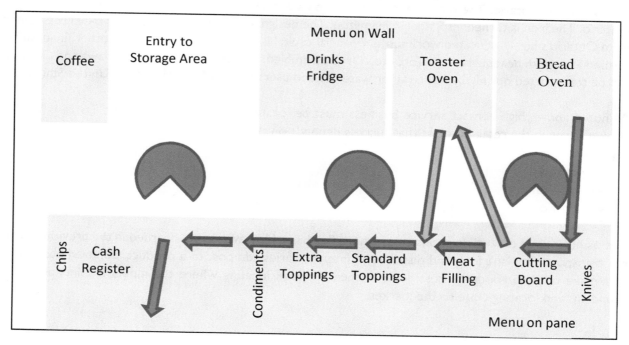

For retail shops, the layout must draw customers in and make it easy and comfortable for them to navigate the entire store. An inviting layout will encourage them to do so.

As a common example, if a grocery store puts carts near the front door, in a highly visible and accessible place, shoppers are likely to grab one. Intuitively, shoppers pushing carts are likely to buy more than customers carrying baskets. Supermarkets often put fruit and vegetables near the front of the store. One widely accepted theory as to why they do this is that once people have selected healthy food items they give themselves permission to buy the snacks, desserts, and junk food found in the middle of the store. Milk and other dairy products are generally displayed at the back. These frequently purchased perishables are often the main item on shoppers' lists. By placing milk at the back of the store, supermarkets draw customers down the length of the aisles where they walk past many items which they may have forgotten to put on their shopping lists, or they spot and buy on impulse. Supermarkets place the most expensive or biggest margin items at eye level, where they are first to be spotted and easiest to grab. Items on sale and low margin items are generally down at floor level, requiring the shopper to bend low to grab them. Finally, the queue to the check-out is lined with gum, candy bars, and magazines. Customers will browse the magazines while waiting in the queue. This provides a pleasant distraction from the wait. In addition, these inexpensive but high margin products are the sort of items that people buy on impulse.

SCHEDULING

Earlier in this book you read how one manager planned a series of activities to accomplish the organisation's goals. She said:

"I've run you a bath. I need you to jump in it, and give yourself a good scrub."

"I'll go downstairs now and make your breakfast. When you are out of the tub, I want you to get dressed. I've ironed your shirt. I've put out your clean shorts. They are on your chair. I've polished your shoes and put them by the front door."

"Can you be standing beside the car at ten o'clock? If you are ready by ten, we can be at your Grandma's house by eleven. Today is her birthday, so we don't want to be late…"

Each one of the activities that she listed would take time to accomplish. Bathing takes time. Getting dressed takes time. Cooking and eating breakfast takes time. Driving from your house to your Grandma's house takes time. Your manager was not just planning, she was performing a management activity called **scheduling**. Scheduling involves determining when an activity should take place so as to accomplish a goal by its target completion date. The schedule will depend on how long each activity takes, and whether one activity is dependent on the completion of another.

Scheduling: Determining when an activity should take place so as to accomplish a goal by its target completion date.

Although the production of goods lacks some of the immediacy of the provision of services, businesses that produce or sell seasonal products need to ensure that the product is available to coincide with customer demand.

Sporting goods stores will significantly change their selection of merchandise depending upon the time of year. Winter sports equipment like skates, hockey sticks, downhill and cross-country ski equipment will dominate the store space in October, November and December. This will give way to the clothing and equipment needed for summer sports, like tennis, golf and water sports, in March, April and May. Sporting equipment manufacturers need to plan for these changes and schedule the manufacture of the appropriate gear for the appropriate season.

Operations managers need to be mindful of **lead times**. Lead time is the gap between the time when a customer wants a product, and when the producer needs to begin the process of creating it.

Lead time: The gap between the time when a customer wants a product, and when the producer needs to begin the process of creating it.

A notoriously bad example of scheduling was the construction of the Olympic Stadium, in Montreal. Although begun in 1969, a stadium which was meant to be ready for the 1976 Olympic Games was not ultimately completed until 1981! The key lesson to scheduling is that, if you want to finish on time you must begin on time.

One of the most common tools used by operations managers to aid their scheduling is the **Gantt chart**. The Gantt chart is named after Henry Gantt, the man generally credited with its invention in its current form. A Gantt chart displays activities, either tasks or events, as a list down the left hand side of a table. Along the horizontal axis at the top is a suitable time scale. This may be expressed in hours, days, weeks, months or years. Each activity is represented by a bar; the position and length of the bar reflects the start date, duration and end date of the activity. The Gantt chart allows planners to see, at a glance:

- The sequence of activities;
- When each activity is scheduled to begin and end;
- The duration of each activity;
- Where two or more activities overlap with each, and may be done simultaneously;

In general, a Gantt chart is intended to show the start and end date of the whole project, and the dates by which certain activities are to be accomplished if the project is to be completed on time. Below, is a simple example of a Gantt chart, which demonstrates the activities that need to be accomplished in order for a male student to get to a 9.00 a.m. lecture.

Time/Activity	6.40	6.50	7.00 a.m.	7.10	7.20	7.30 a.m.	7.40	7.50	8.00 a.m.	8.10	8.20	8.30 a.m.	8.40	8.50	9.00 a.m.	9.10
Alarm rings	▓															
Get out of bed		▓														
Shower			▓													
Shave				▓												
Make coffee				▓												
Make breakfast				▓												
Eat breakfast					▓											
Dress						▓										
Find books							▓									
Leave home								▓								
Walk to bus stop									▓	▓						
Wait for bus											▓					
Sit on bus												▓	▓			
Walk to class															▓	
Sit down																▓

Note from the **Gantt chart** that, if the student wants to shower, shave, make and eat breakfast, and arrive in class on time, he will need to set his alarm for 6.45 a.m. and get out of bed before 7.00 a.m. The chart shows that he can turn on the coffee maker before he steps into the shower. If he fails to do so, he will add ten minutes to the time needed to do everything he needs to do.

Gantt chart: A visual representation of all of the activities required to complete an activity and the time needed to accomplish each activity

SUPPLY CHAIN MANAGEMENT

Very few goods can be assembled or services provided without buying goods and services from other businesses. If your business is to tutor algebra to high school students, you will needs to buy pens, paper and notebooks from Grand & Toy or Office Depot. If one of your clients lives a long way from a bus stop you may have to use a taxi in order to get to his home.

A product as complex as a car is assembled from steel, copper, chrome, rubber, leather, and glass as well as many other materials. The various materials that go into the making of a car had to be purchased from the manufacturers of each of those products.

Operations necessarily involves coordinating the business' interaction with all its suppliers. A fast food restaurant can't make a hamburger unless it has buns. A bakery can't make buns unless it has flour. A flour producer can't make flour unless it has wheat. A farmer can't grow wheat without fertilizer. A manufacturer can't produce fertilizer without phosphate. This long string of dependencies is known as a **supply chain**. A supply chain is the flow of materials and services between all the businesses that provide inputs into a finished product.

Supply chain: The flow of materials and services between all the businesses that provide inputs into a finished product.

When the members of the chain communicate with one another to plan, organise, and schedule as a coordinated system, they are likely to save both time and money. Individual members of the chain won't produce too much or too little, or deliver too soon or too late. The coordinated planning and scheduling, and the flow of information between the various members of the chain is called **supply chain management**.

Supply Chain Management: Managing the flow of information and materials between all the suppliers and customers in a chain,

---

The saved time and reduced costs that businesses enjoy as a result of good supply chain management should lead to greater profits. The concept isn't new and is neatly summarised in a nursery rhyme that dates back at least as far as the 14th century:

For want of a nail the shoe was lost.
For want of a shoe the horse was lost.
For want of a horse the rider was lost.
For want of a rider the message was lost.
For want of a message the battle was lost.
For want of a battle the kingdom was lost.
And all for the want of a horseshoe nail.

SELF-ASSESSMENT QUESTIONS FOR REVIEW

1. Pick a service business that you use from time to time. Explain how the services provided differ from customer to customer. How might the service that you receive be different from the service received by a friend or family member?

2. Services are said to be intangible. Think of a service that you recently purchased. Identify how you benefited or were changed as a result of receiving this service. Did you have anything to show for it, after you had received the service?

3. Think about a business with which you are familiar. It could be a restaurant, a supermarket, or a bookstore. What's good about the business' location? What problems do you see with this location? What recommendations would you make to the owners to make the business easier to get to, or make it easier for you to park?

4. Think about a business with which you are familiar. It could be a restaurant, a supermarket, or a bookstore. What's good about the business' layout? What problems do you see with this layout? What recommendations would you make to the owners to make the business easier to get round in, easier to find products, more spacious, or more welcoming?

5. Have you ever walked past a restaurant with a seating capacity of 120, because there were only 12 diners inside? Did it occur to you that the empty seats meant the food or the atmosphere was bad? Have you ever squeezed into a restaurant with a seating capacity of 20, because the crowded atmosphere made the location seem "cozy" or "lively"?

DEFINED TERMS

- Capacity
- Customisation
- Forecast
- Gantt chart
- High-contact services
- Intangibility
- Immediacy

- Layout planning
- Lead time
- Location planning
- Low-contact services
- Operations
- Operations management

- Production operations
- Purchasing
- Scheduling
- Service operations
- Supply chain
- Supply chain management

PRODUCTIVITY:
DOING MORE WITH LESS

CHAPTER OVERVIEW

In the previous chapter you learned about operations. A business must produce the good or service that it promises: at the right time, at the right place and in the right quantity.

A business needs to manage its operations not only to satisfy customer needs. Careful planning, scheduling, and control are also necessary to ensure that products are made without delay and without waste. A carefully managed business should not have workers standing idle waiting for others to finish their jobs. Storage spaces should not be crammed full because someone ordered the wrong parts, or because those parts don't work.

In this chapter you will learn about productivity, also called efficiency. Productivity is a measure of doing more with less. Highly productive workers accomplish more than their peers. Highly productive businesses make more cars, sell more clothes, and grow more crops in less time, using fewer workers, and in less space than their competitors. As a result they make higher profits.

Satisfying customer needs means giving people what they want, and what they believe they are paying for. If the business can meet customer expectations, they will be satisfied and will return. This is the meaning of quality.

Conversely, if the business disappoints customers it will be harmed in several ways. Disappointed or frustrated customers will bring defective products back. They will demand replacement or repair. Time and effort will have to be put into assuaging their disappointment, apologising and offering compensation. All of this before the business repairs or replace the product. This too eats into profits.

Well managed businesses establish systems and procedures to not just minimise defects, but to eliminate them altogether.

LEARNING OUTCOMES

As a result of reading this chapter you will learn:

- The meaning of productivity as a ratio between inputs and outputs.

- Productive countries are rich because they can produce more goods, services and prosperity for their citizens than other countries.

- National productivity depends on the quality and the quantity of factors of production available. Canada is a rich country because it has abundant, high quality factors.

- Productive businesses are profitable because they can produce more goods and services, using the same quantity, or fewer inputs, than their competitors.

- Individual businesses can control the quantity and quality of their inputs through policy choices and good management.

- The goal of the business is not necessarily maximum output. The goal should be to produce products that satisfy customer expectations.

- Meeting customer expectations is known as quality.

- Making quality products leads to customer loyalty

- Products that don't meet customer expectations lead to complaints, repairs and replacements.

- Time spent dealing with complaints, repairs and replacements is expensive and wasteful and lowers productivity.

- It is better to take care to make a product defect free, and deliver on customer expectations than to spend resources on repairs and replacements.

DOING MORE WITH LESS

Productivity is a ratio. Productivity measures how much gets achieved relative to the inputs used to achieve it. By definition, the more we are able to accomplish while using fewer inputs, the more "productive" we are.

Productivity: A ratio which measures how much gets achieved relative to the inputs that are used to achieve it.

Consider a ratio with which we are all familiar: kilometers per hour. This measure of speed is a ratio which compares the distance travelled, what we are trying to achieve, to the time we spend trying to achieve it. A vehicle that travels at a speed of 80 kilometer per hour will arrive at its destination sooner than a vehicle which travels at a speed of 50 kilometers an hour.

Suppose you wanted to drive from Toronto to Ottawa, a distance of 400 kilometers. If you averaged 80 kilometers per hour you would arrive in Ottawa in five hours. On the other hand, if you averaged 50 kilometers per hour it would take you three hours longer, depriving you of three hours of enjoyment once you got there. In managing a business, the ratio of outputs, or result achieved, relative to inputs is a key measure of good management.

Another word for productivity is **efficiency**. The two terms are synonyms. If a task is said to have been performed with efficiency, it means that it has been accomplished with minimum expenditure of time and effort.

Efficiency: A synonym for productivity. A ratio which measures how much gets achieved relative to the inputs that are used to achieve it.

All resources are scarce. The amount of time, money, and other inputs to create and deliver a product to a customer is finite. Therefore, it is in every business' interest to maximise its productivity or efficiency.

MEASURING PRODUCTIVITY

As you can see from the simple example of the average speed travelled by a car, we use measures of productivity every day. We use measures of productivity in all walks of life. Another example of productivity is the ratio of "bits per second" or "bps", the speed at which data travels. An internet system that works at 30 million bps will allow you to download movies twice as fast as one which downloads at 15 million bps. Productivity is measured commonly in the world of sports. Baseball players are judged by their batting average, the number of times on base divided by the number of appearances at the plate. Basketball players are judged by PPG, the total number of points they have scored divided by the number of games they have played.

You have already learned one important measure of productivity: gross domestic product (GDP) per capita. GDP per capita is the most widely used measure of a country's wealth relative to that of other countries.

	Measure of Productivity				
	Travel Speed	**Download Speed**	**Batting Average**	**Scoring Average**	**National Prosperity**
Output:	kilometers	bytes	hits	points	GDP
Input:	hours	seconds	at bats	games	population

Economic Productivity

In countries around the world, tens of millions of workers make millions of different products. Every country differs in terms of its climate, geography, access to capital, and the education level of the labour force. No two countries make exactly the same products. Because of this, the only sensible way of comparing productivity between countries is to use a single common yardstick that measures value. Typically, when comparing the productivity of different countries, the common yardstick that is used is the US dollar. A measure of productivity that uses dollar value as the measure of output is called **economic productivity**.

Economic productivity: A measure of productivity that uses dollar value as the measure of output.

GDP per capita is a simple measure of economic productivity that is calculated by dividing the total value of all the goods and services produced in a country, by the number of people who live there. GDP per capita allows us to compare the productivity of bankers in Luxembourg, steelworkers in Germany, and autoworkers in Canada.

Twenty Countries with the Highest per Capita GDP
2014 ($US)

Country	GDP / Capita ($US)	Country	GDP / Capita ($US)
Luxembourg	98328	Australia	44612
Norway	64837	Canada	44057
Switzerland	57744	Iceland	43648
United States	54640	Belgium	42987
Ireland	47796	Finland	39987
Netherlands	47635	United Kingdom	39225
Austria	46171	France	38870
Sweden	45113	Japan	36485
Denmark	44835	New Zealand	36401
Germany	44788	Italy	35067

Source: The Organisation for Economic Cooperation and Development (OECD), OECDdata.org

Economic Productivity Influenced by Access to Factors of Production

Canadians, with a GDP per capita of just over $44,000 are wealthier than the citizens of all but a handful of countries. Canada's prosperity is due to the fact that we enjoy plentiful supplies of all of the factors of production. Canada is abundantly endowed with many valuable natural resources. For example, Canada has the world's 3rd largest supply of fresh water. It is the world's 3rd largest producer of aluminum, the 5th largest producer of oil, and of natural gas, and the world's 7th largest producer of wheat. Canada is widely judged to have one of the world's most sophisticated, safe, and well-run banking systems. This gives Canadian businesses easy access to both financial capital, and the technological capital that money can buy. Canada has one of the world's best-educated and best-trained labour forces. Well trained workers, using modern technology and equipment, with plentiful supplies of relatively cheap natural resources can produce a great deal of prosperity.

In contrast, consider Burundi, one on the world's smallest and poorest countries. Burundi is land-locked, resource poor, and has an adult literacy rate of just 67%.[1] Most people in Burundi do not have a bank account, and it is not easy for small enterprises to get loans.[2] It is no great surprise, therefore, that Canadians are a great deal wealthier than the population of Burundi.

So, one source of a country's prosperity is access to a plentiful supply of high quality factors of production. However, what explains the gap between countries that do have resources, developed banking systems and well educated workers? Like Canada, Norway is a sparsely populated northern country with a long seacoast and plenty of oil. But Norway's GDP per capita is nearly 50% higher than ours. The United States, a country with which Canada shares a continent, a language, and a culture has always had a GDP per capita that is 10% - 20% higher. Is it because Canadians don't work hard enough?

PROSPERITY IS NOT THE RESULT OF WORKING LONG HOURS

In fact, working longer hours does not seem to make a country wealthier. The Organisation of Economic Cooperation and Development (OECD) is a multi-national think-tank and research organisation with 34 member countries. The OECD collects and distributes research and data on the wealth creation, economic development and productivity of its members. A scatter plot showing the relationship between hours worked and GDP per capita of the 34 OECD countries shows that as the hours of work decrease the GDP per capita rises! The trend line is shown in green.

---

1 The United Nations

2 Wharton Financial Institutions Center, University of Pennsylvania. Sourced at: fic.wharton.upenn.edu/fic

Hours Worked and GDP per Capita (OECD)

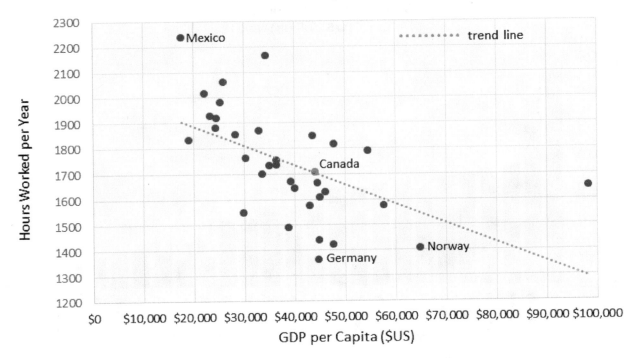

Source: The Organisation for Economic Cooperation and Development (OECD), OECDdata.org

Working long hours is not the key to prosperity. The average Canadian worked 1708 hours in 2014, roughly the OECD average. This is 25% less than the 2236 hours worked by much poorer Mexicans, and 20% more hours than wealthy Germans and Norwegians.

LABOUR PRODUCTIVITY

The key to prosperity lies not in working hard, but in working "smart". Most countries keep data on **labour productivity**. Labour productivity is a ratio that divides a country's GDP, not by the population but, by the total number of hours worked. This gives us a slightly more accurate portrayal of how productive a worker is, when on the job.

Labour productivity: A measure of the productivity of a country's labour force which divides GDP by the total number of hours worked.

In 2014 Canadian workers produced goods and services worth $50.70 per hour. In comparison with our peers in the other OECD countries, Canadian workers are mediocre performers.

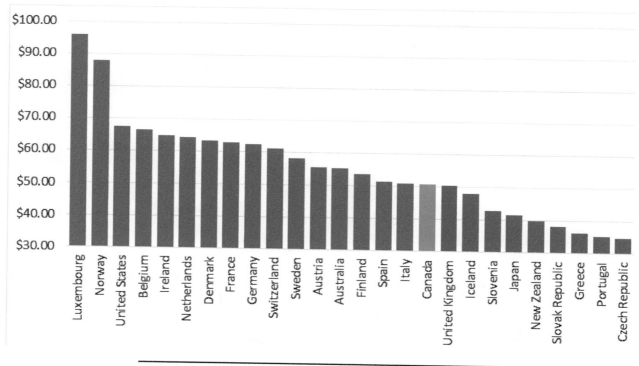

Labour Productivity
GDP per Hour Worked - 2014
(US dollars)

Source: Organisation for Economic Cooperation and Development

The conclusion we must draw: Canadian are rich, but we could be richer.

BUSINESS PRODUCTIVITY

Business productivity is the measure of how much a business produces, relative to the labour, capital and other resources used to produce it. The higher the ratio of output to inputs, the greater is a business' productivity.

$$\text{Business Productivity} = \frac{\text{Quantity or value of goods or services produced}}{\text{Quantity or value of resources used to produce it}}$$

The most common way to look at productivity across different industries and businesses is to measure economic productivity, in other words to use dollar value as the measure of output. In addition however, when two competing businesses make the same or very similar goods, productivity can be measured by **physical productivity**. Physical productivity measures the **quantity** of units produced relative to the inputs. Businesses such as farms can measure their output in bushels per acre. Wine producers can measure output in liters per acre. Manufacturing businesses that produce similar products can measure their physical productivity in units per hour. Automakers typically measure their productivity in terms of the number of hours of labour required to produce a car. An automaker that produces a vehicle in 14 hours is more productive than a rival that takes 18 hours to build a similar product.

Physical productivity: A measure of productivity that uses a numerical quantity as the measure of output.

High productivity gives a company a competitive edge because its costs will be lower. If we assume that all automotive assembly workers make more or less the same wage, a business that can make a car in less time than its rivals will be able to sell its product at a lower price, and gain more market share. Alternatively, it can sell a car at the same price as its rivals, but make a greater profit.

Every industry is different, and the choice of what outputs and inputs use to measure productivity will vary. However, intuition and common sense should allow us to imagine appropriate measures for any given industry.

Productivity in the Restaurant Business

As an example, the purpose of a restaurant is to get customers sitting at tables, and ordering food. The more revenue that a table generates per diner, or per party, or per evening, the more successful it is likely to be. In the restaurant business a meal served to an individual is called a "cover". The average amount that each diner spends is the "check average".

It is easy to imagine two similar-sized restaurants, with comparable prices, located close to each other on the same street. The Italian restaurant has seven tables, five set for four people and two set for two. The French restaurant has six tables set for four people. If the Italian restaurant serves 36 covers in an evening and the French restaurant serves only 27, the Italian restaurant is doing a better job of getting people into and out of its place of business. Similarly, if the check average at the Italian restaurant is $32 per diner, and the $28 at the French restaurant, the Italian restaurant is doing a better job of promoting and selling its product once diners have entered the premises.

Spot the Difference

The French restaurant can take steps to improve its situation. More attractive signage outside the building might entice more people to cross the threshold. More tables for two means that couples dining alone will not occupy only half the capacity of a table. Some changes to the menu might add more dishes that can be prepared and served quickly. Smaller, but tasty portions might entice people to add another course to their order. More training for the wait staff might lead to their selling dessert and coffee with more energy and enthusiasm.

Industry analysts can generate any number of measures of productivity for restaurants. Depending upon what they wanted to understand or improve about a particular business, they could measure:

- Covers per table
- Check average
- Revenue per table
- Revenue per square foot
- Revenue per waiter

A restaurant which consistently, and over an extended period, can get more people inside the door, and spending more per person will enjoy a greater chance of making a profit.

Productivity in the Retail Business

For retail businesses the goal is to get people into the store and then make purchases. Basic measures of productivity in retailing therefore include revenue per customer, revenue per store, and revenue per square foot of store space.

A 2015 survey by CBRE, a Toronto-based real estate business, studied the revenue generated per square foot, by three dozen of Canada's leading retailers. CBRE found that the most productive retailer in Canada is the Apple Store. Apple Stores generate $7,241 in sales for every square foot of retail space it operates in this country. That figure is nearly 2.5 times more than its nearest rival, Lululemon.

Selected Canadian Retail Stores
Revenue per Square Foot, 2014

Apple Store	$7,241
Lululemon	$2,961
Costco	$1,490
Louis Vuitton	$1,224
Dollarama	$238
Sears	$213
Hudson's Bay	$144
Target	$98

Source: CBRE Market Flash, July 2015, Money Talks: Retail Sales Productivity Shows Divergence in Performance

At the other end of the spectrum, the least productive retailer was Target. Canadian Target stores recorded just $98 per square foot. Soon after CBRE conducted its survey, Target's US parent corporation closed its Canadian stores. Also near the bottom of the list were two of Canada's best known department stores, Hudson's Bay and Sears. The managers of these stores have to look carefully at whether department stores aren't focused enough, their stores are too big, in the wrong location, laid out poorly, or perhaps there aren't enough sales people on the floor.

In the preceding pages, you have had very brief examples of productivity in just two industries. But productivity is measured and studied in all industries. Airlines measure revenue per passenger-mile, hotels measure occupancy rates, and so on. Investors, lenders and suppliers all want to know how individual businesses compare to their peers. They look carefully at measures of outputs to inputs when buying shares, making loans, and planning their own future production.

WHAT MAKES WORKERS PRODUCTIVE?

What makes workers productive? To find an answer, let's return to the examples from the sporting world. We have to assume that *all* professional athletes possess the essential physical attributes needed in their field: speed, strength, balance and co-ordination. Why then, are some athletes more productive at scoring goals, shooting baskets, or making runs?

Arguably, the answer is that some athletes train harder, are better coached, and practice more than others. Some athletes think and analyse the game better than others. Finally, some athletes are particularly good at working with their teammates. All of these are compelling reasons why some athletes win scoring titles and championships, while others don't. Training, coaching, practice and thinking increases a player's productivity.

The same line of reasoning applies to workers, businesses and entire economies. A business can increase its total production by hiring more workers. However, this is unlikely to increase productivity. Intuition and common sense tell us that a brand-new hire is unlikely to be as productive as an experienced worker. New employees need orientation and training before they can reach full productivity. A garage mechanic who is just out of school is unlikely to be able to rebuild a car engine as quickly as a mechanic with 20 years' experience.

The senior mechanic will have benefitted from what is known as the **experience** or **learning curve**. The learning curve is the name given to the common phenomenon that the more often a person practices or performs a task, the more adept they become at doing it.

Experience Curve/Learning Curve: The phenomenon that the more often that a person performs a task the more adept they become at doing it.

People build up mastery by repeating a task or an activity over and over again. In this way, the time and effort required to perform the activity drops, it becomes easier, and the performer makes fewer mistakes. Think about the first time you assembled a piece of IKEA furniture. You were probably looking to avoid mistakes rather than minimising the time it took to build. You probably spent several minutes staring at the various pieces in confused apprehension. If you purchased a second piece, you probably assembled it in much less time. After assembling a few pieces of IKEA furniture you became expert. Eventually your productivity, as measured by the time (input) it takes to assemble a piece (output) leveled off, with no further improvements.

Rather than hiring new workers, or building new factories, a business should strive to increase its output by raising the productivity of its existing resources. Businesses can do this through training, coaching, practice, and by investing in the tools and equipment that will help workers to accomplish more in less time.

Increasing Productivity

Increasing productivity means, quite simply, doing more with less. Increased productivity is the result of many factors, and there is no easy or simple formula to accomplish it. If there was a simple formula it would look something like this:

1. Have a clear and credible strategy.
2. Invest in good technology.
3. Create motivated employees.

These are the essential elements of increased productivity.

Improved management means doing a better job of planning, organising, leading and controlling the factors of production. This must begin with the business' strategic leaders. If a business has a very clear mission it should be easy for managers to set priorities, and allocate resources.

Increased productivity also comes from good management within each of the business' functional areas. Good operations management can prevent delay and waste and thereby boost the business' productivity. Good marketing management involves planning products that people want, at prices they can afford, making sure they know about it, and making it easy and convenient to get the product into their hands. A carefully designed marketing mix that addresses every step of the buying decision process should generate increased revenue, without generating additional costs.

In addition, as you will learn in subsequent chapters, productivity can be dramatically increased through good human resource management. Groups of very normal people are able to achieve extraordinary results if they are motivated, well organised, and well led.

QUALITY

By using resources more efficiently, the quantity of output will be greater. Producing more is good. Producing it well is better. But unless the resulting goods and services are of satisfactory quality - the "right" products, consumers will not want them.

Quality means meeting or surpassing the customer's expectations. Note that this definition does not use the term "fancy", "expensive", or "lots of features". The key phrase is "customer expectations".

Quality: Meeting or surpassing the customer's expectations.

A Quality Dining Experience

About 15 years ago, I had an office in downtown Toronto. One Wednesday morning before my afternoon class at UTSC, I went to my office. I had a consulting job coming up, so I wanted to spend a few hours on that, before giving a lecture for the "Introduction to Management" class.

I left the house, early, at maybe 7.15 a.m. I worked in my office until about 1.30 p.m. and then hopped in my car to drive to UTSC. From downtown, I took the DVP North to the 401, and then started driving east along the 401. As I was driving, my stomach started to rumble. All of a sudden, I realised I was very hungry! I had forgotten to have either breakfast or lunch, and I had a class at 3.00 p.m. I felt famished, but it was already 2.15 p.m.

Then, I saw the sign indicating the exit for Neilson, and I remember that there was a fast food restaurant at the corner of Ellesmere and Neilson, just 5 minutes from campus. I exited the 401 at Neilson and drove 1 minute south. There, in the shopping plaza, was a picture of an elderly gentleman wearing glasses, a goatee, and the knotted bow-tie.

I parked outside the restaurant and ran inside. A cheery young woman smiled at me and said "Welcome to the Colonel's. How may I help you today?"

I didn't know what I wanted, so I glanced at the menu on the wall above her head. "I'll have the Happy Combo Value Meal" I said.

Thirty seconds later she produced two greasy pieces of chicken, a small box of soggy French fries, and a watered-down cola drink. She smiled and said "That will be $7.95 please. Have a nice day!"

I paid her, and ate the meal in under two minutes. The chicken was greasy, but tasty. The fries were soggy, but filling. The drink was watery but thirst quenching.

The restaurant had given me exactly and precisely what I was expecting: An inexpensive, filling meal, served quickly and without fuss, by a pleasant young woman who was able to give me change back from $10. I drove to UTSC, contented, and gave my lecture.

Every time I go to that fast food restaurant, I get: two greasy pieces of chicken, a small box of soggy French fries, and a watered-down cola drink.

I've never been served the wrong item. I've never had to wait more than two minutes. I've never been told that they have run out of chicken. Every young man or young woman working behind the counter has wished me a "nice day". Even with inflation, I still get change back from $10. I've never been disappointed. Not once in the 50 or 60 times I've eaten there over the past 15 years.

You can have a quality dining experience at the corner of Neilson and Ellesmere.

If a business gives its customers what they want, it can generate easy additional revenue. A satisfied customer becomes a repeat customer. A business' existing customers are its most profitable customers because they don't need to be enticed or convinced.

Giving the customer what they want leads to reduced costs and increased profits. The business won't have to incur additional costs repairing the product, or replacing the product. In addition, the business will have to devote fewer employees to customer service, listening to complaints, apologising and placating disappointed customers. Repairing and replacing products generates paperwork. So getting it right the first time leads to less bureaucracy.

Why Quality Matters – The Cost of A Product That Doesn't Work

A woman goes to a computer store, where she buys a laptop for $750

The variable cost of manufacturing the laptop was $500, as follows:

10 hours labour x $25/ hr.	=	(250)
$250 raw materials	=	(250)

The laptop selling price of $750 therefore represents a 50% mark-up on the manufacturer's variable cost. The profit margin per unit sold is $33^{1/3}\%$.

The woman takes the laptop home, only to discover that when she first tries to use it, the laptop doesn't work.

The next day, the customer returns to the shop. She is frustrated and disappointed that the product doesn't work. She is also frustrated because this second trip to the store is unnecessary and time consuming. When she is in the shop, she spends half an hour directing her frustration and disappointment to the young woman who works behind the computer shop's Customer Service counter.

The young woman behind the customer service counter promises that the computer will be repaired, within 24 hours, and sent by courier to the customer's home. She then says to the customer "at no cost, of course". That's not true. While there is no cost to the customer, the process of dealing with a complaint, repairing a defective product and sending it by courier will cost the manufacturer $125. The additional cost cuts the manufacturer's profit in half.

Revenue	=	$750

Cost including Repair

Original cost	=	(500)
Complaints Department (1/2 hr. @ $20)	=	(10)
Paperwork, reporting, bureaucracy	=	(10)
Repair Department (1/2 hr. @ $40)	=	(20)
Replacement part	=	(60)
Courier	=	(25)
	=	625

Revised Profit	=	$125
Revised Profit Margin	=	$16^{2/3}\%$

The example probably underestimates the true cost of a production error. Research suggests that 90% of dissatisfied customer don't complain. But they tell, on average, nine other people about their bad experience. Then, they take their business elsewhere. As a result, the business loses all future sales and profits from dissatisfied customers. If you assume that the young woman customer might have purchased 3 more computers from the same store in the next dozen years, the lost profit is likely to be in the vicinity of $2,000 – more than twice the value of the original purchase.

QUALITY MANAGEMENT

As the discussion in the preceding pages reveals, it is no longer enough for businesses to measure productivity simply in terms of the numbers of items produced.

In the decades after the Second World War, American consultant W. Edwards Deming tried to persuade firms in North America that they needed to improve quality at least as much as quantity. He wasn't very successful in the United States. However, Deming's ideas were embraced by the Japanese. In the two decades after the end of the Second World War the words "made in Japan" meant goods that were cheap and shoddily made. However, throughout the 1960s and 1970s Japanese managers worked to improve the quality, reliability and durability of their products. By the 1980s, "made in Japan" became synonymous with well-made dependable products.

The Japanese' reputation for building dependable cars allowed them to take market share from their US rivals. American carmakers had developed a reputation for **planned obsolescence**. Planned obsolescence is a deliberate policy of making a product with an artificially limited useful life, so it will soon become obsolete. The rationale behind the strategy is to generate short-term sales volume by reducing the time between repeat purchases.

Planned obsolescence: A deliberate policy of making a product with an artificially limited useful life, so it will soon become obsolete.

In contrast, Japanese cars acquired a reputation for reliability and durability. Consumers wanted cars that started in all temperatures, didn't rust, and did not have to be taken in for repairs with frustrating regularity.

The Japanese adopted Deming's philosophy that quality improvement needed the participation of all employees, an approach called **total quality management (TQM)**. TQM stresses that every employee including senior management, product designers, engineers, and production workers are responsible for seeing that products work as they should.

Total Quality Management: Involving everyone in the business to ensure that products meet or surpass customer expectations, and that no defects are tolerable.

PRODUCTIVITY AND QUALITY: CONCLUSIONS

Productivity means minimising the time, cost and effort that goes into making a product. Quality is ensuring that customers get exactly what they are expecting, or better. A business must therefore develop methods for determining what customers want, and then direct all of its resources toward fulfilling those needs.

Resources spent making repairs or replacing defects are wasted resources. The overall goal of the well-managed business should be to eliminate all errors by making the product correctly from the beginning.

Businesses must recognise the connection between "quality", i.e. doing it right and meeting expectations, and "productivity", i.e. not spending time and money rectifying defects.

There is an old saying that is used by carpenters and builders "measure twice and cut once". It means that it is cheaper to do a job properly the first time, then to have to do it again.

SELF-ASSESSMENT QUESTIONS FOR REVIEW

1. Give an example of a measure of productivity other than any that have been mentioned in this chapter.

2. In the chapter, the concept of the learning curve was illustrated with the example of assembling a piece of IKEA furniture. Think of an activity that, when you performed it the first time, took a great deal of time and thought but, after you had done it several more times, was accomplished with less time and effort. How much faster were you able to accomplish the task, once you had acquired some practice?

3. If you have ever been disappointed by a meal in a restaurant, did you complain to the waiter or did you just say to yourself "I'll never go there again!"

4. Can you recall an occasion when you felt that a business had let you down by failing to deliver what you were expecting? What did you think you were paying for, and what did you actually receive? What caused the breakdown in understanding or the difference between expectation and result? How could the business have communicated or managed your expectations better?

5. Related to the above, did you complain to the business? Did you express your frustration and disappointment to friends and family? How many people did you tell about your bad experience? What was their reaction when you told them about the business that you felt had disappointed you?

DEFINED TERMS

- Economic productivity
- Efficiency
- Experience curve
- Labour productivity
- Learning curve
- Physical productivity
- Planned obsolescence
- Productivity
- Quality
- Total quality management

MANAGING INFORMATION

CHAPTER OVERVIEW

To satisfy customers, a business must have systems and procedures to find out what customers need and want. This requires research. Knowing what to make, when to make it, and how it is to be made requires that managers have timely and accurate information concerning customer needs.

If a business makes what customers need, and what they are expecting, they will become loyal. If the product disappoints, because it is defective or deficient, customers will complain, demand a repair or demand a refund. Nobody wants phones that drop calls, flights that depart late, or ATMs that are out of order. The resources spent replacing or repairing products raise the business' costs, lower its productivity, and reduce profits.

Knowing how a product has performed, and whether it has met customer expectations requires more research, and the collection of more information.

At the beginning of this book you learned about the essential management activity called control. Control involves setting standards, measuring outcomes and, if the actual performance isn't up to standard, taking action to correct or improve performance.

Knowing when to tighten standards and how to improve performance requires that managers have timely and accurate information about the business' internal operations. Managers must know the quantity and value of inputs that go into creating products, and the quantity and value of the sales and revenues that are the desired result.

Managers need information upon which to make decisions. This chapter concerns the area of the business known as information management.

LEARNING OUTCOMES

As a result of reading this chapter you will learn:

- Why businesses need information.

- The difference between data, information and knowledge.

- The meaning of information technology.

- The meaning of data analysis.

- The most common and important type of management information is accounting.

- Accounting that provides detailed information that is important to the managers operating the business is called managerial accounting.

- Accounting that provides general information about the condition of the business to the wider world is called financial accounting.

- All business are required to produce annual financial statements, at very least to calculate the taxes that are owed.

WHY BUSINESSES NEED INFORMATION

Businesses need information to make decisions, and to take appropriate actions.

Armed with the information as to how much coffee it normally sells at any given time of the day, the staff at the World's Worst Coffee Shop would know when to make more. Keeping the dispensers full of freshly made coffee is the best way that a coffee shop can satisfy its customers.

Having the systems in place to do this requires management planning and forethought.

Previously, you learned that a business can make products efficiently and well if it has high quality factors of production. In recent years, some management theorists have suggested that information should now be considered a factor of production.[1] [2]

The position taken in this textbook, however, is that information on its own is **not** a factor of production. Without a human being knowing what information to ask for, and without that human being putting the information to practical use, columns of figures on their own cannot help a business to succeed. Therefore, information is merely a raw material. To explore this idea further, you must understand the difference between:

- Data
- Information
- Knowledge

Let's begin by looking at these three key concepts.

DATA

In its day-to-day activities a business collects a huge and varied amount of facts and figures. A collection of raw facts and figures are called **data**.

Data: A collection of raw facts and figures

On their own, data are of little value. Examples of data include the following:

- The Ottawa store has 6 sales staff.
- Last month we signed 9 new contracts.
- The Alberta region generated $3.7 million in sales in October.
- The factory produced 15,800 bicycles.

---

1 Financial Times,   Why 'Big Data' is the fourth factor of production, Steve Jones, December 27, 2012

2 The Substitution of Information Technology for Other Factors of Production: A Firm Level Analysis Sanjeev Dewan, Graduate School of Management, University of California, Chung-ki Min, Department of Economics, Hankook University of Foreign Studies, Management Scence, December 1, 1997

Another example of raw data:

- "My midterm mark was 78%"

To the right is an image of a simple piece of paper, similar to dozens that you get handed every week. As customers, we tend to crush these into a ball and throw them into the waste paper basket. But the piece of paper to the right contains a wealth of information to those who know how to use it.

It indicates, among other things:

Which products are selling
Which products are not
Which products need to be re-ordered
Which products don't
When customers are in the store
Whether customers pay by cash, debit or credit card.

Through time, sales receipts like this can be used to measure the effect of advertising, sales promotions, and price changes.

INFORMATION

To be useful, data need to be structured, or put into some context. For example, a single data point can to be compared to all the other data points. Alternatively, the data can be revisited across time periods. Once data has been structured or put into context it becomes useful to people as **information**.

Shelley's
Food Market

Welcome to
Shelley's Food Market
85 King Street N.
Campbellville, Ontario

Lane: 006   Cashier: 106
Date: 08/13/2015   Time: 09:37
Transaction: 6681229

** MEAT **
1 lb. Maple Smoked bacon $3.85

** DELI **
500 gms. Asiago & Artichoke Dip $4.95

** BAKERY **
4 Kaiser Rolls @ $0.55 each $2.20

Sub-Total: $10.00
HST $0.00

Total amount due $10.00

TENDERED
Cash: $20.00
Change: $10.00

Items sold: 3

Thank you for shopping at Shelley's

CUSTOMER COPY

Information: Data that has been structured or put into context so that it becomes useful to people

---

Data becomes information only after a human being says "I know how many cups of coffee we sold today. I need to know how that compares to the number we sold yesterday."

Similarly, the data observation "Yesterday we sold 600 cups of coffee" provides no particular insight unless it is given some context. The coffee shop employee might want to ask:

- How many cups do we sell per hour, at various times during the day?
- How does 600 cups relate to our total capacity?
- How does 600 cups relate to the sales in other stores?

KNOWLEDGE

Through the accumulation of understanding and experience, we can use information to help us to form judgements and make decisions. This is the meaning of **knowledge**.

Knowledge: The accumulation of understanding and experience, to use information to form judgments and make decisions.

A simple example of the display of knowledge occurs when an employee says to herself: "The coffee urns are getting empty. I should make a fresh pot."

MANAGEMENT INFORMATION SYSTEMS

A **management information system** (MIS) is any system for collecting data that can be organised in such a way that it produces information of use to the managers of a business. The purpose of a management information system is to give managers the information they need to organise and control the business more effectively.

Management information system (MIS): Any system for collecting data that can be organised in such a way that it produces information of use to the managers of a business.

Restroom Cleanliness Form

Instructions: Post each form on the back of the appropriate restroom door. Input the week ending date on each form. Inspect, clean and restock the restrooms a minimum of every 60 minutes. Input the time of the inspection and your initials.

☐ Women's Room   ☐ Men's Room   Week Ending

Mon.		Tues.		Wed.		Thur.		Fri.		Sat.		Sun.	
Time	Initials	Time	Initials	Time	Initials	Time	Initials	Time	Initials	Time	Initials	Time	Initials

As a very simple example, a restaurant strives to satisfy its customers' needs, and to meet their expectations. Diners at a restaurant expect that it be clean, and appear to be clean. Therefore, as part of the operations system, a restaurant manager needs to know whether the washrooms are inspected regularly, that the floor is clean, the waste paper baskets have been emptied, and the towel and soap dispensers have been topped-up.

Most definitions of a management information system include the word "computer". That is nonsense. The purpose of a management information system is to supply information to the people who need it in a timely fashion, and in a useable form. A simple, paper based form bearing employees' initials can provide a restaurant manager with information about who has done a necessary job, and when.

The management information process begins when a human manager says "I need information".

Often, the motivation for creating a management information system is to bring order to disorder. For example, a business will want to improve its management information if it discovers that:

- Someone cleans the washbasins and tidies a washroom, and tops up the paper only to be followed five minutes later by someone who does it all again. Doing a job a second time, when it doesn't need doing, lowers productivity.

- Someone forgets to clean and tidy the washroom and there are no paper towels in the dispenser. Disappointed customers will not return to a restaurant with filthy washrooms.

Another example, which you have already seen, is a coffee shop that isn't able to track how much coffee it has sold in the previous hour, so isn't aware when it needs to make a fresh pot!

INFORMATION SYSTEMS AND INFORMATION TECHNOLOGY

An **information system** is any system that allows people to record and store data, to organise the data into useable form, and then transmit information to the people who need it.

Information System: Any system that allows people to record and store data, to organise the data into useable form, and then transmit information to the people who need it.

Any technology that allows people to do these things is an **information technology**.

Information technology: Any technology that allows managers to collect, record, store and organise data.

Once again, many definitions of information technology include the word "computer". Again, this is nonsense.

Carbon and Fibre Information Technology.

You and a friend have heard that a band that you like will be coming to Canada. As yet, no venue or dates have been announced.

Several days later, you are walking past a well-known concert venue in downtown Toronto. You see a poster in Box Office window, confirming that the band is coming. The poster indicates the concert dates, the website where advance tickets can be bought, the phone number for the Box Office, and a range of ticket prices.

You reach into your backpack and pull out a pencil. You tear a sheet of paper out of a notebook and then, in pencil, you **record** all of the relevant data: dates, website URL, phone number, and ticket prices. You then fold the paper in half and put it into your wallet for **storage**.

Later that day you meet your friend, and tell her your news.

"So, what have you learned?" asks your friend, Tina.

"Let me see" you reply, and reach for your wallet. Referring to your hand-written note, you **transmit** the information "They will be playing at the Apollo, for two nights: Thursday, December 14th and Saturday, 16th. I made a note of the ticket prices".

Tina thinks about the dates and then, after a little **analysis** says "The 14th is no good for me. I've got two exams"

"What about Saturday?"

"The Thursday exams are my last. Sure, I can go on Saturday"

"Me too!" you say. "Tickets are $35, $45, and $55 in advance, or $40, $50 and $60 at the door."

"I can't afford the top prices. Do you want to get two, at $45?"

"**Decision** made" you say "I'll get my credit card."

The first requirement of any information technology must be that the data can be recorded. In other words, it can be written down. Then, it needs to be stored in a safe manner.

Among the earliest forms of information recording and storage was to chisel shapes and images onto a stone surface. This storage technology allows the information to be retained for thousands of years. It is a storage system that is impervious to heat and cold, rain and fire. However, the storage medium, a stone slab, is heavy and therefore not very portable.

Sometime during the Han Dynasty (202 BC – 220 AD) the Chinese invented paper. Paper is much lighter than stone, so much more portable. Information could travel further. Nevertheless, paper scrolls need the input of an individual scribe. Handwritten documents can be produced only one at a time. The 15th century invention of the printing press by Johannes Guttenburg revolutionised the spread of knowledge. The printing press allowed books and pamphlets to be printed much more quickly and distributed on a much larger scale than previously.

Today of course, most of the information that we collect is written with a key stroke and stored on a silicon chip. The term **information age** has been widely used to describe the period since the 1970s up until today, when the development of affordable personal computers allowed large quantities of data to be assembled, stored and manipulated by the average person.

Information age: The period since the 1970s when then development of affordable personal computers, allowed large quantities of data to be assembled, stored and manipulated by the average person.

Gordon Moore was an American businessman who co-founded Intel, one of the world's leading makers of microchips. In 1965 Moore observed that, in the previous decade, the number of transistors that could be placed on an integrated circuit board had doubled every two years. Moore predicted that the trend was likely to continue for the foreseeable future. Moore's observation implied that the data processing power of an affordable computer would double every two years. Over the past half century, Moore's prediction has proven to be so remarkably accurate that it has come to be known, popularly, as **Moore's Law.**

Moore's Law: The observation that the amount of data that can be recorded, stored and analysed by information technology doubles every two years.

You will recall that, in the 18th century, the sudden coming together of manufacturing techniques and technologies caused the "Industrial Revolution". In a similar way, the rapid development of information technologies caused the 20th century's "information revolution". These technologies have dramatically increased the ease and speed with which we can record, store and analyse data.

DATA ANALYSIS

Data analysis is any operation that organises data into a form that is useful to the user.

Data analysis: Any operation that organises data into a form that is useful to the user.

The most common form of data analysis involves some kind of mathematical manipulation.

If you have ever used an Excel spread sheet, you may have noticed an icon that looks like the image on the right. This button allows your spread sheet to perform one of the simplest of all mathematical manipulations. It sorts data into alphabetical order.

Other common means of sorting data include:

Statistical analysis involves manipulating the data so as to observe such common statistics as the mean (or average), the median (or mid-point), the range (highest to lowest), or the standard deviation (a measure of dispersion within the group).

Time series analysis involves sorting data points across different dates or times, from oldest to newest. Time series analysis allows the user to spot a direction or trend.

Cross sectional analysis involves looking at a data point for a single representative, for example one store or one sales person, and comparing that result to others in the population.

By far the most commonly used, and important, collection of management information is accounting information.

ACCOUNTING INFORMATION

From time to time, brief articles will appear in the business section of the main newspapers and business periodicals which read like this one, which appeared in The Globe & Mail newspaper, a few years ago:

> "Warner Music Group said yesterday it swung into profit in the fourth quarter, but its results fell short of expectations. Profit totaled $12-million (U.S.), or 8 cents a share, for the three months ended Sep. 30, compared with a loss of $30 million or 21 cents a year ago. Revenue fell 6 per cent to $854-million."

One paragraph articles like this are common in the business section of daily newspapers. A question that one might want to ask, after reading this brief item is "How do we know what Warner Music's revenues and profits were?"

We know these values because Warner Music's accountants tell us. That's what accountants do. Accountants..... count.

Accounting is a system for collecting, analysing, and communicating financial information. The purpose of accounting is to measure a business' revenues, expenses, profits or losses, and taxes payable. This is done so that all the parties who are interested in a business will know how it is performing.

Accounting: The system for collecting, analysing and communicating financial information

---

Accountants are trained how to collect and organise all the financial data that passes through a business. Every day businesses generate revenues and incur costs. Bills come through the post and are paid. Shipments of products are sent out and invoices are sent to customers.

Accountants: Individuals trained how to collect, organise and present financial data

---

Accountants must therefore create and operate systems within the business to ensure that all of these, in some cases millions, transactions are collected, recorded, sorted, and analysed.

They make sure that records are accurate and that taxes are paid properly and on time. Accountants and auditors perform overviews of the financial operations of a business in order to help it run efficiently. On the job, accountants:

- Examine statements to ensure accuracy
- Ensure that statements and records comply with laws and regulations
- Compute taxes owed, prepare tax returns, ensure prompt payment
- Organize and maintain financial records

Accountants then translate all this information into a small number of standardised reports so that the business' managers, and others can use the information to help them make informed decisions.

Accounting also uses performance measures to prepare performance reports for owners, the public, and regulatory agencies. To meet these objectives, accountants keep records of such transactions as taxes paid, income received, and expenses incurred, and they analyze the effects of these transactions on particular business activities.

By sorting, analyzing, and recording thousands of transactions, accountants can determine how well a business is being managed and how financially healthy it is.

WHO USES ACCOUNTING INFORMATION?

There are many users of accounting information:

- The owners of the business, whether a business is a sole partnership or a large public corporation, have invested capital into an enterprise. They want to know whether the enterprise is making profits.

- Lenders, such as bankers, want to know that the business is on a sound footing, using borrowed capital wisely, and capable of repaying the money that it owes.

- Employees and unions use accounting information to negotiate wages and salaries and to plan for and receive such benefits as health care, insurance, vacation time, and retirement pay.

- Managers need to know how well a business is performing, and whether it is financially sound.

- Governments use accounting information to determine whether a business owes tax.

- Government departments and ministries rely on accounting information to fulfill their duties. For example, provincial securities commissions require businesses to file financial information so that potential investors can assess a corporation's financial status.

And, perhaps most crucial:

- Business managers themselves use accounting information to set goals, develop plans, set budgets, and evaluate future prospects.

MANAGEMENT ACCOUNTING

Management accounting is the collection, organisation and presentation of financial information of interest to managers within the business. Management accounting is intended to tell internal users about the business' performance and problems, for planning, decision making and control purposes. Management accounting tends to look at individual products, departments or divisions. Managers need this information in order to make decisions for their departments, to monitor current projects, and to plan for future activities.

Management Accounting: The collection, organisation and presentation of financial information of interest to managers within the business.

FINANCIAL ACCOUNTING

The collection, organisation and presentation of key financial information that is of interest to the public is called **financial accounting**.

Among the users of financial accounting are the business' shareholders, suppliers, lenders, banks, tax authorities, and others who are not directly involved in the business on a day-to-day basis. Financial accounting concerns itself with the performance and condition of the business as a whole.

Financial accounting: The collection, organisation, and presentation of financial information of interest to the public, concerning the performance and financial condition of the business as a whole.

Financial accounting information is collected on an annual basis. The name given to a business' operating year is **fiscal year**. The word "fiscal" means "relating to government revenue", especially the collection of taxes. A business must make an accounting of all of its revenues and expenses, and calculate its profits, so that it can pay any taxes every year.

Fiscal year: A business' operating year for financial accounting purposes especially for the payment of taxes.

A business' fiscal year does not need to coincide with the calendar year. It is the business' owners who choose the date on which the year, for its planning, operating and tax purposes starts and ends.

The table below shows the choice of year end for a number of well-known Canadian businesses and not for profit organisations.

A Business Chooses Its Fiscal Year

Organisation	Dates of Fiscal Year
Walmart Canada	1 February to 31 January
Hudson's Bay Company	Saturday closest to 31 January
Best Buy	1 March to 28 February
Government of Canada	1 April to March 31
University of Toronto	1 May to April 30
Maple Leaf Sports	1 July to 30 June
Canadian Tire	Last Saturday in December
Tim Horton's	Sunday closest to 31 December
Rogers	1 January to 31 December

Often a business will choose its fiscal year end to coincide with the ebb and flow of business activity. Most businesses will experience some seasonality or cyclicality to their revenue. Many businesses experience periods of intense activity followed by periods of less activity. Seasonality is especially observed in Canada, with its extreme weather conditions.

Retail stores, for example, have a strong seasonal pattern. Many see the majority of their revenues generated in just three or four months of the year. The year-end Christmas season tends to be particularly busy. Other businesses, such as ski resorts or golf courses close down altogether for several months.

Many businesses choose, as their fiscal year end, a date several weeks after the end of the period of their busiest activity. Retailers often choose the end of January or February. There are a number of simple, practical reasons for this.

A business wants to looks its best when it prepares its year-end financial statements. In December, retail stores are flooded with customers. A business with strong sales in the weeks before Christmas wants to show its lenders and investors that it has bulging cash registers and empty shelves. This helps public sentiment. At the end of December, many of the business' managers want to take vacation time. Then, in the first days of January, many of the items which the business thought had been sold are returned. Note, from the list above, Walmart chooses its fiscal year end as January 31. The Hudson's Bay Company chooses the Saturday nearest to that date. Best Buy's year end is 28 February.

Maple Leaf Sports and Entertainment, whose main properties are the Maple Leafs and the Raptors, ends its year on 30 June, a few weeks after the end of the hockey and basketball playoffs and therefore during the "off-season".

It is only after the period of intense activity has passed that the organisation's accountants can begin to collect and analyse all of the necessary data. During the relative calm, the business' managers have the time to perform all the necessary photocopying, discussing and explaining of their financial affairs with the business' accountants.

AUDITING

Accountants are also engaged to perform a formal examination of an organisation's financial procedures and financial statements. This is done to determine whether the organisation's procedures are in line with accepted principles and to determine whether the financial statements accurately represent its financial condition. This is known as an **audit**.

Audit: A formal examination of an organisation's financial procedures and financial statements.

It is not just businesses that submit their financial statements to formal examination. Government organisations and not for profit organisations must also submit their procedures and financial statements for review. Like businesses, these organisations are accountable to the people they serve, and to the people who finance them, including taxpayers.

Accountants who perform this role are often referred to as **auditors**. The role of an auditor is to perform checks on the collection, organisation, and presentation of accounting information, in order to prevent fraud and reassure investors and lenders.

Auditor: Someone authorised to perform checks on the collection, organisation, and presentation of accounting information in order to prevent fraud and reassure investors and lenders.

When banks and other lenders are considering making loans, or investment banks are assisting corporations to sell shares, they will require the business to prepare and submit audited financial statements. Since auditors are intended to be qualified third parties, the audit will determine if the firm has controls to prevent errors or fraud from going undetected. Auditors examine the full range of finance related documents: invoices, cancelled cheques, payroll records, and cash receipts records. In the performance of their duty, auditors may be required to physically check inventories, tour warehouses and factories, and inspect the condition of the business' capital equipment.

All businesses must use the same rules and methods. These rules and methods are called **generally accepted accounting principles** (GAAP). One of the auditor's responsibilities is to ensure that the client organisation's accounting systems and procedure adhere to GAAP.

Generally Accepted Accounting Principles (GAAP): The rules and methods that an organisation's accounting system must follow.

In Canada, the generally accepted accounting principles are set by the Canadian Institute of Chartered Accountants, the professional body to which all Canadian accountant belong, and whose mandate is to oversee the education and qualifications of accountants, and to set accounting standards.

FINANCIAL STATEMENTS

A business must prepare and publish income statements and balance sheets at regular intervals. These documents focus on the activities of the company as a whole, rather than on individual departments or divisions.

Financial statements must conform to GAAP. This ensures that all interested users can clearly compare information, whether from many different businesses or from the same businesses at different times.

Financial Statements: The balance sheet and the income statement, documetns that a business must prepare and publish at regular intervals

---

We will consider the two most important financial statements, in detail, in the next chapter.

SELF-ASSESSMENT QUESTIONS FOR REVIEW

1. If you were the manager of a ladies' shoe shop, identify the kinds of information that you would need in order to ensure that your shelves were well stocked, and contained the right assortment of products? How could this information be quickly and easily collected?

2. Although it is not business, the University of Toronto is an organisation that is accountable to the Government and the taxpayers for its funding. What sort of accounting information would be useful to:

    *   Your parents as taxpayers
    *   The Principal of UTSC
    *   The Ontario Minister of Education

3. What information did you collect regarding the Universities to which you applied? Why did you collect this particular data? How did you organise the data to help you make your final decision?

4. When your high school sent you a report card, what did you do with the information? Did the grades and comments contained in the report card cause you to change any aspects of your behaviour or study habits?

5. Best Buy's annual year end is February 28th. During which month(s) or season of the year do expect Best Buy makes the greatest volume of sales? Why do you think these months are Best Buy's busiest period?

DEFINED TERMS

*   Accountant
*   Accounting
*   Audit
*   Auditor
*   Data
*   Data analysis
*   Financial

*   Accounting
*   Financial Statements
*   Fiscal Year
*   Generally Accepted Accounting Principles
*   Information
*   Informatin age

*   Information system
*   Information technology
*   Knowledge
*   Management information
*   Management information system
*   Management Accounting
*   Moore's Law

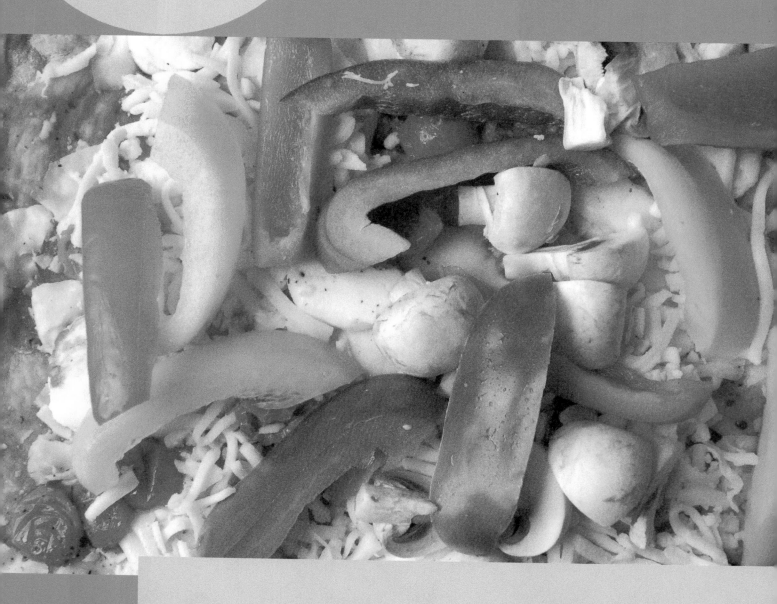

MEASURING PERFORMANCE:
THE FINANCIAL STATEMENTS

CHAPTER OVERVIEW

Managers need information so they can measure and control the business' performance. Armed with information, managers can make sound decisions. Shareholders and lenders need information about the business so they can judge the performance of their investments, or their loans. Suppliers need information so they can decide whether to provide it with raw materials and supplies.

The most commonly collected and widely used management information is accounting: the collection, organisation and presentation of financial information. At the end of each fiscal year, a business must collect and organise the data which are presented to the world as the "Financial Statements".

In this chapter, you will learn about the two most important pieces of management information.

- The income statement shows how well a business performs the fundamental tasks for which it was created, to generate revenues by selling products.

- The balance sheet shows how much capital a business has accumulated, whether from its owners or by borrowing. The balance sheet also shows how the business has used that capital. A business uses capital to buy raw material, parts and supplies, buildings, machinery, tools, and equipment.

- Between them, the income statement and the balance sheet are designed to show interested readers how the business has done, and where the business now stands.

LEARNING OUTCOMES

As a result of reading this chapter you will understand the purpose and structure of the two most important financial statements, the income statement and the balance sheet. Specifically, you will learn:

- The income statement is often compared to a movie, and the balance sheet is compared to a still photograph. You will learn why.

- The income statement reveals the business' ability to generate revenue from selling its product.

- The income statement also breaks down the various costs and expenses that the organisation incurs.

- A business exists in order to make a profit. By showing the reader both revenues and costs, the income statement indicates whether the business has succeeded at one of its principal aims.

- To make and sell products, a business needs capital. The balance sheet shows where the capital has come from.

- Capital put into a business by its owners is called equity

- Capital that is lent to a business is called liabilities

- The money, materials, buildings, technologies and supplies that a business accumulates are called assets.

- The business uses its assets to produce goods and services that its customers need and want.

- A business' total assets, by definition are financed by equity plus liabilities.

- The balance sheet helps the reader to understand the business' ability to raise cash

- The balance sheet helps the reader to understand the risk that lenders are taking by financing the business, in comparison to other businesses.

- The income statement and the balance sheet together tell the reader about the profit made relative to the capital risked.

THE INCOME STATEMENT

One of the key distinguishing characteristics of a business is that, by selling products which satisfy customer needs, it attempts to generate revenues in pursuit of making a profit. The financial statement which shows how well the business has succeeded in this is the **income statement.**

The **income statement** is known by a variety of other names. One of these is the "Statement of Profit and Loss", frequently referred to informally as "the P and L".

The purpose of the income statement is to show how the business performed in the course of the prior year. It shows how much revenue the business generated, and the costs incurred by the business in the course of making and selling products.

Income Statement: The financial statement that shows how much revenue the business generated, and the costs incurred, in the course of making and selling products.

The income statement is occasionally compared to a movie. This is because an income statement has a beginning and an end. It shows information about the business' activities over a period of time. You can recognise this from the fact that an income statement will include in its title some form of words like:

"for the 12 months ending March 31"
"for the year to April 30"
"for the 52 weeks ending 30 September

Look at the example below.

Universal Pizza Company
Income Statement
for the year ended November 30, 2015

Revenue (100,000 pizzas @ $10 per pizza)	$1 000 000
Cost of Sales (100,000 @ $4.00 per pizza)	- 400 ⌐
Gross Profit ⌐	
⌐	

An income statement is laid out in a very logical fashion. It starts with the most obvious indication of business activity: revenue. It then begins to deduct various categories of costs, including the cost of making the goods or services that it sold, the cost of running the business, and any taxes paid. An income statement ends by showing the profit after tax, the net benefit to the owners from operating the business.

REVENUE

The purpose of a business is to sell products or services to customers, in order to satisfy customer needs. Therefore, the ability to generate revenues is evidence that the business is doing **something** right.

The first item on an income statement shows the value of revenues that the business generates by selling its goods and services.

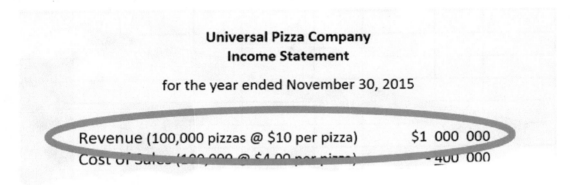

Universal Pizza Company
Income Statement

for the year ended November 30, 2015

Revenue (100,000 pizzas @ $10 per pizza) $1 000 000

Cost of Sales (100,000 @ $4.00 per pizza)   -400 000

In the example above, for illustrative purposes, you are shown more detail than is typical. Below, you can see the Income Statement for Rogers Communications Inc., one of Canada's largest and most diverse businesses. Rogers' revenue comes from a remarkable variety of sources: wireless, cable, advertising on its TV and radio stations, and selling tickets to Blue Jays' baseball games.

SUMMARY OF CONSOLIDATED RESULTS

	Years ended December 31		
(In millions of dollars, except margins and per share amounts)	2014	2013	% Chg
Operating revenue			
Wireless	7,305	7,270	-
Cable	3467	3475	-
Business Solutions	382	374	2
Media	1826	1704	7

REVENUE GROWTH

Most businesses aspire to grow. Canadian and world population is growing. Canadian and world GDP is growing. More people with more wealth want more goods and services. So, most businesses aspire to sell more goods and services to more customers from one year to the next.

If a business' revenue grows through time, it suggests that more customers are buying more products. Falling revenue suggests fewer customers buying less product, or the business is having to reduce its prices to maintain sales.

To judge the business' progress, therefore, its revenues should be viewed in terms of a three to five year trend. Generally accepted accounting principles dictate that businesses must compare their income statement for the current year to the year before, exactly for that reason. Most public corporations will show the 5 year trend for revenue growth, and some other key income statement items which you will learn about below.

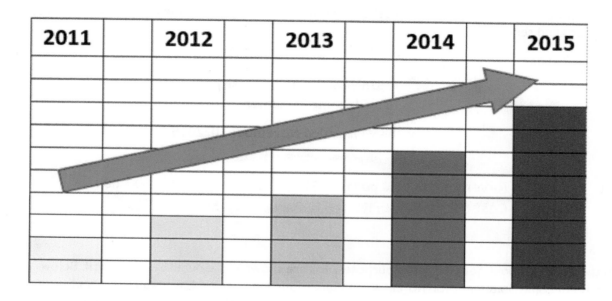

Revenue should grow by at least the growth rate of national GDP. Revenue that doesn't keep up with GDP growth means that the business is growing less quickly than the economy generally.

While revenue growth is good, a business should **not** grow faster than its ability to create and deliver products that maintain their quality. Investors and lenders are suspicious of businesses that promise or display sudden, huge increases in revenue. Unexplained or unexpected spurts in revenue suggests that products may be underpriced, or that sales managers are promising more than the operations managers can deliver. If this is the case, quality will fall.

COST OF SALES

Whenever a business sells a product, whether it is good or a service, it must provide its customer with something in return for the revenue that comes in. Whether the customer walks out with a haircut, a full stomach, a pair of trousers, or a new bicycle, the business has incurred some cost that went into producing or providing the product. Previously, when you learned about how businesses set prices, you learned that the term for this was **cost of sales**.

Cost of sales: The cost of making the product itself, and omits all of the administrative costs of running the business.

GROSS PROFIT

Gross Profit is calculated by deducting the cost of sales from revenue.

Universal Pizza Company
Income Statement

for the year ended November 30, 2015

Revenue (100,000 pizzas @ $10 per pizza)	$1 000 000
Cost of Sales (100,000 @ $4.00 per pizza)	- 400 000
Gross Profit (profit from selling pizzas)	600 000
Operating Expenses (fixed cost of business)	- 100 000
Operating ... profit ... EBIT)	500 000

Gross profit shows whether the business is making a profit from selling its products. In the example, the Universal Pizza Company makes and sells pizzas. It is fundamental to the Universal Pizza's survival that it sell pizzas for more than they cost to produce.

Gross Profit: Revenue minus cost of sales. The profit that comes from selling products.

If Universal Pizza fails to make a gross profit, its managers must either raise the price, or reduce the cost to making pizzas.

A price rise could be managed with more effective promotion. Advertising could raise the product's profile. Sales promotions, like coupons, could get more people to come into the pizzeria and try the product. But these tactics have costs.

The other option is for the business to attempt to reduce the cost of the pizzas by buying cheaper ingredients. Tinned tomato paste may be cheaper than fresh. Thin crusts use less material than thick crusts. The "all dressed pizza" need not include mushrooms. However, a thinner pizza with fewer toppings is unlikely to be compatible with a price rise.

OPERATING EXPENSE

Operating expense is the cost of running the business organisation, as opposed to the cost of making the product itself. Operating expense is known by a variety of other names, including "general and administrative expense".

Operating Expense: The cost of running the business organisation, as opposed to the cost of making the product.

Universal Pizza Company
Income Statement

for the year ended November 30, 2015

Revenue (100,000 pizzas @ $10 per pizza)	$1 000 000
Cost of Sales (100,000 @ $4.00 per pizza)	- 400 000
Gross Profit (profit from selling pizzas)	600 000
Operating Expenses (fixed cost of business)	- 100 000
Operating Profit (or EBIT)	500 000
Interest Expenses ($500,000 loan @ 10%)	- 50 000
Profit Bef T	

Previously, when you learned about break even analysis, you learned that operating expenses are also called "fixed" expenses. This is because operating expenses should not vary, whether the pizzeria makes ten pizzas or ten thousand. If the business doubles its revenue by selling twice as many pizzas the manager's salary shouldn't double, and the pizzeria shouldn't have to pay twice as much rent.

As a business grows, it is likely to take on more employees. It's also likely that a manager who can double the business' revenues will be rewarded with an increase in salary. However, these increases to operating expenses don't happen instantly, automatically, or in direct proportion to the growth in revenue.

A clever manager who can double sales deserves a raise. However, few would suggest that a 20% raise plus a 20% bonus would be a poor reward. A business that doubles its revenues may need to hire an Assistant Manager. However, the Assistant Manager will earn a salary that is lower than that of the Manager.

Lenders and shareholders tend to monitor a business' operating expense carefully, because the ability to control costs is a sure way to attain profits.

OPERATING PROFIT

The gross profit less operating expenses produces the **Operating Profit**. The operating profit has other names, most commonly "Earnings before Interest and Taxes" or "EBIT".

Universal Pizza Company
Income Statement

for the year ended November 30, 2015

Revenue (100,000 pizzas @ $10 per pizza)	$1 000 000
Cost of Sales (100,000 @ $4.00 per pizza)	- 400 000
Gross Profit (profit from selling pizzas)	600 000
Operating Expenses (fixed cost of business)	100 000
Operating Profit (or EBIT)	500 000
Interest Expenses ($500 000 loan @ 10%)	50 000
Profit Before Tax	450 000

Remember, "gross profit" indicates whether the business makes a profit from selling products. Operating profit indicates whether the owners are making a profit from operating business that sells products.

Operating profit: The profit made from operating a business that sells products.

As mentioned above, if a pizzeria fails to make a gross profit from making and selling pizzas, its options are limited. It can try to raise its selling price or it can try to find ways to cut the cost of sales.

On the other hand, a pizzeria that makes a positive gross profit but fails to make an operating profit has a few more options available to it. The business can, of course, try to raise its prices and cut the cost of sales. In addition, if the business isn't profitable because its fixed costs are high, it can attempt to reduce those. Senior managers and other staff who aren't involved with making pizzas can take salary cuts. If senior managers are located in an office not located above the shop, they could move to a smaller, cheaper premises. The advertising budget can be slashed.

Alternatively, the business could *increase* its market budget. More advertising and more effort devoted to other promotional activities could raise the volume of sales. The product may be making a positive contribution, but the quantity of sales hasn't reached break-even. Selling more pizzas may lead to profitability.

INTEREST EXPENSE

Capital, whether it is in the form of sophisticated technology and equipment or simply in the form of cash, is neither plentiful nor free. When a business borrows money, it must pay interest on its debt. Interest paid on borrowed money is a cost of doing business. The income statement shows this cost as the **interest expense.**

The cost of borrowing money does not include the loan itself. If a business borrows $500,000 it will eventually have to repay that amount. The loan is neither revenue, nor is it a cost. However, the interest that the business pays, some negotiated percentage of $500,000, is an expense.

Universal Pizza Company
Income Statement

for the year ended November 30, 2015

Revenue (100,000 pizzas @ $10 per pizza)	$1 000 000
Cost of Sales (100,000 @ $4.00 per pizza)	- 400 000
Gross Profit (profit from selling pizzas)	600 000
Operating Expenses (fixed cost of business)	- 100 000
Operating Profit (or EBIT)	500 000
Interest Expenses ($500,000 loan @ 10%)	- 50 000
Profit Before Tax	450 000
Taxes	130 000

Interest Expense: The interest costs of borrowing money to finance the business.

PROFIT BEFORE TAX AND TAX

Every individual and organisation in Canada that earns an income or makes a profit must pay tax. It's the law. Revenue Canada wants to know how much profit a business has made. So, the business has a legal obligation to tell them.

Sole proprietors will treat any income derived from their employment as personal income, and pay tax at their marginal personal rate. Likewise partners in a general partnership will each pay taxes at their personal rate.

Corporations are separate legal entities from their owners. Therefore, corporations pay taxes in their own name. The corporate tax rate varies from province to province. In addition, some industries benefit from special tax programs and a variety of incentives. As a result, there is no one universal tax rate which is payable by all Canadian businesses. In 2015, most Canadian corporations pay taxes at a rate between 25% and 30%

NET PROFIT

Net profit is often called, informally, "the bottom line". This is because net profit is, literally, the bottom line of the income statement. Net profit is the result after all of the business' costs and expenses are deducted from its revenues. Net profit represents the benefit, or the return, from owning a business.

Universal Pizza Company
Income Statement

for the year ended November 30, 2015

Revenue (100,000 pizzas @ $10 per pizza)	$1 000 000
Cost of Sales (100,000 @ $4.00 per pizza)	- 400 000
Gross Profit (profit from selling pizzas)	600 000
Operating Expenses (fixed cost of business)	- 100 000
Operating Profit (or EBIT)	500 000
Interest Expenses ($500,000 loan @ 10%)	50 000
Profit Before Tax	450 000
Taxes (approx. 25% - 30%)	- 130 000
Net Profit	320 000

Net Profit: The result after all of the business' costs and expenses are deducted from its revenues. Net profit represents the benefit, or the return, from owning a business.

A business that makes a net profit has managed to bring in more money than goes out, after making and selling the product, after the cost of operating the organisation, after paying interest on borrowed capital and finally, after sending the tax man his share. What remains belongs to the business' owners, to spend, to re-invest in the business, or to start a new enterprise. The net profit is theirs.

THE INCOME STATEMENT – SUMMARY AND CONCLUSION

The purpose of the income statement is to show how the business has performed its fundamental task, making and selling products in pursuit of profit.

The structure of the income statement is simple and logical. It begins by showing how much revenue came into the business. It then shows the various costs and expenses that had to be incurred in running the business. First comes cost of sales, the costs incurred to make and sell the product. This is followed by operating expense, the cost of operating the organisation. Then comes interest expense, the cost of borrowing the capital needed to create the organisation. Finally, the income statement shows the cost of complying with the laws of Canada.

The net profit shows the owners of a business whether the rewards were worth all of the effort, and all of the risk. Remember, the owners of a business invest their capital and put it at risk. The next financial statement that you will learn about shows how much capital is at risk, and it shows just what resources, materials, machines and equipment the capital has been used to acquire.

THE BALANCE SHEET:
RAISING CAPITAL AND BUYING POSSESSIONS

A business needs capital. The purpose of the **balance sheet** is to show how much capital a business has accumulated, and to show how the business' has used that capital.

Balance Sheet: The financial statement that shows how much capital has been made available to the business, and how the business has used that capital.

To a growth-seeking organisation the ability to raise capital, and to acquire useful resources is a measure of its financial condition. The term used for the resources that a business acquires is **assets**. An asset is any resource owned or acquired by an organisation from which benefits are expected to flow.

Assets: The resources owned or acquired by an organisation from which benefits are expected to flow.

Assets include things that can be sold or can be used to create products. An asset therefore represents a potential future source of cash. For this reason, assets are generally good things to have.

To give you a simple example: A submarine sandwich business owns a variety of assets. The kitchen will contain toasters, ovens, coffee makers, and fridges. The walk-in fridge will contain several hundred freshly baked buns, boxes of lettuce and tomatoes, packages of cheese, and a variety of sliced meats. Over the course of the next day, the business will turn all of these inputs into finished sandwiches and sell them. The fridge, the other appliances, and all of the food items are necessary parts of the business. Every one of these assets will be used in the production of meals to be sold to hungry customers. The balance sheet puts a value to these assets.

The Balance Sheet is often likened to a snap shot. Like a snap shot, a balance sheet provides information about the business at a single moment in time. Ten minutes after we have our photograph taken we might remove our shoes, mess up our hair, or go from standing to sitting.

Similarly, our assets change from one day to the next. One day we buy a pair of shoes. The next day we take cash from the bank in order to buy a sweater. The things we own are in a constant state of flux. For this reason, a balance sheet always displays the particular date for which it has been presented. In the example below, the balance sheet has been prepared on "November 30, 2015".

Universal Pizza Company
Balance Sheet
as at November 30, 2015

The word "asset" has crept into everyday vocabulary. In popular use, "assets" means any positive attribute or advantage. Thus, people will say "her education will be an asset to her career" and "his positive attitude is a real asset". In accounting terms, an asset is an item that has financial value. If you own a car, and it has a value of $15,000, it is an asset. You are at liberty to sell that car at any time in the future. You can use the money to pay your university tuition, go on a round the world vacation, or make a deposit on the purchase of a house. Let's begin by looking at a common list of assets that might be possessed by ordinary people:

Rachel, a 36 year old marketing analyst for a software business, might list her most valuable assets as follows:

- 3 bedroom Bungalow $420,000
- Fiat Punto   18,000
- Cash in savings account   6,500

Lynn's job is to manage customer loyalty programs at a large retail clothing chain. Lynn lives in a condo, but drives a more expensive car than Rachel. She has a small amount of cash in the bank, but she prefers to take whatever cash she has to buy art.

- 2-bedroom city centre condo $340,000
- Car   32,000
- 3 limited edition art prints   15,600
- Cash in Bank   1,200

Martin, 43, is married with four kids. Martin and his wife need a home that is big enough to accommodate the kids, and they need two cars. They don't have a lot of spare cash. In fact, they have a small overdraft. With four kids and a dog, they have neither the time nor the interest to go to art galleries. At the top of Martin's list of assets are the following:

- 5 bedroom house $680,000
- Cottage   286,000
- Ford Escape   28,600
- Subaru Forrester   24,500
- Cash in bank   0

Of course, these individuals own a variety of other possessions. Between them, their assets include a 4-year old mountain bike, a 32-inch TV, sofas, printers, and other items which each has acquired through the years. Like most people, many of their possession are aging or used. Seven years ago Martin spent $2,300 on his dining room set. Since then, Martin's kids have given the table a few knocks, and one of the 6 chairs is broken. Rachel spent nearly $1,200 on a bridesmaid's dress. It doesn't fit her anymore, and the colour is no longer in style. In accounting terms, the value of an asset is the amount that it could realise in the payment of a debt.

The term that accountants use for the gradual decline in an asset's value, due to age, use or obsolescence is **depreciation**. If Martin were to do a quick search of an internet auction site, he would discover that the dining room set for which he paid $2,300 seven years ago now has a value of one tenth of that, due to depreciation.

Depreciation: The gradual decline in an asset's value, due to age, use or obsolescence.

Happily for their owners, some assets can increase in value. Although Martin's house is now worth $680,000 in the real estate market, he and his wife paid only $375,000 when they bought it 14 years ago. The name for this, the increase in the market value of an asset is **appreciation**.

Appreciation: The increase in the market value of an asset

	Martin **Balance Sheet** **as at October 31, 2015**	
Assets		**Liabiliti**
House	680,000	Car Lo
Cottage	286,000	Mort
Ford Escape (new = $38,000)	28,600	
Subaru (new = $34,000)	24,500	
Other miscellaneous	12,000	Equ
Kids	(not an asset)	Ir
Total Assets	**$1,031,100**	

Note that an asset must be a resource that is **owned**. While a well-trained, well-educated, and hard-working employee is a benefit to a business, in accounting terms people are not assets. An employer cannot sell an employee to another business, like a slave. An employee sells his or her services to the employer voluntarily, and expects to be fairly compensated.

Professional athletes *appear* to get bought and sold all the time, or traded for other athletes. The difference is that the Leafs, Blue Jays and Raptors do not own players, they own the contracts which players have willingly signed. In these contracts, athletes agree to sell their services to the owners of the contract. A player is not an asset, the contract is the asset. A sports organisation that needs to raise money can selling a player's contract to another team.

With the basic concept of asset in mind, let's take a look at the types of assets commonly owned by most businesses.

Cash: Businesses need cash with which to buy other assets, and with which to pay their bills. Apple, one of the world's largest corporations, has accumulated US$137 billion (CDN $170 billion) in cash.

Accounts receivable: Many businesses do not expect or demand immediate payment from their customers. When you call a plumber or an electrician, he will typically send you bill. You will pay it – eventually. If you are like most people, it will take you a week or two to get around to paying your bills.

Most businesses therefore have a significant asset called **accounts receivable.** This is the name given to money that a business is legally owed, and is expecting to receive.

Accounts receivable: Money that a business is legally owed, and is expecting to receive.

Most accounts receivable are not due from consumers. Accounts receivable are mostly due from other businesses in a supply chain. As an example: An agricultural supplies store sells 600 kilograms of cattle feed to a dairy farmer. The dairy farmer promises to pay for the feed at the end of the month. The dairy farmer produces 2,000 litres of raw cream and sells it to a maker of ice cream. The ice cream maker promises to pay the dairy farmer at the end of the month. The ice cream maker sells 3,000 half-litre cartons of ice cream to a grocery store. The grocery store promises to pay the ice cream maker at the end of the month. The grocery store sells a carton of ice cream to your mum. Your mum pays the grocery store in cash. The agricultural supplies store won't get paid for several weeks, only after your mum takes the ice cream home, and everyone else gets paid.

Raw Materials: Businesses need to acquire raw materials before they can make them into something else. Warehouses full of parts, supplies, and natural resources have value.

Finished Goods: Once built or assembled, a business hopes and intends to sell finished products to someone else. Until they do so, products spend time sitting on the shelves of stores and warehouses, waiting for customers to come along. In mid-2015 The Hudson's Bay Company, Canada's largest department store owned more than $2.4 billion worth of finished goods or **inventory** ready to be bought by someone.

Inventory: Finished goods ready to be bought.

Machinery and capital equipment: A business can't operate without machinery plant and equipment. While some of this can be rented or leased, in most cases the business owns the capital with which to make its products. By the end of 2014, Magna International, a Canadian corporation based in Newmarket, Ontario, had invested more than $15 billion into property, plant and equipment. After depreciation (drills, stamps, and metal cutting machines soon wear out) all of this factory equipment is worth more than $6 billion.

Buildings and real estate: While many businesses rent or lease their offices, factories or warehouse space, many others own their own premises. For example, Rogers owns the Rogers Dome, the home of the Toronto Blue Jays.

Intangible Assets: Earlier, you learned that a hockey team does not own the players who work for it.

Rather, the team owns each player's contract. The contract itself, just a few pieces of paper, is an **intangible asset**. An intangible asset is a resource or possession that has little or no tangible value itself, but which can be expected to bring financial benefit.

Intangible Asset: Any resource or possession that has little or no tangible value, but which can be expected to bring financial benefit.

Other examples of intangible assets include trademarks, patents, copyrights, customer lists, broadcast rights, and trade secrets. Among the most famous and valuable intangible assets in the world are the Coca-Cola trademark and, intriguingly, the secret formula used to make the world's best-selling soft drink. Coca-Cola generates a great deal of publicity from the fact that its recipe is not written down, but parts of it are carried in the memories of a small group of very senior employees. On its balance sheet at the end of 2014, Coca-Cola valued these and other intangible assets at more than US$12 billion.[1]

Valuing an Intangible Asset

To see why a few pieces of paper may have considerable financial value, consider that the Pittsburgh Penguins own a contract signed by Sidney Crosby. The contract states that, for a period of several years, Mr. Crosby will play hockey only for the Penguins.

Thanks to the contract, the Penguins have the exclusive right to employ the 2-time NHL scoring champion, 2-time NHL Most Valuable Player, the Captain of Team Canada, and the man who scored an Olympic Gold Medal winning goal.

The year before Mr. Crosby began his career in Pittsburgh the team averaged less than 12,000 spectators. In the following year, attendance increased by nearly 4,000 spectators, and the heightened demand allowed the Penguins to increase the average ticket price by $10. In season ticket revenue alone, Mr. Crosby's contract is arguably worth:

Additional season ticket price:	11,750 tickets x 40 games x $10	=	$4,700,000 per year
Additional seasonal attendance:	4,000 tickets x 40 games x $50	=	$8,000,000 per year
	Total additional revenue	=	$12,700,000 per year

This calculation omits any additional revenues that might come from another intangible asset, the right to broadcast Penguin games on local TV and radio stations.

So, the assets component of a typical balance sheet might look something like this:

---

1 United States Securities and Exchange Commission, Form 10-K For The Coca-Cola Company, December 2014, p. 39

Mollie and Abbie Dog Toys Limited Balance Sheet as at November 30, 2015		
Assets		
Cash in bank	20,000	
Finished goods	100,000	
Work in progress	60,000	
Raw materials	40,000	Useful resources available to the business: cash, goods for sale, raw materials, office equipment, parts and supplies, trucks, machinery, factories, etc.
Accts Receivable	80,000	
Parts and supplies	50,000	
Delivery trucks	50,000	
Machinery	100,000	
Factory	250,000	
Total Assets	$750,000	

Now that you understand assets, you need to understand the other elements of the balance sheet: owners' equity and liabilities.

OWNERS' EQUITY

A business begins when an entrepreneur has an idea. Without capital, most ideas remain just that: ideas. So, one of the first things an entrepreneur must do is find capital. The first, and most obvious, source of a business' capital is its founders. Many small businesses are entirely financed by their founders.

However, the founders' personal capital is usually limited. Once the entrepreneurs have exhausted their own capital they must find other backers: investors who believe in the idea and are willing to provide financial support. This is why business founders look for partners, limited partners or shareholders.

A potential investor should not be surprised if an entrepreneur has limited financial resources. But every entrepreneur should be expected to invest as much capital as they reasonably can, or "put their money where their mouth is". The first question that any would-be investor or lender should ask an entrepreneur is "How much of your own money will YOU invest?"

The name given to the value of the capital that is put into a business by its owners is **owners' equity.** If you were to start a tutoring business, and you bought a $400 colour printer, the money that you paid for the asset represents your financial commitment to the business. It is your owners' equity.

Owners' Equity: The value of the capital put into a business by its owners

When your parents bought their home, they were obliged to make a down payment. They may have used their savings, a family inheritance, or sold some other asset to supply their portion of the purchase price. In Canada, banks typically insist that home buyers contribute a minimum of 25% of a home's purchase price. If the owners provide that much equity, the banks will normally finance the rest with a mortgage loan.

A balance sheet shows the owners' equity in two components. First, it shows the **paid-in capital**. As the name suggests, this is the capital that the business' owners actively invest in the business. Sole proprietors or partners will buy assets with their own money. In this case the balance sheet will show the words "owners' capital". Shareholders will buy shares, and the corporation will use the capital to buy assets. In that case, the balance sheet will read "share capital".

Paid-in Capital: Capital that business owners actively pay in to the business.

In addition, owners' equity includes an item called **retained earnings**. As a business grows, and begins to make profits, it does not keep its profits locked up in wooden chests, sealed in a vault. Profits, earned every day, and on every sale, are used to buy more raw materials, newer equipment, bigger factories, more delivery trucks, and to hire new employees. Retained earnings accumulate as the business grows. These are used to create a bigger business capable of making more profit in the future.

Retained earnings: The profits that a business accumulates as it grows. These are used to buy more assets, hire new employees and create more profit in the future.

A pizzeria that makes a pizza for $4 and sells it for $5, has a dollar of gross profit with which to buy a new bread oven, a bigger toaster, or put up a bigger sign.

At the end of each fiscal year, when accountants prepare a business' financial statements, they calculate the profits for the year. At that point, the owners of the business have every right to take the profits in cash. Every partner, limited partner, or shareholder could demand that they take their money and spend it on a vacation cruise, buy a new car, or blow it all on champagne and cigars.

They could. But most don't. You will recall that the definition of an **investment** is a decision not to spend one's capital for immediate consumption, but to put it to work so that it might produce more capital in the future.

Investment: A decision not to spend one's capital for immediate consumption, but to put it to work so that it might produce more capital in the future.

Business owners not only put capital into a business. Their usual intent is to keep capital in the business, as long as it continues to grow and produce more profit in the future.

Mollie and Abbie Dog Toys Limited Balance Sheet as at November 30, 2015			
Assets			
Useful resources available to the business: Cash, goods for sale, raw materials, office equipment, parts and supplies, trucks, machinery, factories, etc. These must be paid for.	**Owners' Equity**		
	Share capital	Capital **put** into the business by the owners
	Retained Earnings	Capital **kept** in the business by the owners

LIABILITIES

Finance, you will remember, is the activity that involves finding, packaging and distributing money. Financial intermediaries help to connect entrepreneurs and business managers with savers and investors.

The assets on a balance sheet show where a business has put its money. The other half of the balance sheet shows where the money came from. When a business raises capital it can come from only two sources. One source of a business' capital is the business owners. If the owners can't raise enough capital to carry out their plans, the other source is to borrow capital from others. Money that a business has borrowed or money that it owes is known in accounting terms as **liabilities**.

Liabilities: Money that a business has borrowed or money that it owes

---

Liability, is another way of saying loan, obligation or debt. Incurring a liability is one of the two ways that a business can acquire the capital to pay for assets. A simple example of a liability is a mortgage. When your parents bought their home, an asset, it is likely that they obtained a mortgage from the bank. Perhaps their home cost $380,000. Perhaps their savings were $120,000. So they borrowed $260,000 to acquire your family home. Likewise, you might own a car for which you paid $18,000. If you had only $6,000 when you bought the car, you would have obtained a car loan from the dealer, or from a bank.

With the basic concept of liabilities in mind, let's take a look at the types of liabilities commonly owed by most businesses.

Bank line of credit: Banks lend money, that's why they exist. Many of the loans that banks make are for very short duration. A **line of credit** is an agreement between a bank and a borrowing customer that the customer can withdraw money up to an agreed limit, as long as the loan is repaid in full at some point during the year. From time to time, as the business grows, the bank and the customer will review and renegotiate the limit.

Line of credit: An agreement between a bank and a borrowing customer that the customer can withdraw money up to an agreed amount as long as the loan is repaid in full at some point during the year.

Lines of credit are used by businesses that have to make large purchases from time to time, but don't want to negotiate a separate loan each time. Your personal credit card is a line of credit. You can make larger purchases whenever you like, and the bank provides the payment. However, the bank expects that you will repay the balance at the end of the month.

Accounts payable: You will recall from the discussion just a few pages back, many businesses do not expect or demand immediate payment from their customers. When you call a plumber or an electrician, he will typically send you bill. Most businesses therefore have a significant asset called **accounts payable**. This is the name given to money that a business legally owes, and is expecting to have to pay.

Accounts payable: Money that a business legally owes, and is expecting to have to pay.

You will also recall from the earlier discussion that accounts payable are mostly due to other businesses in a supply chain. As an example: The grocery store promises to pay the ice cream maker. The ice cream maker promises to pay the dairy farmer. The dairy farmer promises to pay agricultural supplies store. They are all owed money by somebody else, and nobody will get paid until your mum pays the grocery store in cash.

Taxes payable: This is money owing to a municipal, provincial or federal government.

Loans payable: These are loans that are due to be repaid in the next 12 months.

Term Loans: These are loans that must eventually be repaid, but not within the next 12 months.

Mortgages: These are loans to pay for buildings like warehouses, offices and factories. The borrower is bound to hand over ownership of the building if payments on the loan are not made.

Mollie and Abbie Dog Toys Limited Balance Sheet as at November 30, 2015			
Assets		**Liabilities**	
Cash in bank	20,000	Bank – line of credit	7,000
Finished goods inventory	100,000	Accounts Payable:	
Work in progress	60,000	Suppliers	40,000
Raw materials	40,000	Wages owed to employees	30,000
Accounts Receivable	80,000	Tax owed to Revenue Canada	8,000
Parts and supplies	50,000	3 year GMC Truck loan	35,000
Delivery trucks	50,000	5 year term loan	100,000
Machinery	100,000	Mortgage on factory	150,000
Factory	250,000	**Owners' Equity**	
		Share capital	200,000
		Retained earnings	180,000
Total Assets	**$750,000**	**Total Liabilities + Equity**	**$750,000**

THE ACCOUNTING EQUATION

Having briefly explained the three main components of the balance sheet we can now put them all together.

Remember, assets are the useful resources that a business has purchased with its capital. Also remember there are only two sources of capital. Capital can be invested by the business' owners or capital can be lent by others, like banks. Everything that a business owns, had to be paid for. The balance sheet is called what it is because the value of the assets has to be equal to the value of the owners' equity and the liabilities. The two sides, the uses and the sources, must balance.

This equation, assets being equal to owners' equity plus liabilities, is commonly known as **the accounting equation:**

The Accounting Equation: Assets = Owners' Equity + Liabilities

Mollie and Abbie Dog Toys Limited Balance Sheet as at November 30, 2015	
Assets	**Liabilities**
Useful resources available to the business: Cash, goods for sale, raw materials, office equipment, parts and supplies, trucks, machinery, factories, etc.	Money borrowed from financial intermediaries and money owed to other creditors and suppliers
	Owners' Equity
	Money put into the business and kept in the business, by its owners
Total Assets =	Total Liabilities + Owners' Equity

INTERPRETING THE BALANCE SHEET – LIQUIDITY

Remember, a balance sheet shows the assets available to a business. It shows their value, at a single moment in time. The balance sheet also shows the reader how the assets were acquired. If the capital was borrowed, the business has liabilities. If the capital was put into the business by its owners, the value of the assets thus acquired is their equity.

A balance sheet can tell us, from the types of assets and liabilities that a business has, whether the business has the ability to raise the cash to pay its bills. As noted above, since assets can be sold, they represent a potential, future source of cash.

Some assets can be turned into cash instantly. Some assets take a while to sell, their value subject to change. Some assets may be very hard to sell, and their value unknown. The ease and speed with which an asset can be converted into cash is called **liquidity**.

Liquidity: The ease and speed with which an asset can be converted into cash

---

The reason that liquidity is important is, at the end of the day an organisation needs cash. While machinery and buildings are a store of value they can't be used to pay tax, pay salaries, or buy raw materials. Assets are used to generate revenues, but most assets aren't cash and can't be used to buy things. A business needs cash to pay day-to-day bills. That's why we care about "current" assets & "current" liabilities.

CURRENT ASSETS

Current assets are assets that an organisation hopes or expects to convert into cash within the "current" fiscal year, in other words within the next twelve months.

Current assets: Assets that an organisation hopes or expects to convert into cash within the "current" year, in other words within the next twelve months.

The most liquid asset is cash itself, followed by any short term bank deposits. Cash, of course, is instantly useable to pay bills or buy things. A $10 bill can be used to buy groceries, pay for a taxi ride, or tip a waitress. If you don't have the cash in your wallet, money in your bank account should normally be accessible in the time it takes to find an ATM.

Other assets can be converted into cash reasonably "soon", if not instantly. Accounts receivable, money owed to you by your customers, are normally due to be paid within 30 days. A few of a business' customers may be strapped for cash, and take a little longer. But even these customers may make partial payment in the current month, and endeavour to pay the balance in the month after that. Rogers Communications Inc. Canada's largest internet, cable and mobile phone service business takes, on average 43 days to collect the money it is owed.[2] Maple Leaf Foods, one of Canada's largest diversified food manufacturers, takes, on average 37 days[3].

---

2 Rogers Communications Inc. Annual Report 2014
3 Maple Leaf Foods Annual Report 2014

The list of current assets includes:

- Cash: By definition cash is a perfectly liquid asset.
- Accounts receivable: Money owed to the business is normally due within a month.
- Finished goods inventory: These are products which are ready and available for sale.
- Work in progress: These are products that will soon be available for sale.
- Raw materials: Inputs to products which are scheduled to be created and made available for sale.

There are other assets which the business is not intending to sell. Machinery and equipment, parts and supplies, delivery trucks, and buildings are assets because they are all used in the creation of products. They help to turn the raw materials into finished goods, get those finished goods to market, and eventually generate cash. But these assets generate cash indirectly. They can't or won't easily be sold because they are bolted down, or immobile. For this reason, assets which aren't intended for immediate sale are referred to as long term assets or **fixed assets**.

Fixed Assets: Assets that aren't intended for immediate sale.

Mollie and Abbie Dog Toys Limited Balance Sheet as at November 30, 2015			
Assets		**Liabilities**	
Current Assets		Assets that can be turned into cash today.	
Cash in bank	20,000		
Account Receivable	80,000	Assets that can be turned into cash, for reasonably certain value, within a month.	
Finished goods inventory	100,000		
Work in progress	60,000	Assets that can be turned into cash, after some work, within a few weeks.	
Raw materials	40,000		
Long Term or Fixed Assets			
Factory	250,000	Assets that aren't intended to be turned into cash. They help generate cash by turning other assets into finished products.	
Machinery	100,000		
Delivery trucks	50,000		
Parts and supplies	50,000		
Total Assets	$750,000		

You will notice, as you go down the above list, that each successive asset is one step, a few days or a few processes, further away from being converted into cash.

Some raw materials may get wasted, or spoiled. Some work in progress may be defective, or rejected at some stage along the assembly process. Some finished goods may get damaged in transit. Some others may not sell. Some accounts receivable may not be collectable. A business may find that one of its customers fails and goes out of business while still owing money.

So, while we can say with almost perfect certainty that two $10 bills can be used to make a $20 purchase, the same cannot be said about $20 worth of accounts receivable or $20 worth of finished goods inventory. Thus, while all assets represent a possible future source of cash, the precise value of that cash becomes less certain as the time it takes to realise increases.

Suppose you go out for the evening with friends. At the end of the evening it is cold and dark. The nearest subway station is 12 blocks away. You are tired, so you decide to take a cab. Just before you call for a taxi, you look in your wallet and it's empty of cash! The fact that you own a bike worth $700 is of no concern to the cab driver.

CURRENT LIABILITIES

As you see from above, not all assets are the same. The same can be said about liabilities.

Some debts are repayable immediately. Some debts don't need to be repaid until the end of the month, giving us a week or two to come up with the cash. Still other debts may not be due for several months, or years. If you get a car loan, your first payment may not be due for 6 months, and the entire loan will be repaid on a schedule that lasts 3 to 5 years.

Mollie and Abbie Dog Toys Limited Balance Sheet as at November30, 2015		
	Current Liabilities	
To be repaid immediately or on demand	Bank Line of Credit	2,000
Bills and debts to be paid within the month.	Accounts Payable:	
	Bills Payable to Suppliers	40,000
	Wages owed to Employees	30,000
To be paid this year	Taxes due to Revenue Canada	8,000
To be repaid after this year (e.g. 3 – 5 years)	**Long term Liabilities**	
	Bank Loan	100,000
	GMC Truck loan	40,000
To be repaid over 25 years	Mortgage – factory	150,000

If you obtain a mortgage on your house, while there are small payments to be paid every month, the entire loan is not scheduled to be repaid for 25 years.

MEASURES OF LIQUIDITY

The quickest, surest source of liquidity is **cash**. This is followed by having access to a bank account. Virtually every business therefore keeps some cash in the bank. It's always useful to have some cash. So, the simplest and most obvious measure of a business' liquidity is its cash balance.

Cash: The quickest, surest source of liquidity.

Shareholders do not expect the businesses in which they invest to always sit on mountains of cash. Investors expect the managers of a business to put the cash to good work. However, this has to be balanced with the need for the business to have sufficient cash to pay its bills as they come due. A business with $2 million in the bank can pay more bills, more quickly than a business with $1 million.

In addition, having lots of cash gives a business the ability to seize sudden or unforeseen opportunities. Apple's managers have spent many years proving that they can run a business profitably and well. As a result, there doesn't seem to be a growing chorus of shareholders complaining that they are wasting the $137 billion they have accumulated in the bank. On the contrary, this huge source of liquidity allows Apple's managers to buy almost any internet start-up, hardware maker or software developer they choose, when the time is right.

Another very common measure of liquidity is **working capital**. Working capital is calculated by subtracting the organisation's current liabilities from its current assets. This calculation gives the difference between an organisation's anticipated cash inflows and its expected cash outflows, over the next twelve months. The calculation of working capital is intended to aid the organisation in understanding its ability to pay its bills, during that period.

Working Capital = Current Assets minus Current Liabilities

Working Capital: The difference between current assets and current liabilities, or anticipated inflows and outflows, over the next twelve months.

To put the calculation of working capital into personal terms, suppose you had a job that paid you $2,600 after taxes every month. You are normally paid on the 30th day of the month. Sometime during the month you sit down at your kitchen table and open up your accumulated mail. In the mail are your VISA card statement, your Home Depot credit card statement, and the monthly bill from your internet and cable provider. In addition, you receive a reminder that your rent is due on the 25th. You also have a monthly car loan repayment. You know that you have $400 in your savings account.

This gives you working capital, for this month, as follows:

Current assets:	Paycheck	$2,600
	Saving account	400
Current liabilities:	VISA card	$1,100
	Home Depot card	250
	Rent	650
	Cable and internet bill	100
	Car loan – monthly payment	300

Can you pay your bills? In this example, you can. Your working capital for the month is $3,000 minus $2,400 or $600.

While working capital measures the absolute difference between current assets and current liabilities, the **current ratio** shows the relative difference between them. Current ratio is calculated by dividing current assets by current liabilities.

$$\text{Current Ratio} = \text{Current Assets} \div \text{Current Liabilities}$$

Current ratio: Current assets divided by current liabilities.

The purpose of calculating the current ratio is the same as the purpose behind calculating working capital: to aid the organisation in understanding its ability to generate cash and pay its bills, during the current year.

Using the personal example above, if your anticipated income is $3,000 and your expected bills and required payments are $2,400, your current ratio is $3,000 / $2,400 = 1.25 times.

Between working capital and current ratio, the latter is perhaps a more useful measure for managing short term cash flows. A business which anticipates raising $3,000,000 from its current assets and needing to pay $2,999,400 in current liabilities has the same working capital as you do, just $600. However, it has very little "wiggle room" when it comes to paying its bills. If it fails to collect just 1/10 of 1% of what it is owed it will have scramble to pay its own debts.

INTERPRETING THE BALANCE SHEET - LEVERAGE

As you have learned, in order to buy the assets that it needs, a business needs capital. The first source of capital is owners' equity. If the owners of a business aren't willing to put their capital at risk, why should anyone else?

Banks and other financial intermediaries exist to make loans. They provide loans in combination with business owners' equity capital, to make plans and projects come to realisation. How much a bank lends, the length of the loan, and the interest rate to be paid all depends on an assessment of the business' plans, its ownership, leadership and management, and the nature of the project.

Another important consideration to lenders is the amount that a business has already borrowed relative to the amount of equity that the owners have contributed. A business that borrows very heavily can acquire a lot of assets, and grow. The ratio of how much borrowing a business does, relative to the owners' equity is called **leverage**.

Leverage: The ratio of how much borrowing a business does, relative to the owners' equity.

Leverage matters because, while borrowing allows the business to buy useful assets, it also means the business will have to pay more interest. In addition, the more capital that a business' managers decide to borrow, the more they are asking others to take the risk.

When looking at a balance sheet most readers will want to consider the liabilities to owners' equity ratio, more commonly called the **debt to equity ratio**. The debt to equity ratio is simply the product of total liabilities divided by total owners' equity.

Debt to Equity Ratio: Total liabilities divided by total owners' equity.

This ratio is important because banks and other lenders place limits on what the ratio should be. It was noted previously that Canadian banks will lend home buyers only 75 per cent of the purchase price of a property. They limit the debt to equity ratio on mortgage lending to 75%: 25% or 3:1.

While there are no formal or fixed rules regarding how much leverage that a business can put on its balance sheet. It is most unusual for banks or other lenders to provide more than 80% of the capital, a leverage ratio of 4:1, to any enterprise, no matter how well established, well-run, or profitable.

The image below shows the debt to equity ratio for five large and well-known Canadian businesses, over the past five years.

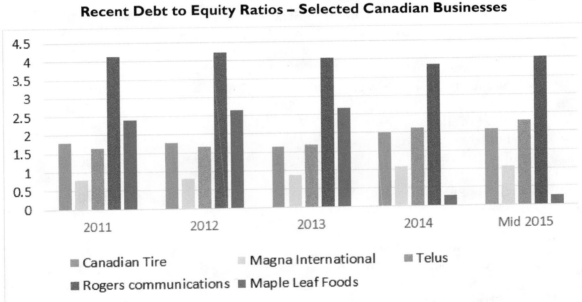

Recent Debt to Equity Ratios – Selected Canadian Businesses

Only Rogers Communications, barely, borrows $4 dollars for every dollar of owners' equity.

RETURN ON INVESTMENT

The final important piece of information to be taken from the financial statements combines information from the income statement with information from the balance sheet.

Return on investment (ROI) measures the profit generated by a business relative to the amount of capital invested by the owners at the beginning of the year. ROI is usually expressed as a percentage.

The return on investment formula is:

$$ROI = (Net\ Profit\ /\ Owners'\ Equity) \times 100\%$$

Return on investment (ROI): The profit generated by a business relative to the amount of capital invested by the owners.

To give you a very simple example, suppose you decided to establish a business tutoring algebra. You have limited savings, but you invest $600 into a new printer, stationery, and supplies. Your upfront investment is your owners' equity. During the year you deliver 80 hours of tutoring at $25 per hour. Your total revenue is $2,000. Your cost of sales, the costs incurred to deliver your service, consists mostly of bus and taxi fares. In addition you used your printer a good deal. It's a bit more beat up after the end of the year than when you first took it out of the box.

The income statement for your sole proprietorship will be as follows:

Scarborough Math Tutoring
Income Statement
September 1, 2014 to August 31, 2015

Revenue	
80 tutorial hours x $25 per hour	$2,000
Cost of Sales	
Bus fares	180
Taxi fares	200
Gross Profit	**1620**
Operating Expenses	
Depreciation of printer	100
Miscellaneous office supplies	20
Interest expense	nil
Taxes	nil
Net profit	1500

The positive return, the benefit that came to you from risking $600, was $1500. Your return on investment is calculated using the formula shown on the previous page:

$$\text{Return on Investment} = \frac{\$1,500}{\$600} = 250\%$$

You earned 250% more than you risked. Normally, the profit or loss on a business investment is calculated so as to show an annual return.

SELF-ASSESSMENT QUESTIONS FOR REVIEW

Consider the balance sheets of two businesses in the same industry.

Consolidated Magnox Balance Sheet as at						
Assets			**Liabilities**			
Current:			Current:			
Cash	50		Overdraft	40		
Inventory	150		Employees	50		
Receivable	30		Suppliers	60		
Fixed Assets:			Term Liabs:			
Machinery	100		Bank loan	80		
Factory	150		Mortgage	120		
Parts	20					
			Equity			
			Shares	100		
			Profits	50		
Total Assets	**500**		**Liabs + Equity**	**500**		

International Comcorp Balance Sheet as at				
Assets			**Liabilities**	
Current:			Current:	
Cash	10		Overdraft	70
Inventory	210		Employees	70
Receivable	40		Suppliers	60
Fixed Assets:			Term Liabs:	
Machinery	80		Bank loan	90
Factory	130		Mortgage	130
Parts	30			
			Equity	
			Shares	50
			Profits	30
Total Assets	**500**		**Liabs + Equity**	**500**

Which of these two firms has the most cash?

1. Which of these two firms appears to have the smaller amount of unsold product?

2. Which of these two firms appears to have the bigger (or newer) plant and equipment?

3. Which of these two firms appears to be slower in paying its bills?

4. Which of these two firms is more heavily reliant on bank debt?

5. Which of these two firms has raised less initial capital from its shareholders?

6. Which of these two firms has, through time, accumulated less profit?

DEFINED TERMS

- Accounting Equation
- Accounts payable
- Accounts receivable
- Appreciation
- Asset
- Balance sheet
- Cash
- Cost of goods sold
- Cost of sales
- Current assets
- Current liabilities
- Current ratio
- Debt to Equity Ratio
- Depreciation
- Fixed assets
- Gross profit
- Intangible asset
- Interest expense
- Income statement
- Inventory
- Investment
- Leverage
- Liabilities
- Line of credit
- Liquidity
- Net profit
- Operating expense
- Operating profit
- Owners' equity
- Paid in capital
- Retained earnings
- Return on investment
- Revenue
- Share capital
- Statement of earnings
- Statement of profit and loss
- Working capital

MANAGING CAPITAL:
THE FUNCTION OF FINANCE

CHAPTER OVERVIEW

Businesses need capital to buy the raw materials, parts, machinery and equipment that go into creating products. But capital is neither plentiful, nor free. Managers need regular and systematically collected information about the sources, uses, and the profitable use of the capital at their disposal.

The balance sheet shows the sources of capital, the owners' equity and liabilities. The balance sheet also shows how the capital was used, to buy assets. The income statement shows whether the assets were put to profitable use, by generating more than enough revenue to cover all of the expenses.

The activity that involves planning, organising, leading and controlling capital is financial management. Financial managers plan the business' use of the capital by making budgets. They organise the raising of capital by being the primary contact between the business owners and lenders. Financial managers also appraise and prioritise the various new plans, projects and opportunities that compete for business' finite supply of capital. Finally, finance managers exercise control by setting standards, measuring performance, and taking corrective action to improve performance

LEARNING OUTCOMES

As a result of reading this chapter you will learn:

- Why businesses need finance.

- The purpose of making a budget.

- The advantages and disadvantages of equity finance.

- The advantages and disadvantages of debt finance.

- How financial managers appraise projects.

- The key role played by financial managers in communicating with suppliers of capital.

FINANCING THE ENTERPRISE

At one time or other you have engaged in financial management. If you have ever planned a foreign vacation, you've had to calculate what the plane tickets, hotels and rail journeys were going to cost. Based on research performed using online travel sites, you have had to forecast whether you could afford your planned vacation. If you couldn't afford it, you had two choices:

- Adjust your vacation plans.
- Borrow from your parents.

Remember, finance is the function of business that involves locating, collecting, packaging, and redistributing capital. **Financial management** therefore involves planning, organising, leading and controlling the finding and using of capital.

Financial management: Planning, organising, leading and controlling the finding and using of capital.

Without capital, a business cannot buy or rent office space. Without capital, it cannot purchase office equipment, machinery and supplies. Without capital, a business cannot pay its employees. Therefore most business, once they grow beyond a handful of people, hire dedicated employees to manage the finance function.

The raising of capital is a sufficiently strategic activity, essential to the business' long term growth that the individual who heads the finance function typically also sits on a corporation's Board of Directors. The most common North American title for the most senior financial manager is **Chief Financial Officer (CFO)**.

Chief Financial Officer (CFO): The senior manager responsible for overseeing the financial management of the entire organisation.

The CFO is typically one of the two or three most senior and influential people in any organisation, whether a business or a not for profit.

A Conversation with the Chief Financial Officer

You are sitting at the dining room table one evening when your sister looks up and says "Daddy, I want to buy a car!"

There is silence from the end of the table for several seconds. Then, your father says with unnerving calm "I see. Why do you want to buy a car?"

Your sister says "Well, my friend Mary has a car. She can drive to the mall whenever she likes. Whenever I want to go the mall I have to ask Mummy if I can borrow hers. She always says she needs it. So I always have to take the bus, and we live in the sticks. So it's not fair!"

Your father says "I see. Do you know how much a car costs?"

You can see from the expression on your sister's face that she hasn't got a clue (about how much a car costs). So, to be helpful, you contribute "You should be able to pick up a 5-year old Honda Civic for about $10,000."

Your father looks at you like you ought never to open your mouth in public again. He says, very quietly "Thank you. We do not need your help." He then turns to your sister and asks.

"Where will you get the money to buy a car?"

"Well" says your sister "I was hoping maybe I could borrow the money from you and Mummy."

"Your mother and I thought you were going to go to University next year"

"What's that got to do with it?" your sister asks.

"Well, we had set aside the money to pay for your university tuition. We can't afford to pay your school fees and buy you a car."

"Oh, you wouldn't be buying me a car. It would only be a loan. I could get a job!"

"Yes, you could get a job." says your father. "Do you have a job in mind?"

"No."

"Have you been looking for a job?"

"Not yet. But I could start real soon."

"Do you know how long you would need to work, in order to pay for a car?"

"No."

"I see."

"It's not fair" your sister says, and then starts to hyperventilate.

Previously, when you learned about how businesses were created, you learned some of the basic concepts involved in the field known as finance. Finance owes its existence to two simple assumptions:

- There are people who have ideas and ambitions, plans and projects that they would undertake - if only they had the capital.

and

- There are people who have capital but, for the time being, have no immediate need or desire to spend it.

Those who need capital include not just the owners of businesses and entrepreneurs, they include managers within businesses. The simple story above, involving the purchase of a car, includes all of the key issues that concern finance managers:

- An individual or a department within an organisation proposes a project.
- The project needs to be justified.
- An estimate needs to be made of the project's cost.
- The project must be evaluated and prioritised against alternative projects.
- If the capital is available, and the project is consistent with the organisation's mission, it can proceed.
- If the capital is not readily available sources need to be identified and approached.
- One source of capital is investors, people who will share ownership in the enterprise.
- Another source of capital is lenders.

Financial managers estimate the business' capital needs, an activity called budgeting. They appraise the various plans, projects and opportunities that are proposed, an activity called investment appraisal. From understanding the current balance sheet and the financial forecasts, they decide how best to raise any additional capital that growth or opportunity requires. To do this, financial managers communicate with and provide information to both lenders and investors. Finally, finance managers are responsible for ensuring that everyone in the organisation is mindful of the organisation's financial limits and standards.

What Financial Managers Do

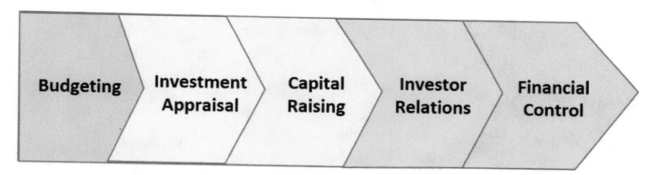

Before taking a closer look at these activities, let's first consider why businesses need finance.

WHY BUSINESSES NEED FINANCE

Businesses need finance because they absorb capital. A business must spend money to establish itself, long before it is in a position to sell anything.

Even before it opens its doors for the first time, a business will need to incur all sorts of costs. The business' founders will need to hire lawyers, to draw up a partnership agreement or to incorporate. They will need to hire the first few employees, perhaps to do market research, or to complete the development of the product. Employees need a place to do their work, so office or factory space will need to be rented.

The business will need to acquire and install machinery and equipment as well as tools and supplies. All of this money will be spent just to get the business to the point where it is in a position to start production. It's true "You have to spend money before you can make money."

A Business Must Spend Money Before It Can Make Money

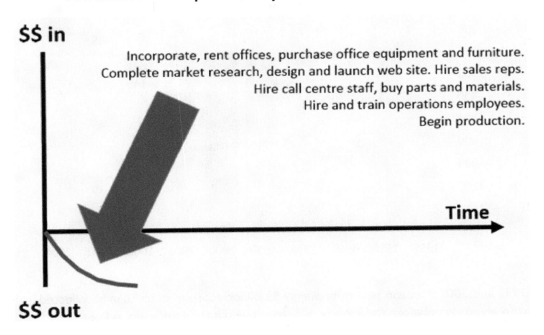

$$ in

Incorporate, rent offices, purchase office equipment and furniture. Complete market research, design and launch web site. Hire sales reps. Hire call centre staff, buy parts and materials. Hire and train operations employees. Begin production.

Time

$$ out

Even the smallest and simplest of businesses needs to spend capital before it can supply the goods or the services it intends to sell. An entrepreneur who is considering starting a math tutoring business will need to incur bus fares, just so he can travel to meet with his former high school teachers to discuss the idea. A pack of photocopy paper will need to be purchased from an office supplies store, so that posters and flyers can be made. Pens, graph paper and binders will need to be acquired. None of these individually may cost a great deal, but as the business grows it may need a better quality colour printer, a website, and so on.

A math tutoring business requires little capital. On the other hand, larger or more complex businesses might incur a huge array of costs incurred for months, or even years, before the product is ready to be launched. Remember that prior to opening Disney World, Walt Disney's business had to purchase 25,000 acres (40 square miles) of Central Florida, and then build a Magic Kingdom. From conception to grand opening, the process took nearly a decade.

Few businesses become successful overnight. Many entrepreneurs naively imagine that they can realise the phenomenal growth rates experienced by Facebook. Amazon, founded in 1994, did not make its first annual profit until 2003.

Apple – Accumulated Loss and Profits 1995 - 2004

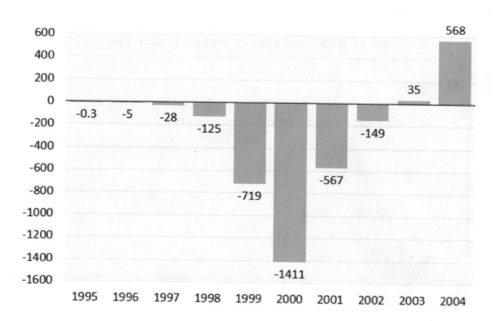

Between 1995 and 2002 Amazon paid out roughly $3 billion more in costs than it collected in revenue. It took Amazon seven years before the volume of sales allowed it to break even. All of this had to be paid for.

Break-Even Does Not Occur Instantly

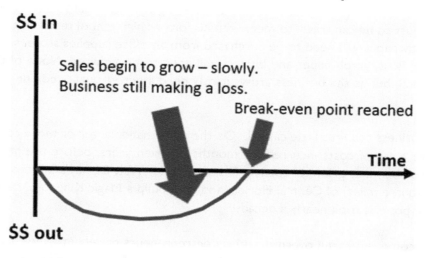

Until a business attains its break-even quantity of sales, it must rely on the owners' deep pockets or borrowed money, to survive.

At this stage of the young business' life, borrowed money may be hard to obtain. Banks are often reluctant to lend to unprofitable or unproven businesses. Remember, a bank is never lending its own capital, the money that banks lend belongs to depositors. Therefore, most young businesses must rely on owners' capital exclusively, at least until they break even.

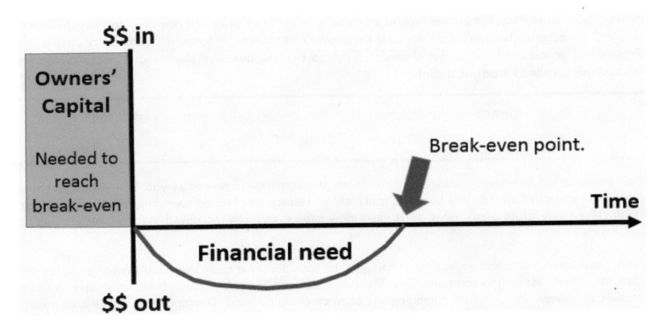

Only **after** a business has broken even can it realistically hope to raise capital by borrowing. Banks want to lend, but only to organisations with a track record and a demonstrable ability to grow, make profits, and therefore repay loans.

The CFO and other financial managers must therefore ensure that they have raised enough owners' equity at the outset. They must also manage their relationship with suppliers, who may be more willing to provide credit than banks. The CFO must exercise rigorous control at this point, ensuring that no department over-spends.

FINANCIAL PLANNING – BUDGETING

The financial management process begins by planning the anticipated financial needs of the business. A financial plan is called a **budget**. A budget (the word is derived from the old French word for purse) is a forecast of the cost of the plans and projects that the organisation wants to carry out in the coming period.

Budget: A forecast estimate of the cost of the plans and projects that the organisation wants to carry out in the coming period.

When your father asks your sister "Do you know how much a car costs?" he is asking her to provide a budget.

The word budget is most frequently heard when Canadian federal or provincial Finance Ministers prepare and announce the government's budget for the coming fiscal year. Finance Ministers announce the government's plans and spending priorities. These may include, for example, more money for schools and hospitals, less money for transportation, and a change in the rules for providing welfare benefits. The Minister then provides a discussion of what these policies will cost and where the government will find the money.

In the case of a business, the budget will be a careful forecast of all expected revenues and expenditures. Unlike Governments, businesses do not have the power to set taxes. A business cannot force customers to purchase products. If the budget shows that the cost of the business' plans and projects exceed its inflows, this is called a **budget deficit**.

Budget Deficit: When the cost of an organisation's business' plans and projects exceed its inflows.

If an organisation forecasts a budget deficit, it has the same two choices as you have when planning a trip that you can't afford. The business must either reduce its planned spending, by scaling back or eliminating some of its plans, or it must raise new capital through increased owners' investment or borrowing.

A budget is intended to force a business' managers to consider what their various plans and projects will cost. In popular use, when someone says "I'm on a budget" what they mean is that they have a finite amount of money, and that their spending has been carefully planned. Overspending in one area means they will have to cutback elsewhere.

If a budget shows that the cost of the organiisation's plans and projects will be less than expected inflows, this is called a **budget surplus.**

Budget Surplus: When an organisation's inflows exceed the cost of its plans and projects.

A business with a budget surplus can build up its cash balance, it can repay some of its outstanding debt, or it can reward its owners by sending them a dividend.

FINANCIAL PLANNING - INVESTMENT APPRAISAL

Alongside the cost of this year's plans and projects, a business will be looking further down the road to future projects. The role of the finance function is to appraise and prioritise these.

Remember, an investment is a decision to commit capital to an enterprise that could generate more capital in the future. Businesses are faced with investment opportunities routinely. These might include any of the more obvious examples:

- Develop a new product.
- Expand into a new geographic market.
- Expand capacity to better serve an existing market.
- Buy a competitor, a supplier or distributor.

The responsibility of financial managers is to assess the relative attractiveness of each of these competing investment opportunities, an activity known as **investment appraisal**.

Investment Appraisal: The assessment of the attractiveness of competing investment opportunities.

While many factors will influence the decision to make a major investment, some of the more fundamental considerations will be:

- Size
- Length
- Return
- Risk

Size of Investment: Even the largest of businesses have finite amounts of capital. Facing a limit to how much money there is available, the financial manager's first question might be: "How much will it cost?"

Put into a simple personal example, your parents can afford either to send your sister to university or to buy her a car. The cost of the car is roughly the cost of a year of university education, about $10,000. They cannot afford to do both.

Length of Investment: An investor may be willing to invest in a project if the returns are expected in the near future. As an example, you are prepared to invest four years getting a degree. Thereafter, you anticipate that you will get a well-paid job.

Consider how you would view a university education if a degree took seven years to complete instead of four. During the additional time, more change can happen. The jobs you hoped to get when you started may no longer exist. The greater the length of any investment, the greater is the risk.

Because of this, finance managers appraise the length of time until an investment starts to generate return. The time in which the cash generated by a project is expected to exceed the initial outflow is called the **payback period**.

Payback period: The time in which the cash generated by a project is expected to exceed the initial outflow.

Investments with a shorter payback period are often preferred because they involve fewer unanticipated changes in the business environment.

Return on Investment: Payback period alone isn't enough to separate the most attractive projects from others that are less so. Some investments involve long term commitments and small but steady returns. University education is an investment with a long payback period. However, after 40 years the return on investment is high.

Remember, return on investment compares the profit or benefit from the investment against the capital that was put at risk. If you invest in a university education, for four years after high school you put $10,000 per year towards tuition fees, lab fees and books. In addition, as a full-time student you can't work.

Your starting salary after graduating, $42,000, will be higher than you would be earning in a job that requires a high school education – but not hugely so. The returns from a university education are initially small, but they are steady and continuing over the long term.

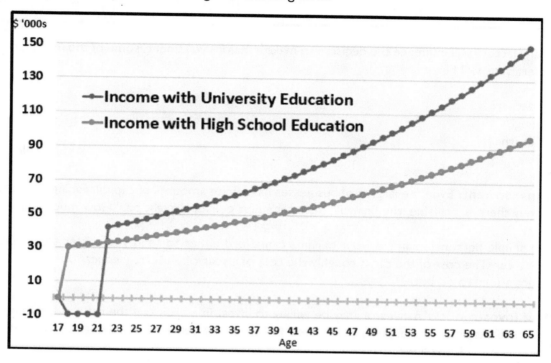

Your total lifetime earnings are unlikely to catch up to those of a high school graduate until you are in your mid-30s. However, thereafter your income starts to pull away swiftly. Because of your higher education and broader range of skills, you are likely to get more promotions and larger raises in pay. By the age of 65, normal retirement age, the average university educated individual will have earned $1 million more over her lifetime than those without a degree. Recall that one of the most important measures of an enterprise' success is return on investment. The return, or profit, from the enterprise is compared to the capital that was put at risk.

There are formulas that allow finance managers to calculate the returns coming from long term investments involving returns that change from year to year. These are beyond the scope of this introductory text. Your professor has done one of these calculations for you. Assume that a high school graduate earns $30,000 at age 17, and gets an average pay rise of 2.5%. Assume that a university graduate, invests $40,000 in her degree, earns $42,000 beginning at age 21 and gets an average pay rise of 3.0%. The return on investment, until retirement at age 65, is roughly 8.3%.

Risk of Return: Risk, you will remember, is defined as the range of possible outcomes. Since investments are intended to realise returns in the future, financial managers must make forecasts about the profit that will come from an individual project or investment. These forecasts will be based on a variety of assumptions about, for example, the cost of materials, the size of the market, growth in the market, and the actions of competitors.

These forecasts are often presented using several scenarios, which show a variety of possible outcomes. This "scenario analysis" might typically consist of:

- Base or expected case: The investment performs largely as expected.
- Best or optimistic case: One or two things go better than expected.
- Worst or pessimistic case: One or two things go worse than expected.

The purpose is to understand the **risk of return**. Risk of return means the range of possible returns from an investment, if it doesn't perform exactly according to the forecasters' assumptions.

Risk of Return: The range of possible returns from an investment, if it doesn't perform exactly according to the forecaster's assumptions.

In the two charts below the base or expected cases are identical. A planned investment should produce a profit of $10 million for the business, after 5 years. However, the two opportunities show widely differing risk profiles.

An investment whose return will not vary much between best and worst case (the chart on the left) is low risk. If the future were to resemble the pessimistic case, the business will still make a profit, albeit a smaller one. An investment where the range of possible returns is large, even if the best case looks attractive (the chart on the right) is high risk. If some key assumptions prove to be wrong and one or two aspects of the project don't work out, it makes losses early, and never gets off the ground.

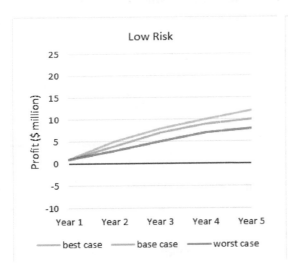
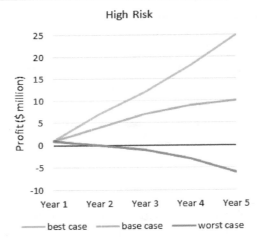

Investment appraisal necessarily requires that finance managers balance the possibility of making large profits against the possibility of making losses. Businesses are typically managing a variety of projects at once. A single business may be building a new factory in the Middle East, expanding a sales force in China, and negotiating to buy one of its competitors, all at the same time. Financial managers have to ensure that no more than one of these projects resembles the chart on the right.

FINANCIAL ORGANISATION - CAPITAL RAISING

Managing involves organising: Assembling all of the necessary resources to accomplish a task. In the case of financial managers, once the organisation's various projects have been appraised and prioritised, the job turns to raising the necessary capital from the available sources.

To raise capital, a business has a variety of options. A sole proprietor can take on a partner, or incorporate. A partnership can look for additional general partners, or limited partners. It too can incorporate. A private corporation can invite its existing shareholders to buy additional shares. A public corporation can invite existing shareholders to invest more, or – with the help of an investment bank – make new shares available to the general public. Of course, with willing lenders, any type of business can raise capital by borrowing.

Raising capital through debt, or "liabilities" in accounting terms, has advantages and costs. So does increasing the owners' equity. The choice of how best to raise the necessary capital will depend on the relative merits and costs of each source and type of finance. The combination of the debt and equity capital that a business chooses to use in order to finance its operations and growth is called its **capital structure**.

Capital structure: The combination of the debt and equity capital that a business chooses to use in order to finance its operations and growth.

Equity financing

For the growing business, an obvious source of capital is the existing owners. The owners of a business can choose to invest more. If some owners choose not to, or have no more capital to invest, the business can look for new investors. New investors can bring not just capital, but can bring skills, ideas, and contacts to the enterprise.

However, the injection of new capital dilutes the ownership of the existing owners. Remember, **dilution** means a decrease in the proportion owned by existing partners or shareholders after new investors put capital into a business.

Dilution: A decrease in the proportion owned by existing partners or shareholders, after new investors put capital into a business.

In the simple example illustrated in the pie charts below, a business begins with three shareholders, A, B and C. Shareholder A owns 30 shares, as does shareholder B. Shareholder C owns 40 shares. Suppose each share represents $1,000 of capital invested.

If the existing owners want to expand the business, but can't afford to put more money into the business themselves, they can invite new investors. In this case the new shareholder, "D" is invited to put new capital into the business.

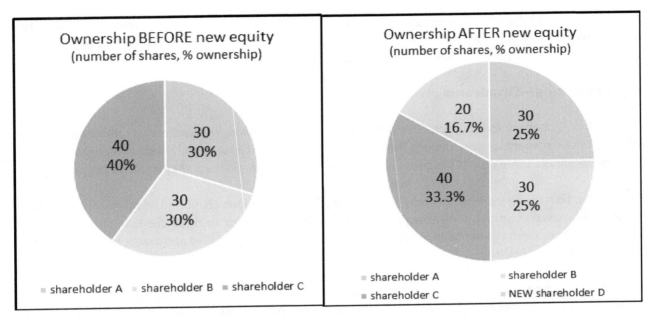

The result of the new equity is a business with more capital. The pie will be bigger. However, the original owners now each have a smaller portion of the bigger pie. Investors A, B and C who previously owned 30%, 30% and 40% of the business, now own a smaller share of future profits.

A larger business, with more assets, more employees, and more capacity, should generate more profits for all of its owners. However, the business should not take on 20% more shares unless the projects thus financed generate at least 20% more profit.

Equity Financing - Disadvantages

The people who start businesses, in other words entrepreneurs, tend to be independent and achievement oriented. Some entrepreneurial personalities are not comfortable with sharing decision making, or even explaining themselves. This may lead to irreconcilable disagreements with other investors.

The most famous example of this involved Steve Jobs, the founder of Apple. Jobs was a genius, but a perfectionist with a reputation for being difficult to work with. During the late 1970s and early 1980s, Jobs and his Apple co-founder Steve Wozniak needed more and more capital with which to bring their ideas to fruition. Apple raised capital, on several occasions, by selling more and more shares to new investors. These investors took increasing control of Apple's ownership and of the Board of Directors. In 1985 Apple's Board of Directors decided that, while brilliant, Jobs was too young and too temperamental to run the growing business that he had founded. So, Jobs was fired from the business that he no longer controlled. Happily for Apple, as history now shows, a wiser, more mature Steve Jobs was invited to return to Apple 12 years later.

Debt Finance - Advantages

The obvious advantage of borrowing is that the owners of the business don't need to dig deeper into their own pockets. Nor do they have to find new investors. By choosing to borrow rather than look to the owners for capital, a business can grow, without changing its existing ownership.

A borrower's only duty to a lender is to make the required loan repayments, plus interest, on time. The interest expense, as you learned in the previous chapter, is regarded as a cost of doing business. Interest expense reduces the profit on which tax is payable.

Debt Financing – Disadvantages

The obvious drawback to incurring debt is that a loan must be repaid, with interest, within a fixed period of time. In this respect lenders are less flexible than owners. The owners of a business recognise that the enterprise entails some risk. If the business is less profitable than planned, they must be patient.

In addition, borrowing increases leverage, as discussed in the previous chapter. The more capital that the business borrows, the more profit the project must generate in order to repay the loan plus interest. An over-reliance on debt makes the business vulnerable to loans being recalled and assets seized by lenders, if revenues and profits fall.

Debt finance suits some businesses better than others. An electric utility has a steady customer base, and a reasonably predictable stream of revenue. Customers will not suddenly decide that they no longer need or want electricity. Therefore, electric utility businesses can borrow reasonably heavily. On the other hand, a technology start-up, with uncertain future revenue but lots of potential, will most likely rely on owners' equity.

Most businesses opt for a blend of both equity and debt financing to meet their needs when expanding a business. The two forms of financing together can work well to reduce the downsides of each. The right ratio will vary according to the type of business, the profits it expects, and the amount of capital that the business needs to grow.

FINANCIAL LEADING - INVESTOR RELATIONS

The management activity known as "leading" means guiding and inspiring others. All business activity involves human interaction and communication. "Leading" in the finance sphere means developing and maintaining good relationships with suppliers of capital, and keeping them informed.

The activity that involves communicating the business' financial results, strategy and plans to everyone who has an interest is called **investor relations**. While the word "investor" may imply that investor relations is concerned exclusively with those who invest equity, like shareholders and partners, investor relations is equally concerned with maintaining good, open communication and good relationships with lenders and suppliers.

Investor Relations: Communicating the company's financial results, strategy and plans to everyone with an interest in a business' activities.

Remember, most businesses finance a great deal of their activity using credit from suppliers. The "accounts payable" on a balance sheet represents money owed to other businesses for goods and services received. It is important that these suppliers be kept advised, informed and reassured.

Well-handled relationships with banks, investment dealers, individual shareholders, and suppliers allow these stakeholders to have a full appreciation of the business' activities, strategy and prospects. As a result, they are more likely to be supportive when the business needs to raise capital.

Investors and lenders must be kept advised through regular meetings and updates. Finance managers should ensure that all interested parties are provided with quarterly, as well as annual balance sheets and income statements.

Increasingly, larger businesses schedule video conference calls. During these video conferences the CFO will highlight the business' successes, and calm any fears. Businesses typically conduct conference calls immediately following the release of quarterly financial statements. These allow the business to provide an overview of the major issues that affected the company's performance in the preceding quarter, and to preview what can be expected in upcoming quarters.

Investor relations also call for formal presentations, colloquially called "road shows", when a business is attempting to sell shares to new investors. Finance managers will travel to the major cities to give presentations to investment dealers, pension fund managers and other potential investors. The "road show" is intended to generate excitement and interest in the upcoming share offering.

FINANCIAL CONTROL

The final responsibility of finance managers is control. **Financial control** involves establishing a standard, measuring performance, and taking action to improve or regulate the raising and spending of capital.

Financial Control: Establishing a standard, measuring performance, and taking action to improve or regulate the raising and spending of capital.

The budget is the business' financial standard. The budget is intended to put a limit on expenditure by various departments and divisions of the business, and set goals for revenue generation. Examples of financial standards are:

- "The advertising budget for the next quarter is $3 million"
- "In the next fiscal year, our stores in Alberta are expected to deliver $20 million in revenue and $3 million in profit."

The second stage of the control process is to measure the actual performance of the activity. The quarterly financial statements are the tools of measurement. Remember, the purpose of the accounting function is to collect, organise and present financial information so that those responsible for leading the business can make informed decisions. Quarterly income statements and balance sheets, although not audited like year-end financial statements, nevertheless allow the business to compare the business' financial performance against its forecasts and goals. An examination of the cash balance, working capital, and current ratio help the business to manage its liquidity. The leverage ratio indicates whether the business has continued scope to borrow from lenders. The income statements indicate the level of sales, cost of sales and operating expenses.

Finance managers can look at these statements and compare actual performance against the budget:

- "Operating expenses were 10% higher than we forecasted, due largely to overspending on advertising by the marketing department."
- "The income statement for the first half of the year shows revenues of $13 million in Alberta."

The final stage of the control process is for managers to take action to improve or correct performance, and to bring it into line with the standard. If the business appears to be running out of cash, managers can take action to reduce current spending. The business can re-double efforts to examine items on the budget, and to differentiate between discretionary ("nice to have") and essential ("have to have") spending. The former need not be cancelled altogether. Some can be postponed. A decision to reduce marketing expenditure can save cash in the short term.

- "We will need to cancel the planned TV advertising campaign. That will save $600,000 from the marketing budget".

Of course, if the standard is being met, people can be rewarded and further encouraged:

- "Our sales people in Alberta are working hard. Revenues for the first six months are 30% above forecast. Let's thank them, and give them a bonus."

The purpose of the control function is to get people and other resources to perform in a manner that will achieve the organisation's goals.

FINANCIAL MANAGEMENT - SUMMARY AND CONCLUSION

The management of the financial activities do not differ fundamentally from the management of any other function of a business. Marketing managers plan and organise product development, pricing, promotion and distribution. Operations managers plan and organise inputs to create products. In the same way, financial managers plan and organise capital: money or the machines and technologies that money can buy.

Effective financial management will ensure that the business has the capital that it needs to carry out the plans that will contribute positively to the future growth of revenues, profits and return on investment.

SELF-ASSESSMENT QUESTIONS FOR REVIEW

1. Prepare a budget for yourself for the upcoming academic year. Be sure to include: tuition, ancillary fees, books, and accommodation costs if you are not living at home. In addition to these items are their other sources of expenditure that you anticipate as a result of your decision to spend the year studying at university? What is your total financial need?

2. Make an estimate of all the revenue that you are expecting over the next academic year. Include income from part-time and/or summer employment, money withdrawn from your savings, scholarships, bursaries or grants. What is the difference between what you expect to spend and what you can supply from your own resources? Will you need additional funding from your family or from OSAP?

3. Evaluate the costs to yourself, to your siblings, and to your parents, of getting financial assistance from your family. Evaluate the difference in how it might affect you, your parents and your siblings if any money received from your family is a gift, or a loan.

4. Evaluate the cost if you borrow money under OSAP. What rate of interest will you pay? How many years will it take you to repay your student loan?

5. If you were planning on working during the academic year, evaluate the impact of earning only three-quarters of what you have budgeted to earn. Could you make savings by spending less in some areas?

DEFINED TERMS

- Budget
- Budget deficit
- Budget surplus
- Capital structure
- Chief financial officer
- Dilution
- Financial control
- Financial management
- Investment appraisal
- Investor relations
- Payback period
- Risk of return

CHAPTER 11

HIRING AND KEEPING THE BEST PEOPLE: MANAGING HUMAN RESOURCES

CHAPTER OVERVIEW

A business, you have learned, requires managing the marketing, operations, accounting and finance functions. However, thus far in this book, there has been an implied assumption that:

- "someone" conducts market research, so as to determine customer needs;

- "someone" performs the operations to create the products;

- "someone" collects and organises data, so managers can make informed decisions; and

- "someone" sets budgets, appraises investment opportunities, and raises capital.

All of these "someones" underline the essential importance of the business hiring and keeping the right people. A hiring decision is among the most important decisions a manager can make. Without the right people - appropriately qualified, experienced, trained, and motivated people - no business can survive.

In this chapter you will learn what managers and business owners need to know about planning, organising, leading and controlling the human resource.

LEARNING OUTCOMES

As a result of reading this chapter, you will learn:

- Human resource management, like any other function within a business, involves planning, organising, leading and controlling.

- Human resources planning begins with determining the jobs to be done, and the activities that a job involves. Then, a job specification documents the knowledge, education, experience and characteristics that are essential to the individual who will be hired to perform a job.

- Human resource organising begins with recruiting: Attracting interested and appropriate applicants to fill a position.

- Human resources organising continues with screening and selection: Sifting through the applications to find the individual who will be most suitable.

- Employees must be compensated. Compensation involves much more than offering a basic salary. Bonuses, benefits and profit sharing are all important components of most employees' compensation package.

- Orientation makes new employees welcome, and brings them on board to be contributing members of the organisation. Orientation brings significant benefits to the employer too.

- People need to have clearly defined goals and objectives in their work. A manager's job is to help determine those objectives.

- Human resource control means setting standards, measuring performance, and providing appraisal and feedback.

- A good human resource system does not stop with hiring new employees, it should oversee existing employees' training and development, in line with their abilities and aspirations.

- The effort that goes into human resource management is not motivated by altruism, or strictly by concern for the employee. Unhappy, unmotivated employees quit, or stay home. Happy, motivated employees are loyal and productive.

MANAGING HUMAN RESOURCES - INTRODUCTION

Earlier in this book, you learned about the management of raw materials and natural resources, and the business function known as operations. In recent chapters, you learned about the management of capital. All of the factors of production need managing, including labour. A business needs to plan how many people it needs. It needs to organise their hiring. It needs to lead their training and development. Finally, people are happy to be controlled, if this involves telling them what is expected of them. The name given to the planning, organising, leading and controlling of an organisation's people is **human resource management**. It is frequently referred to by its acronym: HRM.

Human Resource Management (HRM): The activities involved with planning, organising, leading and controlling a business' people.

DETERMINING THE JOBS THAT NEED TO BE DONE

Particularly as an organisation grows, new jobs openings are created. If you were to establish a math tutoring business, in the first months of its existence you might find yourself, as the sole proprietor, designing posters, printing them, phoning prospective customers, scheduling meetings with parents and teachers, buying stationary and teaching aids, delivering tutoring sessions, preparing invoices, and so on. You would be responsible for 100% of the business strategy, marketing, operations, and management information.

A year later, with success under your belt, you might want to take on an employee. In response to customer needs, you determine that it would useful for your business to have someone tutor chemistry.

Hiring, like most other business activities, is a process. Before you approach any friends who might be suitable to teach chemistry, you would be wise to sit down and write a **job analysis**. A job analysis is a careful breakdown of all of the mental and physical activities that a job involves.

Job Analysis: A careful breakdown of all of the mental and physical activities that a job involves.

A job analysis should be a list of precise activities and actions, for example: "preparing half-hour long chemistry tutorials", "writing chemistry problem sets", "travelling to students' homes" and "meeting one-on-one with high school students".

Probably the best way to write a job analysis is to have a conversation with someone who is already doing the job, or one very much like it. The purpose of a job analysis is to understand what is involved in doing the job, not to describe the ideal person to do it.

The ideal person to do the job is described by the **job specification.** A job specification documents the knowledge, education, experience and characteristics that are essential to the individual who will be performing a job.

Job Specification: The knowledge, education, experience and characteristics that are essential to the individual who will be performing a job.

A job specification for a position as a chemistry tutor might include the following:

Knowledge: Must be proficient in all aspects of organic and inorganic chemistry.

Education: Must have completed Ontario OAC with grades of 90% or better. Must be enrolled in an accredited Ontario university. Must have completed first-year university courses in chemistry with grades of A or better.

Experience: Minimum 2 years demonstrated experience in a teaching or leadership capacity working with teenagers or high-school students. Examples might be camp counsellor or section head, coaching athletes in team or individual sports, peer tutoring or mentoring experience in high-school or university. Summer employment or work experience in a hospital, industrial or pharmaceutical lab.

An individual's personality and interpersonal skills are often relevant to the performance of a job. Understanding the necessary behaviours and interpersonal traits may be essential to the hiring decision. Accounting and finance positions may require candidates who are demonstrably careful, and detail-oriented. For a sales position, highly extroverted personalities may be appropriate. A job specification for a tutoring position might also include the following specification:

Characteristics: Must have demonstrably excellent interpersonal skills and patience. An aptitude for teaching, training or guiding others is essential.

RECRUITING

Having understood the job to be done, and identified the qualities of the "ideal" candidate, the hiring process now turns to **recruiting**. Remember, organising is defined as assembling the necessary resources to accomplish a task. The purpose of recruiting, therefore, is to attract interested and appropriate applicants to fill a position.

Recruiting: Attracting interested and appropriate applicants to fill a position.

Note the inclusion of the word "appropriate" in the above definition. While recruiting should cast the net wide, the purpose is to attract only candidates who are appropriately qualified, and who will fit into the organisation.

The business then prepares a **job description**. A job description should provide prospective employees not just with the job specification, but should also provide an idea of the organisation's environment and culture, and describe the job's place within the organisation.

Job Description: A description of an organisation's environment and culture and of the position and atmosphere of the job within the organisation.

A job description should attract candidates that will fit into the business, while deterring otherwise qualified applicants who do not see themselves fitting in. To do this, a thorough job description is likely to include, and distinguish between some of the following variables:

Job title: Words such as "senior" or "executive" will attract different applicants than "assistant", or "associate".

Location: The location of the job, whether in a large metropolis, small city, town, suburban or rural environment will affect applicants in a variety of ways. The job location will affect housing costs, commuting times, access to schools, hospitals and cultural institutions as well as the ability for individuals to network and make occupational and professional connections.

Size of the organisation: Businesses range in size from multinational public corporations to entrepreneurial sole proprietorships. The size and legal structure of the business will affect promotion opportunities, job mobility, and individual's profile within the organisation.

Level of seniority: A graduate of UTSC once told the author of this book that he quit his job at a world famous corporation when he realised that the founder and largest shareholder of the business was his boss' boss' boss' boss' boss' boss' boss' boss' boss' boss' boss. He quit to start his own business.

Number of colleagues: Some people have a high need for affiliation, others prefer to work alone.

Degree of autonomy: This may vary from meeting with a supervisor daily, to jobs where the employee is asked to report back at end of the following week.

Conditions: Engineers, accountants, and consultants often spend weeks at a time living in hotel rooms, working away from home. In contrast, university faculty often work from home 3 or 4 days a week.

Hours of work: The staff in the branch of a bank tend to work Monday to Friday, from 9 to 5. Emergency room physicians are on call 24 hours a day, and will often do their most important work at 2 a.m. on a Saturday or Sunday morning.

In the autumn of 2015, Rogers was recruiting for the position of Wholesale Billing Analyst. Here's the job description.

The Wholesale Billing Analyst position will be based in downtown Toronto at 1 Mount Pleasant and will report to the Manager, Wholesale Operations. The Analyst will be responsible for supporting wholesale customers with a focus on billing including monthly reconciliation and billing discrepancies.

Responsibilities:

Billing Analysis/ Invoicing Management /Reporting
- Perform accurate and timely billing for wholesale customers; monthly reconciliation and controls
- Monthly and ad-hoc reporting to ensure Wholesale is on track to meet objectives and key performance metrics
- Reporting models for Wholesale to use in analyzing Rogers wholesale performance to industry benchmarks
- Monitoring and management of wholesale billing file controls for accuracy
- Reporting and trend analysis to assist in improving operational efficiency and accuracy
- Ensure all analysis/reporting is accurate, reasonable, comprehensible and completed in a timely manner

Day-to-Day Responsibilities
- End-to-End support of wholesale customers including:
- Customer on-boarding and training
- Subscriber activation and maintenance
- Inquiries, network testing & troubleshooting
- Liaison with Rogers help desk organizations

Process Improvement
- Document business requirements, customer price plans and process mapping to evaluate opportunity for operational efficiency/quality improvements
- Support Wholesale account and project management initiatives

Qualifications:
- Post secondary education in business related discipline
- Financial reporting/analysis experience; minimum 2 years
- Proficient in MS Office; excellent Excel & modeling skills
- Strong analytical, problem solving and multi-tasking skills
- Strong interpersonal and communication skills with the ability to interact with both external customers and internal support staff in a professional and businesslike manner
- Self motivated team player with strong work ethic
- Experience in Oracle Financials, SQL, Cognos and Amdocs billing systems an asset
- Strong multi-tasking, negotiation and decision making skills are required
- Strong time management and organizational skills with the ability to prioritize work in order to meet deadlines
- A dynamic and pro-active individual with a sense of urgency for resolution of issues

Schedule: Full Time
Shift: Day
Length of Contract: Not Applicable (Regular Position)
Work Location: 1 Mount Pleasant (083), Toronto, Ontario
Travel Requirements: None
Posting Category/Function: Reporting and Analytics & Analyst

Recruiting is a promotional activity. Like any promotional activity, the intention of recruiting is to make potential, qualified applicants:

- Aware of the opportunity;
- Knowledgeable about the opportunity;
- Interested in the opportunity; and
- Persuaded to apply.

Again, like any promotional activity, businesses can use a variety of promotional methods including both advertising and personal selling.

A business that is hiring may choose to place ads in local or national newspapers, in trade and professional publications, and on the internet. They may also promote job opportunities through personal selling at on-campus graduate recruitment events and fact nights, or by sponsoring conferences attended by potential employees.

Increasingly, businesses are augmenting their recruiting efforts by using social media. LinkedIn, particularly, is a widely used source for finding job candidates. At the other end of the technology spectrum, a "Help Wanted" sign in a store window is a recruiting tool.

Some larger businesses perform their own in-house recruiting, using dedicated recruiting personnel. However, most small and medium-sized businesses use **recruitment agencies** or search firms, popularly known as **head hunters.** Head hunters are recruiting intermediaries. Just as financial intermediaries put together people who have capital with those who need it, head hunters locate prospective candidates on behalf of employers looking to fill vacancies.

Recruiting agency / Head hunters: Businesses that act as intermediaries in locating prospective candidates on behalf of employers with vacancies.

Head hunters must maintain large numbers of contacts. They do so through networking, cultivating relationships with businesses, maintaining large databases, and cold calling prospective recruits.

INTERNAL VERSUS EXTERNAL RECRUITING

A choice that any organisation has to make when it is looking to fill a vacancy is whether to give preference to current employees. If the policy is to do so, this is known as **internal recruiting** or **hiring from within.**

Internal Recruiting / Hiring from Within: When looking to fill a vacancy, giving preference to current employees.

Like any choice, the decision to give preference to current employees brings both benefits and costs. Many organisations argue that recruiting from within saves time and money. People with a current knowledge of how the business operates will need less training and will fit in more easily. This maintains continuity. Another perceived benefit from internal recruiting is that promotion opportunities act as incentive to employees, and help to sustain morale.

There are costs to internal recruiting, of course. One cost is that a business risks becoming stale without the occasional injection of fresh ideas from outside. When an entire management team has come through the ranks, there is a tendency toward "groupthink" and a reluctance to stray from established ways of doing things. If a business has a problem with a lack of new ideas and fresh thinking, searching outside the ranks of current employees is probably best.

Generally, recruiting from within is regarded as the preferred choice. It tends to pay off in retention and productivity. Good people want to work for a business where they can learn, grow and find career advancement.

SCREENING

If the recruiting process has been successful, the business will have attracted a large field of candidates. Not all of these will necessarily be suitable, so the next process in the HR system is **screening**. Screening involves sifting through a large number of applications so as to determine a much shorter list of those who appear most suitable. This is most frequently done by reviewing the written submissions received from the candidates.

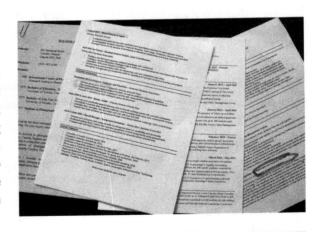

Screening: Sifting through a large number of applications so as to determine a much shorter list of those who appear most suitable.

The written submissions are most likely to consist of job applications, resumes, and curriculum vitae (CVs). The primary difference between a **resume** and a **CV** is the length. A resume is a one or two page summary of an individual's skills, education and experience. A resume is intended to be concise.

Resume: A one or two page summary of an individual's skills, education, and experience.

A CV is longer. It will typically include more detailed information about an individual's skills and accomplishments, educational and academic background, awards, honors, and professional affiliations. Young graduates are unlikely to have had the time or opportunity to develop the accomplishments typically included in a CV. CVs are more typically required for senior management positions or when the position to be filled is in an academic, highly technical or scientific field.

CV: A longer, more detailed portrayal of an individual's skills, accomplishments, education, and experience.

Generally, following the screening of the written documentation, employers draw up a list of candidates who they wish to interview. Interviews are important for two reasons. First, they offer an employer an opportunity to learn about a candidate's **soft skills**. Soft skills is the term given to the array of manners, social graces, charm, confidence and other interpersonal traits that people possess.

Soft skills: The array of manners, social graces, charm, confidence and other interpersonal traits that people possess.

Soft skills are important if the job for which the candidate is being interviewed involves influencing or leading others. Soft skills will be necessary if the job involves dealing with the public, in a role such as sales. No matter how intellectually bright or technically competent an individual may be, people will not respond well to someone who lacks soft skills.

The interview also allows the employer to see how a candidate responds to a situation which undeniably puts people under stress. Interviews can be stressful when you are hoping to get a job, and trying to make a good impression.

EMPLOYMENT EQUITY AND NON-DISCRIMINATION LAWS

As you have already learned, in a liberal, market-based economy like Canada, the government attempts to encourage the private sector economy by imposing a minimum of laws and regulations. However, all Canadian employers must comply with such laws and regulations as do exist.

An essential responsibility of any business' human resource function is to stay abreast of, and ensure compliance with, Canadian laws relating to employment equity and human rights.

The Employment Equity Act requires employers to provide equal employment opportunities to four designated groups: Women; aboriginal peoples; persons with disabilities; members of visible minorities. The purpose of the act is to achieve equality in the workplace so that "no person shall be denied employment opportunities". The act applies to all private sector employers and specifies that employers have the duty to identify and eliminate employment barriers against persons in those designated groups.

The Canadian Human Rights Act makes it discriminatory to refuse to employ, continue to employ, or differentiate toward any individual on the grounds of race, national or ethnic origin, colour, religion, age, sex, sexual orientation, marital status, family status, disability and conviction for an offence. In addition the Act specifies that it is a discriminatory "to use any form of application for employment, or to publish any advertisement that expresses or implies any limitation, specification or preference" based on any of the prohibited grounds.

SELECTION

Ultimately, the purpose of all the planning (performing a job analysis, writing a job specification) and organising (recruiting and screening) performed by human resource managers is to put the business into a position where it can offer a position to the best candidate to fill a vacancy. The process of choosing the best person to fill a job is known as **selection**.

Selection: The process of choosing the right person for the job

Once the business has selected the best candidate, best practice is to inform the successful candidate by phone. This adds a personal touch to the hiring, and allows the hiring manager to convey a sense of enthusiasm and excitement. The phone call should be followed immediately with written confirmation. The letter should include written confirmation of all the elements of the offer: job title, location, and of course all elements of the selected candidate's pay and other compensation.

PAYING FOR WHAT YOU GET

Employees don't work for free. Therefore, once the decision has been made to hire, an employer must find the right combination of pay and other forms of reward in order to attract, retain and motivate their people. The term **compensation** refers to all forms of reward going to employees arising from their employment.

Compensation: All forms of reward going to employees and arising from their employment.

Typically, employee compensation comes in four forms:

- Guaranteed pay
- Bonuses and commissions
- Benefits
- Profit sharing

Guaranteed pay is the employee's fixed monetary reward. This is paid on an hourly, daily, weekly, or monthly basis. Many countries dictate a minimum base salary or a **minimum wage** that an employer must legally pay.

Minimum wage: The lowest hourly wage that an employer must legally pay.

In Canada, responsibility for setting the minimum wage rests with the provinces and territories. In 2015, the minimum wage ranged from $10.20 per hour in Saskatchewan, to $12.50 per hour in the North West Territories. In Ontario, the minimum was is $11.00 per hour. Some provinces allow lower wages to be paid to those who wait on table in bars and restaurants, because it is assumed that they will earn tips.

BONUSES AND COMMISSIONS

Many Canadian businesses offer their workers some form of variable pay, based on the attainment of targets or some other measure of performance. Some plans give incentives to individuals while others reward teams.

The most common form of bonus is **gain sharing.** Under gain sharing, an employer agrees to share any increase in the business' profits that result from improvements suggested or initiated by employees.

Gain sharing: An employer shares any increase in profits that result from improvements suggested or initiated by employees.

Gain sharing is most common in manufacturing plants, where increases in productivity or quality are relatively easy to track and measure. Consistent with the concept of Total Quality Management (TQM) gain sharing works best when employees themselves are responsible for the quantity and quality of output, and are encouraged to improve the way the product is made.

The other common form of variable pay is the **sales commission**. Sales commissions are awarded to salespeople for successful selling. A share of the revenue generated by the salesperson is paid, as a reward for their efforts.

Sales Commission: The reward paid to sales people, based on a percentage of the revenues generated by their efforts.

Many salespeople draw a low base salary, and the commission is an incentive that is directly tied to their role within the business. In some businesses, commissions make the top-performing sales people the highest paid employees.

From the business' perspective bonuses and commissions have two obvious benefits. Bonus plans allow an employer to pay employees more in 'good times' and less when revenues and profits are reduced. In addition, bonuses and commissions are intended to drive employee performance. If an employee knows that his remuneration depends on the business' performance, he or she will have incentive to improve performance.

A disadvantage of variable pay schemes is that many capable, hard-working people are risk averse. They prefer the security and certainty of knowing how much they will earn in a given year. A common criticism of variable pay is that bonuses often end up rewarding the wrong kind of behaviour. If bonus schemes drive managers to work toward achieving short-term financial results, they may be neglecting the long term interests of the business as a whole. Poorly designed bonuses may also encourage managers to take more risks than they otherwise would, because they don't share in downside pain. Although it is certainly not the only industry to have failings, the banking industry has received much adverse publicity in recent years for the high bonuses paid to employees who, it was subsequently revealed, engaged in dubious or illegal practices.

BENEFITS

Employee benefits are non-financial forms of compensation offered in addition to cash salary.

Employee Benefits: Non-financial forms of compensation offered in addition to salary in order to reward and enrich employees.

The standard and traditional list of benefits offered by employers includes paid vacation time (beyond the minimum two weeks mandated by Canadian law), a pension plan, and life insurance. Beyond these, the variety of benefits that may be offered to employees is limited only by the imagination of the employer. Nothing prevents a business from offering its employees pony rides, and trips to the circus, if that is what they desire.

A growing trend in employee compensation is for employers to offer a long menu of benefits, from which employees can pick and choose, up to a financial limit. Employees with children can choose to have employer financed child care. Younger workers can choose tuition reimbursement or car loans. Older employees can choose to have the employer increase its contribution to their pension.

In 2004 when Google's founders, Sergey Brin and Larry Page, made the decision to sell shares in their business to the wider public they wrote a "Founder's Letter" to prospective shareholders. On the subject of employee benefits, Brin and Page wrote:

"We provide many unusual benefits for our employees, including meals free of charge, doctors and washing machines. We are careful to consider the long-term advantages to the company of these benefits. Expect us to add benefits rather than pare them down over time. We believe it is easy to be penny wise and pound foolish with respect to benefits that can save employees considerable time and improve their health and productivity."

PROFIT SHARING

Many businesses offer some form of **profit sharing** with their employees. The purpose of profit sharing is to encourage employees to understand how their work affects the company's performance. Most businesses begin by forecasting expected profits for the year, and then allocating a percentage of this to a pool to be shared by employees.

Profit Sharing: A form of compensation that allocates a percentage of profits to a pool to be shared by employees.

The common range for the profit sharing pool is 5% to 10% of pre-tax profits.[1] The business must then define triggers, based on objectives such as a target level of sales or profits, to determine whether the profit pool will be paid out. Without clearly defined triggers, profit sharing will fail in its intent to be a form of performance incentive.

The business must also develop a methodology for allocating the profit sharing. This must be clear, logical and fair. If the allocation isn't seen by employees to be clear, logical and fair the profit sharing plan may backfire, by creating rivalries and jealousies between employees who receive large bonuses and those that don't.

BRINGING THEM ALONG:
LEADING AND CONTROLLING EMPLOYEES

ORIENTATION

As students, you wll remember the orientation program that you went through prior to your first classes at university. If you are a first year student, it will still be fresh in your mind. Of course you remember all of the social events, the games and the silly chanting. However, for the organisation, the purpose of orientation is both practical and serious.

Orientation, sometimes called induction, is the process of introducing new or inexperienced people to an organisation.

Orientation/Induction: The process of introducing new, inexperienced, and people to the organisation

The purpose of an orientation program, whether at a university or a business, is to introduce newcomers to their new environment, make them comfortable, and provide them with the knowledge they need to become fully participating and effective members of the community.

Employers recognise that orientation isn't just a nice gesture. Research shows that orientation programs lead to higher job satisfaction, better job performance, and greater commitment to the organisation from employees who have been through one.[2] By the way, the research also shows that students who attend Frosh Week are less likely to drop out![3]

The specific benefits of orientation include:

- **Reducing Learning Time.** Orientation helps the employee get up to speed quickly, reducing the costs associated with learning how to do a job.

- **Reducing Anxiety.** Anybody, when put into a new situation, will experience anxiety. This anxiety can impede his or her ability to learn to do the job. Orientation helps to reduce that anxiety. A new employee will receive guidelines for their behavior and conduct, so he or she doesn't have to experience the stress of guessing what to do.

- **Reducing Turnover.** Employee turnover increases if employees feel they are not valued. The time and effort that an employer puts into orientation shows the employee that their arrival is valued. This helps to prepare the employee to succeed in the job.

- **Saving Management Time.** The better the initial orientation, the less likely that managers and coworkers will have to spend time teaching the new employee at a later date.

2 "New Comer Orientation Training in Manufacturing Industry: A Comparison Analysis Between Indonesian Company and Japanese Company", Liao, Wen-Chih; Handayani, Sulistio; Chien, Szu-Min. American Journal of Economics and Business Administration 3.4 (2011): pp. 610-617.
3 "Will They Stay Or Will They Go? Predicting The Risk Of Attrition At A Large Public University", Miller, Thomas E Miller, College and University 83.2 (2007), pp. 2-7

SETTING STANDARDS AND GOALS

Having brought a new employee on board, the business' managers must set standards of performance and define clear goals.

Peter Drucker is widely regarded as one of the 20th century's pre-eminent thinkers about management. In his 1954 book "The Practice of Management" Drucker outlined the concept which he termed **Management by Objectives (MBO)**. Drucker believed that a business can best improve its performance when managers and employees sit down together, to define objectives that are agreed by both parties.

Management by Objectives: A theory which suggests that a business can best improve its performance when managers and employees define objectives that are agreed to by both parties.

By being part of the objective setting process, employees will understand what is expected of them. Having a say in what the results should be ensures more commitment from employees to achieve those results.

An important aspect of having agreed standards and objectives, an employee's performance could then be fairly measured and evaluated.

PERFORMANCE APPRAISAL

Performance appraisals, also called reviews, evaluate an employee's achievements and growth, or lack thereof. Businesses use performance appraisals to give employees feedback on their work and to justify pay increases and bonuses.

Performance Appraisal: An evaluation of an employee's achievements and growth, or lack thereof.

Because businesses have a limited pool of capital from which to award raises and bonuses, performance appraisals help determine how to allocate those funds. They provide a way for businesses to determine which employees have contributed the most to the business' growth so that high performing employees can be appropriately rewarded.

The performance appraisal should not be the only time during the year that managers and employees communicate about the employee's contributions. Frequent conversations help to keep everyone on the same page, develop a stronger relationship between employees and managers, and make the formal annual review less stressful.

TRAINING & DEVELOPMENT

Performance appraisals allow employees and their managers to create a plan for employee training and development. Training and development differ. **Training** is aimed at increasing an employee's skills to enable them to do a particular job more efficiently.

> Training: Activities aimed at increasing an employee's skills to enable them to do a particular job more efficiently.

Employee training is the responsibility of, and primarily serves, the interests of the employer.

Employee development is aimed at increasing an employee's general skills and knowledge, coupled with career planning. Employee development goes beyond the scope of the employee's current position, and is intended to groom an employee for increasing responsibility within the organisation.

> Employee development: Activities aimed at increasing an employee's general skills and knowledge, coupled with career planning.

Employee development is a shared responsibility of management and the individual employee. The responsibility of management is to provide the right resources and an environment that supports the employee's development needs and aspirations.

There are many ways that businesses can provide employees with learning opportunities, including:

Job expansion. Once an employee has mastered the requirements of his or her job and is performing satisfactorily, he or she may want greater challenges. Giving an accomplished employee new or additional duties is a means of grooming them for promotion and keeping them challenged.

Job rotation. This involves giving employees the opportunity to work in a different area of the business on a temporary basis. The employee keeps his or her existing job but exchanges responsibilities with another employee

Job shadowing. If an employee wants to learn what someone else in the business does, he or she can follow that person and observe him or her at work.

Peer-assisted learning. Two employees share their knowledge or skills with each other. Both employees should have an area of expertise from which the co-worker can benefit.

Coaching. This involves an agreement between an experienced manager and his or her employee. The role of the coach is to demonstrate skills and to give the employee guidance, feedback, and reassurance while he or she practices new skills.

Mentoring is similar to coaching. Mentoring occurs when a senior, experienced manager provides guidance and advice to a junior employee. The two people involved have usually developed a working relationship based on shared interest and values.

> Mentoring: A senior, experienced manager provides guidance and advice to a junior employee.

Classroom training. A business can offer opportunities to attend courses, seminars, or workshops that are offered either internally or externally.

EMPLOYEE RETENTION

Over the past 14 pages, you have read of the extensive efforts that a business must go to in order to define, describe, and promote jobs, to screen and select candidates, and then compensate, control and develop employees. Why go to so much trouble? The simple and compelling answer is: The cost of hiring the wrong person, or losing the right one, is enormous!

The activities that a business goes through, in order to keep and manage its people is called **retention**.

Retention: The activities that a business goes through, in order to keep and manage its people.

In 2013, the latest year for which data is available, 7.3% of Canadian workers left their jobs. This average disguises a wide range between industries. More than 20% of retail workers quit their job that year.[4] The term used for this is **turnover**.

Turnover: The percentage of employees who leave their jobs in a year.

Turnover does not include workers who leave because they retire at normal retirement age. But it does include those who quit to take a job with another organisation. It includes those who quit to go back to school, to travel, or simply to stay at home. Turnover measures the percentage of an organisation's work force who, therefore, would rather be doing something else.

Not all turnover is necessarily bad. A business can benefit when a poorly performing employee leaves. The departure of an employee that hasn't fit in gives a business an opportunity to inject new blood. However, turnover is expensive. A recent report in the UK placed the cost of replacing a white-collar employee at £30,000 or $60,000.[5] A similar report in the United States put the average cost at US$49,500 or $65,000.[6]

---

4 The Conference Board of Canada,

5 HR Review Tuesday, February 25, 2014

6 De Paul Center for Sales Leadership, 2011 - 2012 Sales Effectiveness Research, http://www.salesleadershipcenter.com/research.html

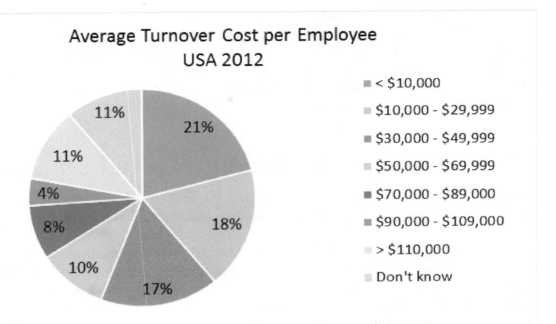

Average Turnover Cost per Employee USA 2012

- < $10,000
- $10,000 - $29,999
- $30,000 - $49,999
- $50,000 - $69,999
- $70,000 - $89,000
- $90,000 - $109,000
- > $110,000
- Don't know

There are two main factors that make up the cost of replacing a departed employee:

- The cost of lost output while a replacement employee gets up to speed
- The logistical cost of recruiting and absorbing a new worker

Even for minimum wage jobs that seemingly require little skill, the cost of replacing a worker who leaves is surprisingly high. In Canada, the Government of Alberta worked with a hotel to calculate the cost to replace just one housekeeping room attendant. It calculated that the direct and indirect cost to replace just one employee, earning $12 an hour, to be $4,000[7]. This is equivalent to two months of the employee's salary.

It doesn't matter whether an employee leaves a job voluntarily or whether they were fired. It will cost the business to replace that employee.

The other problem with unhappy employees is sometimes they just don't bother to come to work. This is a problem called **absenteeism**. Absenteeism is defined as an employee's absences from work due to illness, or personal or family responsibility.

Absenteeism: an employee's absences from work due to illness, or personal or family responsibility.

This definition disguises the fact that, in many cases, sick days are taken by people who aren't really sick. They are demotivated.

---

7 Finders and Keepers, Alberta Human Resources and Employment, Government of Alberta, 2003

8 StatsCan. Cansim Table Table 279-0029 Work absence statistics of full-time employees, for Canada, provinces and census metropolitan areas (CMA), and by sex.

In Canada in 2014 the overall absenteeism rate was **8.8** days per employee.[8] That's an average. This means there are likely to be businesses that averaged fourteen absentee days, in addition to those that reported only three days. These lost days mean lower production and therefore lower productivity. An employee who doesn't show up means the business will have to find someone to fill in. Presumably the "fill-in" has less experience, and less knowledge of the business' operations. Output suffers, morale suffers, and the problem could become a vicious spiral.

HIRING AND KEEPING THE RIGHT PEOPLE: CONCLUSIONS

Throughout this chapter there has been a common theme. The time and effort that goes into planning, organising, leading and controlling a business' human resource is an investment that pays off.

Hiring the wrong person to do the wrong job is an expensive and unsatisfactory way to start. Failing to make people feel welcome and wanted makes them less productive. Without carefully and thoughtfully designed compensation packages jealousies will occur, morale will fall, and good workers will leave. Finally, people stay with businesses that demonstrate they value – and care for – their employees. For businesses trying to do this, financial reward is not always the answer. In the next chapter, you will learn a good deal more about this.

SELF-ASSESSMENT QUESTIONS FOR REVIEW

1. Every semester, the Department of Management needs to hire a number of Teaching Assistants to help with the management of this course. Prepare a job analysis, in other words, a list of the activities that a Teaching Assistant for this course would be required to do.

2. Prepare a job specification for the position of Teaching Assistant for this course. What knowledge, education, experience and characteristics do you think your Professor would look for?

3. When the Department of Management is recruiting for applicants to TA this course, how and where do you think it tries to make the position known? Where would you look, or who would you speak to if you were interested in being a TA for this course?

4. Students who work as Teaching Assistants get to put that experience on their resume. Usually, they can rely on the Professor for whom they worked to provide a letter of reference or recommendation to other potential employers or to graduate schools. Do you think that this is an important consideration to students who apply for TA jobs? Do you think that these things can be considered "benefits" from the job?

5. If you attended Frosh Week orientation, what did you learn about UTSC? Did you meet any member of the UTSC faculty or staff who might prove helpful or useful to you in your career as a student? Did your feelings about attending UTSC change? How did they change?

DEFINED TERMS

- Absenteeism
- Compensation
- Curriculum Vitae (CV)
- Employee benefits
- Employee development
- Gain sharing
- Head hunter
- Hiring from within
- Induction
- Internal recruiting
- Job analysis
- Job specification
- Job description
- Management by objectives
- Mentoring
- Minimum wage
- Orientation
- Performance appraisal
- Profit sharing
- Recruiting
- Recruiting agency
- Resume
- Retention
- Sales commission
- Screening
- Selection
- Soft skills
- Training
- Turnover

CHAPTER 12

GETTING PEOPLE TO TRY HARD:
MOTIVATION

CHAPTER OVERVIEW

You have learned that leading and managing do not involve the arbitrary exercise of power. Dictators and bullies can make people bend to their will. Leading and managing involve getting others to want to work to get things done.

The resources at a business owner's disposal are natural resources, capital, and labour. Effective management of the business, therefore, includes getting people:

- To try hard.
- To "want to".
- To care.

Having committed and motivated workers is so key to the success of a business that it has been a major object of study by researchers and management theorists for more than a century. To see that this is so, you need only to go to your local bookstore. There, on the shelves, you will find dozens of books on the subject of employee engagement, team-building, morale, and motivation.

There is a vast array of theories, models, and approaches to how a business can get the most out of its people. In this chapter you will learn several of the most frequently used, most widely studied, and most influential of these theories.

LEARNING OUTCOMES

As a result of reading this chapter you will learn:

- Why motivation is important.

- Why managing the human resource probably needs more time and care and thought and effort than managing capital or natural resources.

- There are many theories, models and approaches as to how a business can get the most out of its people. Some are better known and more widely discussed than others. The key theories that you will learn:

    The Classical Theory suggests that people are motivated only by the pursuit of money. If this theory was ever true, it is probably much less true today than in the past.

    The theory of scientific management proposed that worker productivity could be increased through rigid control over standardised work routines. The principles of scientific management appear to work to a limited extent, but not over the long term. Bored and alienated workers will begin to lose their motivation.

    The Hawthorn studies were designed to test the effect of the environment on worker productivity. What the researchers discovered surprised them. The unexpected findings of the Hawthorn studies helped move the study of human resource management in a new direction.

    McGregor's Theory X and Theory Y built on the findings of the Hawthorn studies. These theories challenged businesses and managers to examine their attitudes toward employees and the beliefs that shaped their behaviour toward workers.

    Maslow's theory of the hierarchy of needs suggests that there is no one thing that motivates people. Rather, people are motivated to satisfy a variety of different needs. Once a need has been satisfied, it no longer acts as a motivator.

    Herzberg's motivation-hygiene theory also suggests that people have a number of motivators. Herzberg also identified factors within a job that they find dis-satisfying and potentially demotivating. The theory suggests that managers attempt to mitigate or minimise negative factors, while improving or accentuating the positive factors that increase motivation.

    Adam's equity theory proposes that people have an innate sense of what is fair, or equitable. Workers will compare the circumstances of their job with work colleagues and peers. While workers do not necessarily expect that everyone will receive the same compensation or treatment, they expect that they will be treated equitably.

WHY MOTIVATION IS IMPORTANT

By definition, a business is made up of a **combination** of the four factors of production, no business can survive without some quantity of each of them. Students sometimes ask "Are there businesses where one factor of production is more important than the others?" Certainly it can be argued that in some industries, the quality of one factor might be more important than the others. In agriculture, a poorly educated farmer, using obsolete capital equipment, might still be able to produce a good crop, if the farm has exceptionally fertile soil. Similarly, a law firm may have poor equipment but can thrive because of the experience and expertise of the human resources who walk through its door each day.

A related question is "Does one factor of production need to be managed with more care and effort than the others?" The answer to this question is "Yes". Labour, the human resource, needs more care and attention to manage than natural resources or capital. This is because humans, unlike natural resources or capital, have emotions.

Natural resources like lumps of coal or pieces of lumber can be left in a warehouse or a yard for months or years, and they will suffer no deterioration and harm. Financial capital is scarce, and shouldn't be wasted. But a cost overrun in one month can be offset by a tighter budget, or less expenditure in the next.

Human resources are different. Unlike natural resources or capital, human beings have feelings and memories. People will react if they are taken for granted, overlooked, or treated badly. They will stop trying. They will stop caring. As you saw in the last chapter, some workers simply won't show up. Others will quit.

The internal process that gives an individual the energy and desire to act or behave in a particular way is called **motivation**. The question of what motivates people to go to work each day has been studied by management theorists and social psychologists for decades.

Motivation: The internal process that gives an individual the energy and desire to act or behave in a particular way.

Despite the attention of researchers, and the known costs of absenteeism and turnover, recent research shows that 40% of American workers feel that they working for "bad bosses"[1]. The survey showed that

- 39% of respondents reported that their supervisor had failed to keep a promise.
- 37% indicated that their boss failed to give credit when due.
- 27% said that a supervisor had made negative comments about them to other employees.
- 23% reported that their boss had blamed others for their own mistakes.

It's hard to imagine someone wanting to put effort into a job if this is how they are being treated! It's important to stress, not all bosses are bad bosses. The research indicated that these comments applied to a minority of supervisors, just 40%. It's also probable that some of the incidents reported were misunderstandings, or exceptional incidents when one of the people involved was having a bad day. Nevertheless, the research highlights the need for managers to be vigilant in how they interact with colleagues and co-workers and how they are perceived.

---

1 Hochwarter, Harvey and Stonertate University, as reported in "Who's afraid of the big bad boss? Plenty of us, new FSU study shows" Barry Ray, FSU News, Florida State University, December 2006

Let's now consider seven of the most widely studied theories about motivation.

CLASSICAL THEORY OF MOTIVATION

One of the earliest, and simplest theories of motivation is the **classical theory**. The classical theory of motivation holds that workers are motivated only by money.

Classical Theory of Motivation: Workers are motivated only by money.

The word "classical" means traditional, or long lasting. The classical theory therefore, has been with us for a long time. The basic premise to this theory is that everyone needs money, simply to survive. Someone in a position of power or authority, therefore, could bend others to do their bidding simply by offering money. Positive behaviour, or compliance, could be reinforced by offering more money.

In a work environment, the logical consequence of the classical theory is that people will work harder, and be more productive if offered more pay. According to this theory, money is both a reward for past performance, and incentive to work harder still.

The classical theory dominated management thinking up until the early years of the 20th century. One hundred and fifty years ago, standards of living were much lower. No social safety net of unemployment insurance, welfare benefits and free universal health care existed.

During the middle of the nineteenth century in Britain, children as young as four were employed as "climbing boys", chimney sweeps who climbed naked into chimney stacks to scrub it clean of soot. Chimneys were as small as nine by fourteen inches. Children occasionally became stuck and suffocated to death.

Similarly, girls as young as eight were employed to crawl, on their hands and knees, in the dark, dragging wagons through coal mines.

Happily, in much of the world, employment laws, health and safety regulations, and attitudes have changed. In developed countries, desperate people no longer have to do just about anything to earn the money they need to buy food. Ask yourself, have you ever had a summer or part-time job to which you would never return, even for more pay? We now live in a world where people can afford to have a little more choice. The classical theory, if it was ever true, no longer works.

TAYLOR'S THEORY OF SCIENTIFIC MANAGEMENT

One of the earliest theorists to study motivation and productivity was Frederick Winslow Taylor. Taylor wanted to improve the efficiency of workers. In 1909, Taylor published "The Principles of Scientific Management."

Taylor's interest was not what motivates workers. He subscribed to the classical theory of motivation. He started from the position that workers are motivated by money. Taylor's interest was in how to use workers' motivation to make money to get them to produce more.

Taylor promoted the idea of "a fair day's pay for a fair day's work." In other words, if a worker didn't achieve enough in a day, he didn't deserve to be paid as much as another worker who was highly productive. He proposed a means to increase productivity.

Taylor began by performing time and motion studies on workers' complex tasks. He used those time and motion studies to break every complex job into a number of simple, separate tasks.

Taylor designed experiments to determine the best way to do things. In one of his more famous experiments, he designed a shovel that would allow workers to shovel for several hours without getting tired. With bricklayers, he experimented with the various motions required and developed an efficient way to lay bricks. Taylor found that by calculating the time needed for the various elements of a task, he could develop the "best" way to complete that task.

Previously, workers had been left on their own to produce the necessary product. There was no standardisation, and there was no incentive to work as quickly or as efficiently as possible. Taylor reasoned that by giving workers a small number of simple, repetitive tasks, which they would perform over and over again, he could remove any inefficient use of their time.

Taylor's four principles are as follows:

- Replace working by "rule of thumb," or simple habit and common sense, and instead develop standard methods which are the most efficient for doing each job.
- Select workers to match a specific job, and train them to work at maximum efficiency.
- Monitor worker performance, and provide instructions and supervision to ensure that they are using the most efficient methods.
- Divide the work between managers and workers so that the managers spend their time planning and training, and workers concentrate on performing tasks.

These principles are also known simply as "Taylorism".

Scientific Management / Taylorism: Managing the business by applying principles of efficiency derived from time-and-motion studies.

Around the same time that Taylor started experimenting with his theories, Henry Ford was developing his now famous automobiles. Ford named each successive model in alphabetical order. His most successful car was the Model "T", which began production in 1908.

During the early days of automobile manufacturing, the body of the car would be fixed into a stationary position and workers would bring and add individual parts to the vehicle. Each car was built by a small team of skilled labourers working together. They spent about 12 hours building each car. Ford wanted a way to produce a larger number of cars in a shorter period time. So, Ford hired Taylor to help map out possible solutions. At that time the price of a Model T was $825.

During the following year, Taylor observed Ford's workers to determine the most efficient and time-saving methods for increasing their productivity. Ford began to adopt Taylor's ideas of scientific management.

Ford determined that the larger parts of the car should remain stationary, while the smaller parts should be brought to the vehicle as needed. This sped up the production process significantly.

To further reduce assembly time, Ford had his workers remain stationary as the body of the car was pulled, by rope, past their workstations. Each worker performed his specified task before the car was moved to the next station. This process was repeated until the car's construction was complete.

Ford continued to improve and streamline the process, and in 1913 he introduced a completely power-driven assembly line. From 12 hours in 1908, average production time for a Model T dropped to 93 minutes five years later. As a consequence Ford was able to lower the price of the vehicle down to $575. By 1914, Ford had captured 48% of the US automobile market.

In the early days of 1914, Ford raised the wages that he was paying his workers from $2.83 for a 9-hour day to $5.00 for an 8-hour day. As a result, Ford greatly improved worker morale and further grew his potential customer base. By 1924 Ford had managed to sell over 10 million cars.

CRITIQUES OF TAYLORISM

Scientific management is based on the idea that there is one "right way" to do something. The "right way" minimises, delay, indecision and wasted movement. Workers specialise at a simple, repetitive task, thereby becoming good at doing one thing. As a result, productivity should rise. This is indeed what happened at the Ford production plant.

The problem with scientific management is, by giving workers a limited number of simple tasks to perform, management is treating them as though they are machines. Tasks that lack any challenge and complexity will eventually become boring. Boredom leads to **alienation**.

Alienation is a concept that was first described by Karl Marx. Marx, you will remember, was among the most prominent and influential critics of the capitalist form of business organisation. Alienation means a worker's loss of the ability to control his or her own life, to make decisions, or to take responsibility for his or her own actions. People who are not interested in or challenged by their jobs will become bored and alienated.

Alienation: An individual's loss of the ability to control his or her own life, to make decisions or take responsibility for his or her own actions.

The specialisation and repetition that Taylor promoted is at odds with modern ideas of how to provide a motivating and stimulating workplace. Think for a moment about your own experience. Are you happier and more motivated when you're feeling tightly controlled, or when you're working using your own judgment?

Bored, unmotivated workers are more prone to illness and absenteeism. This explains why, in the longer term, some of the productivity gains that Taylor and Ford achieved were reversed.

THE HAWTHORNE STUDIES

The **Hawthorne studies** are one of the most famous series of experiments in business history. The studies were conducted by Elton Mayo, a professor of industrial research at the Harvard Business School. A series of research studies took place between 1924 and 1932, at the Western Electric Company's Hawthorne Works in Chicago. The Hawthorne studies take their name from the factory complex where they took place.

Hawthorne studies: a series of research studies designed to examine the relationship between the work environment and worker productivity.

The Western Electric Company manufactured telephones. In the early 1920s its Hawthorne Works employed 12,000 workers. In 1924 Western Electric provided a site to cooperate on a series of tests that were intended to determine the relationship between light levels and worker productivity.

The idea was to vary the levels of illumination on the factory floor. It was expected that as light levels increased, productivity would increase too. In another test room, light levels were dimmed in the expectation that output would decrease. However, the one conclusion the researchers discovered was that there was no correlation between lighting levels and product output. Indeed, to the surprise of the researchers, productivity continue to improve whenever the lights were dimmed further still!

A second set of tests were designed to evaluate the effect that rest periods would have on total output. A number of the factory's women employees volunteered to take part in the study. After six months, the women were given additional rest periods. As the tests continued, other changes followed, including shorter work days. As the women were given more rest periods and shorter days, worker productivity climbed. Again, this was not what the researchers had expected. Over two and-a-half years, worker productivity increased more than 30 percent, and remained steady for the duration of the tests.

In addition, periodic physical examinations showed that the workers' health was improving. Absenteeism at the factory began to fall. By their own testimony, the women expressed increased satisfaction with all aspects of their jobs.

The researchers began to realise that it was not the changes in physical conditions that were affecting the workers' productivity. Rather, it was the fact that someone was concerned about their work and their workplace. The women volunteers welcomed the opportunity that the experiments gave them to discuss changes before they took place. The researchers concluded that factors such as lighting, rest periods and hours of work affected output, but the interest, morale and motivation of the employees were having a much greater effect.

The Hawthorne Studies marked a change in thinking about work and productivity. Previous studies, like Taylor's experiments with scientific management, had focused on ways in which an individual's performance could be improved. In contrast, the Hawthorne studies showed that worker attitudes and behavior was key. The studies also set workers in a social context. That is, they determined that an individual employee's performance is influenced by their surroundings and by the people that they are working with as much as by their own abilities.

The legacy of the Hawthorne studies was the rise of a concept now known as the **Hawthorne Effect**. The Hawthorne effect is the tendency for workers' productivity to increase when they feel they are doing something important, their work matters to someone, and they are worthy of receiving special attention.

Hawthorne Effect: Workers' productivity will increase when they feel they are doing something important, their work matters, and they are worthy of receiving special attention.

For managers, the implication of the Hawthorne effect is very simple. Workers will respond positively if a manager takes an interest in them, and takes an interest in their work.

THEORY X AND THEORY Y

Douglas McGregor was a Professor of social psychology at MIT. Building on what researchers had learned from the Hawthorne studies, during the 1960s McGregor developed two contrasting theories about motivation and the way in which managers treat their human resources. He called these two theories: Theory X and Theory Y.

Theory X assumes that employees are unmotivated and dislike working. To overcome this resistance to work, managers must adopt an authoritarian style of management. In other words, managers must actively and frequently intervene to ensure that things get done. This style of management assumes that workers:

- Dislike work.
- Avoid responsibility.
- Need to be directed.
- Need to be supervised, with lots of controls in place.
- Need to be bribed to produce results.

Theory X: Assumes that employees are unmotivated and dislike working. This encourages an authoritarian style of management.

Theory X is consistent with Taylor's theory of scientific management. It assumes that workers perform best in highly controlled work environments. Businesses that adopt this style of management tend to have many supervisors, to control every step of operations.

In contrast, **Theory Y** assumes that employees are hard-working, self-motivated, and enjoy responsibility. It assumes that workers:

- Are motivated to fulfill goals.
- Seek and accept responsibility.
- Do not need much direction.
- Solve problems imaginatively.

Theory Y: Assumes that employees are hard-working, self-motivated, and enjoy responsibility.

Organisations and individuals that subscribe to Theory Y are willing to delegate, and to give people at lower levels of the organisation responsibility, and the freedom to take decisions.

Theory X	Theory Y
Assumes that people:	Assumes that people:
are lazy	are energetic
lack ambition	are ambitious
dislike responsibility	seek responsibility
are self-centered	can be selfless
resist change	want to contribute to change
are not very bright	are intelligent

In expounding these two theories, McGregor was not prescriptive. In other words, he did not write that Theory X is "bad" whereas Theory Y is "good". In fact, he acknowledged that there probably are workers who fall into the description offered by Theory X. He also understood that there may be some operating environments, for example business that do large scale mass production, where rules and procedures may be inevitable. However, McGregor believed that businesses and individuals to whom Theory X applied were in the minority.

McGregor advocated that business organisations and, in particular, individual managers should examine the assumptions that they make about their workers. In the previous chapter you learned of the careful way in which most businesses analyse, specify and describe their human resource needs, and of the efforts that they make to recruit, screen and select the right people for the job. Having gone to all of that effort to hire people that the business perceives to be bright, well-qualified, and capable, it only makes sense to manage them according to the precepts of Theory Y.

MASLOW'S HIERARCHY OF NEEDS

Abraham Maslow (1908 – 1970) was a Psychologist at Columbia University. Like Taylor, McGregor and Mayo before him, Maslow was interested in what motivated people. He would undoubtedly have been aware of the accumulated body of prior research. People need to eat and to put a roof over their heads, so he would have been aware of the motivation of money. The Hawthorne experiments appeared to suggest that a pleasant work environment, at least initially, positively effects output. The unanticipated finding from the Hawthorne experiments was that people want to feel that their work is valued and important. Maslow's principle contribution to the study of motivation was to argue that people have a **variety** of different needs. In 1954 Maslow introduced the Hierarchy of Needs theory for which he is now most famous.

Maslow argued that people have different needs. Some needs, for example the need to put food into our bellies, are more basic than others. However, as our income, education, and other forms of well-being increase, and we are increasingly able to satisfy this most basic need, we start to aspire to different things. Maslow identified 5 needs. Once people have attained a certain amount of satisfaction with one form of motivator, they begin to look toward the next one. A need that is already reasonably well-satisfied is not a powerful motivator.

Everyone needs food, water, and shelter. These are the most basic requirements to survival. Maslow called these the **physiological needs**.

Physiological needs: Food, water, clothing and shelter are the most basic requirements to survival.

Maslow therefore reckoned that every worker needs to earn a basic living wage. In other words, a salary that is adequate for a worker to pay rent and buy groceries. If a job offers to pay any less than that, the individual's time would be better spent stealing or foraging.

Once we have enough pay to meet our most immediate physiological needs, we start to worry about tomorrow. Our concern moves from "How can I afford to feed myself today?" to "What will I do when I get old, and can no longer work?" and "What if I get sick?"

Maslow argued that people need to know that their family or community will continue to care for them after they can no longer provide for themselves. Maslow called this need for physical and emotional support our need for **security**.

Security Needs: The need for physical and emotional support when we are too old or ill to provide for ourselves

---

In the employment context, people will surrender salary in order to obtain more job security during their working lives, health insurance in case they become ill, and a pension plan to provide income during their retirement years.

Once we know that we will be able to feed ourselves and have shelter for the duration of our lives, we need to feel the love and affection from friends and family, and a sense of belonging from our community. Maslow called these our **social needs.**

> Social needs: The need for love and affection from friends and family, and a sense of belonging from our community.

It is often said that "money can't buy happiness". In the context of work, most people will surrender a high salary or job security if they can work with nice people, develop friendships on the job, and feel that they are part of a team.

For those who have satisfied their social needs, the next step in the hierarchy is to acquire respect and status. Within the community, those who have satisfied the other needs aspire to become the "Captain" or "Chief". They want to sit at the head of the table, or be accorded other forms of recognition. Maslow called these our **esteem needs**.

> Esteem Needs: The desire to be given respect, status or recognition.

In the context of work, our esteem needs are met through being given ever more impressive job titles. "Senior" Vice-President or "Executive" Director confer more status than Vice-President or Director. In lieu of pay, people will be happy to be given a private office, a good parking spot, or privileged access to dining or washrooms that are not accessible to others.

The final rung on Maslow's hierarchy is **self-actualisation**. This term means the ability for an individual to grow and develop, whether emotionally and intellectually, or by learning new skills or acquiring new experiences.

> Self-Actualisation: The ability to grow and develop by learning new skills or acquiring new experiences.

People self-actualise by accepting new or interesting challenges, and by doing things that they find fulfilling. A business can satisfy this need by offering employees new and challenging opportunities that will help them develop new skills. This might involve an overseas posting, where the employee can experience a new culture and learn a new language.

Maslow's five needs are normally depicted as a pyramid, with a wide base and a pointed top. It is shown in this shape because **everyone** needs to satisfy the needs at the bottom. These are basic. Fewer people manage to satisfy each subsequent level. For this reason, Maslow's theory is known as the **hierarchy of needs**. The name suggest that some needs are more basic and more universally sought after than others.

> Hierarchy of Needs: According to Maslow's theory some needs are more basic and more universally sought after than others.

Maslow's Hierarchy of Needs

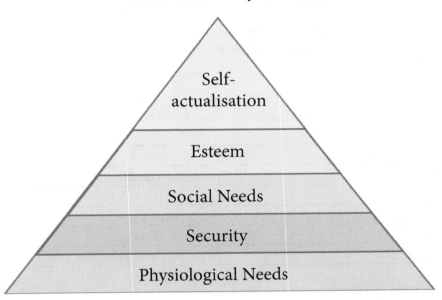

It is only a lucky few who have more than adequate salary, pension plan and heath care plans that will keep them comfortable for life, a friendly and supportive work community, an impressive title that brings recognition and respect, and finally, a job that is constantly interesting and, challenging.

Maslow's theory of the hierarchy of needs points to the fact that there is no "one size fits all" approach to motivating people. Employers must respond to employee needs in a variety of ways, so that workers of all dispositions and abilities are encouraged and enabled to fulfil their own potential. On this, Maslow himself once said "If the only tool you have is a hammer, you tend to see every problem as a nail."

Maslow's theory has its critics. One criticism is that the arrangement of the various needs may not apply to all cultures. For example, the satisfaction of esteem needs may be unimportant in less individualistic cultures that that of the United States or Canada. Another criticism of the theory is that it implies that the various needs must be satisfied in a step-by-step fashion, one after the other. More recent research suggests that, while we may have a patchwork of needs, these do not need to be satisfied one at a time, or in the precise sequence that Maslow envisioned.

HERZBERG'S MOTIVATION-HYGIENE THEORY

Frederick Herzberg (1923 – 2000) taught psychology at the University of Utah. Herzberg was the author of "One More Time, How Do You Motivate Employees?" the most requested article in the history of the Harvard Business Review.

Herzberg's interest was what people liked about their work, and also what they disliked. In 1959 Herzberg surveyed several hundred engineers and accountants on this subject. He found:

They Liked	They Disliked
responsibility	working conditions
recognition	policies and rules
the work itself	supervisors
achievement	pay and security
advancement and growth	interpersonal relations

The findings themselves are perhaps not terribly surprising.

However, upon looking at the two lists together Herzberg noticed that what people liked about their jobs was not opposite of what they disliked. Herzberg's key finding was that the sources of satisfaction and dissatisfaction were not extreme ends of a single range, but two entirely separate lists. "Responsibility" is not related to "working conditions", "recognition" is not related to "policies and rules".

Herzberg recognised that the aspects of work and employment that dis-satisfy people are things that the business cannot do without. If an accountant's job requires that he work long hours at the end of a client's fiscal year, or spend time away from home, there's not a great deal that an accounting business can do to change that. Working conditions, in some cases can't be much altered. Accountants may not like supervision, or business policies and rules, but a business organisation needs some form of managerial control. The things that dis-satisfy people he called **hygiene factors.**

Hygiene factors: Aspects of a job that dis-satisfy workers.

Herzberg recognised that most people don't particularly like being supervised. Therefore, the best that an employer can do is make the supervision as positive, and unobtrusive as possible. People will always aspire to receive more pay. Therefore, the best that an employer can do is ensure that compensation is adequate, and in line with the pay offered for similar jobs at similar employers.

A business has to manage the hygiene factors to make them – at best – tolerable and acceptable.

Herzberg recognised that the aspects of work that people liked are things that the business can increase or improve, often at little cost. Since people like responsibility, a business can offer employees more responsibility. This will increase job satisfaction. Since people like recognition, a business can offer employees more recognition. This too will increase job satisfaction. The things that satisfy people and add to their job satisfaction Herzberg called **motivating factors.**

Motivating factors: Aspects of a job that satisfy and motivate workers.

Motivating factors are desirable, and their presence makes people happy. To increase worker satisfaction, a business should aim to increase or improve the motivating factors.

The existence of these two sets of factors has led Herzberg's theory to become known as both the **motivation-hygiene theory** and also the **two factor theory**.

Motivation-Hygiene Theory / Two Factor Theory: A theory which differentiates between the factors which contribute satisfaction and dissatisfaction to employment.

EQUITY THEORY

Equity theory was developed in 1963 by Jon Stacey Adams, an American behavioral psychologist. Adams asserted that employees want a fair balance between what they perceive themselves bringing to a job, and the rewards that they receive in return.

Like Maslow and Herzberg before him, Adams acknowledged that an individual's relationship to his work and to his employer was measured through many subtle and variable factors. Employees provide an employer with skills, hard work, commitment and enthusiasm. They want this to be returned in salary, benefits, recognition, esteem and so on. Adams theorised that individuals will compare their own input to outcome ratio against the perceived inputs and outcomes of their co-workers. If they believe they are being treated fairly they will be contented and motivated. Adams called this **equity theory**.

According to equity theory, people value fair treatment. An individual will perceive that he is being treated fairly if he perceives the ratio of inputs to rewards to be equivalent to those around him.

Equity Theory: An individual will perceive that he is being treated fairly if he perceives the ratio of inputs to rewards to be equivalent to those around him.

Thus, it is acceptable that a more senior colleague receives higher compensation, since the value of her experience - the input - is greater. The way people judge their satisfaction with a job is to make comparisons between themselves and the people they work with.

$$\frac{\text{Individual's outcomes}}{\text{Individual's inputs}} = \frac{\text{Co-workers outcomes}}{\text{Co-worker's inputs}}$$

If an employee notices that another person is getting more recognition and reward, when both have done the same amount and quality of work, the employee will feel underappreciated. If employees are rewarded equally, the employer will be perceived as fair, observant, and appreciative.

Inputs are defined as each participant's contributions to the relational exchange and are viewed as entitling him/her to rewards. Inputs typically include any of the following:

- Time
- Education
- Experience
- Effort
- Loyalty

- Commitment
- Flexibility
- Enthusiasm
- Personal sacrifice

Outcomes are the rewards that the employee receives. Outcomes can be either tangible, most obviously through pay and benefits, or intangible, through many of the motivators identified by Maslow and Herzberg:

- Job security
- Recognition
- Responsibility

- Sense of achievement
- Praise
- Sense of advancement/growth

Equity theory has implications for business managers in the area of compensation. People measure the totals of their inputs and outcomes. This means a working mother may accept lower monetary compensation in return for more flexible working hours.

Other implications of equity theory include:

- Different employees place different value to various forms of input and outcome. Two employees who have equal experience and qualification, who perform the same work for the same pay may have quite different perceptions of the fairness of the deal.

- Employees can adjust rewards to local conditions. Thus a worker in rural Quebec may accept lower compensation than a colleague in Toronto, if his cost of living is different. A worker doing the same job in a remote African village may accept a totally different pay and benefits structure.

- Although it may be acceptable for more senior staff to receive higher compensation, employees can find excessive executive pay demotivating.

Like other motivation theories, equity theory points to the fact that there is no "one size fits all" approach to motivating employees.

GETTING PEOPLE TO TRY HARD: CONCLUSIONS

The theories described in the preceding pages are just several among many dozens of theories, models, and approaches for getting and keeping workers interested and engaged in their work. The great array of these theories serves to highlight the importance that managers place upon employee motivation. In contemporary businesses, motivation is seen as the key to raising and maintaining productivity.

Previously, when you learned about leadership, mission and strategy, you were reminded that victorious athletes are often heard to say "we had a plan, and we stuck to it". Then, earlier in this book you were reminded that the very best athletes increase their productivity by training harder and practicing more than others. Finally, in this chapter we looked at the important role played by managers as coaches and motivators.

SELF-ASSESSMENT QUESTIONS FOR REVIEW

1. Have you ever had a job to which you would not return, even for more money? Without the income from that job, how would you pay your rent or buy groceries? Do you think that the Classical Theory holds true?

2. Have you ever had a job where you did the same thing all day long? Did you get bored? Did you lose focus? What did you do to keep yourself interested and engaged?

3. During your high school or university career do you recall when a teacher or professor showed particular interest in you or your work? What did they do or say? What was your reaction?

4. Can you provide an example of someone who, rather than take a raise in pay, took a job or made a career move that gave them greater employment security, or more status? Do you think their choice was the right one?

5. Make a list of the things that you dislike about being a university student. Then, make a list of the things you like about being a university student. Comparing the two lists, do they relate to the same things or are they completely separate lists of advantages and disadvantages, costs and benefits?

DEFINED TERMS

- Alienation
- Classical theory
- Equity theory
- Esteem needs
- Hawthorne effect
- Hawthorne studies
- Hierarchy of needs
- Hygiene factors
- Motivation
- Motivation-Hygiene Theory
- Motivating factors
- Physiological needs
- Scientific management
- Security needs
- Self actualisation
- Social needs
- Taylorism
- Theory X
- Theory Y
- Two factor theory

INDEX